Repeating

Žižek

SIC

A

series

edited

by

Slavoj

Žižek

SIC stands for psychoanalytic interpretation at its most elementary: no discovery of deep, hidden meaning, just the act of drawing attention to the litterality [*sic!*] of what precedes it. A *sic* reminds us that what was said, inclusive of its blunders, was effectively said and cannot be undone. The series SIC thus explores different connections to the Freudian field. Each volume provides a bundle of Lacanian interventions into a specific domain of ongoing theoretical, cultural, and ideological-political battles. It is neither "pluralist" nor "socially sensitive." Unabashedly avowing its exclusive Lacanian orientation, it disregards any form of correctness but the inherent correctness of theory itself.

Repeating Žižek

With an Afterword
by Slavoj Žižek
Agon Hamza, ed.

sic **9**

DUKE UNIVERSITY PRESS   Durham and London 2015

© 2015 Duke University Press
All rights reserved

Typeset in Sabon by Tseng Information Systems, Inc.
Printed and bound by CPI Group (UK) Ltd, Croydon, CR0 4YY

Library of Congress Cataloging-in-Publication Data
Repeating Žižek / Agon Hamza, ed.
pages cm — (Sic series)
Includes bibliographical references and index.
ISBN 978-0-8223-5905-0 (hardcover : alk. paper)
ISBN 978-0-8223-5891-6 (pbk. : alk. paper)
1. Žižek, Slavoj — Criticism and interpretation.
2. Philosophy, Modern — History and
criticism — 21st century. I. Hamza, Agon, 1984–
II. Series: SIC (Durham, N.C.)
B4870.Z594R474 2015
199′.4973–dc23
2014042425
ISBN 978-0-8223-7547-0 (e-book)

Cover art: © David Levene/*The Guardian*

Contents

Acknowledgments

This book is the result of a collective work of friends, comrades, and colleagues.

I want to particularly thank Adrian Johnston, Frank Ruda, Sead Zimeri, Gabriel Tupinambá, Henrik Jøker Bjerre, Geoff Pfeifer and Agon Hamza for spending a great deal of time discussing numerous aspects of this volume from its beginning.

I thank Courtney Berger and Erin Hanas from Duke University Press for their help and guidance.

Finally, I want to thank Slavoj Žižek. While his books remain, undisputedly, the best introduction and commentary to his own work, serving as one of the few examples today of what it means to partake in the public use of Reason, Slavoj's philosophy has given us both a cause to think and to return to the truly philosophical questions of today, as well as a cause to organize ourselves and come together.

I dedicate this book to Stojan Pelko.

Introduction:

The Trouble

Agon Hamza **with Žižek**

This volume is a collection of critical analysis of the philosophy of Slavoj Žižek. It is a timely intervention, especially now that Žižek's work has been introduced in many places and disciplines of thought; many books, conferences, and journals have been devoted to his project, and he is currently engaged in a substantial reworking, or rather expanding and further developing, of his main positions, especially as presented and elaborated in his *Less Than Nothing*.

To begin with, I want to argue what this volume *is not* about. That is to say, every determination is a negation, in the sense that it involves the negation of other particular determinations. This volume gathers various thinkers, whose chapters do not constitute the standard approach of a pupil who develops further the master's thought or system in a more coherent manner, or maintaining a blind fidelity to the position of the master. Further, this volume is not meant to be a *defense of* Žižek. In this regard, it is not meant to be either an introductory reader's guide to Žižek or a comprehensive monograph. Neither is it a dialogue with Žižek. Since this volume aims to be a philosophical book, we must bear in mind that "philosophy is not a dialogue,"[1] but "every true philosophical dialogue, is an interaction of two monologues."[2]

The ordinary approach to Žižek's thought is that it is polemical and controversial—meaningless and flat terms that at best present a tautological statement. We know already from Kant that philosophy is a *Kampfplatz*, a battlefield of positions that in itself involves polemics, albeit its peculiar character. Another recurring approach is one that bases itself on the diagnosis of a lack of any system in his thought, which at its best would make him a postmodern philosopher; at its worse, he is reduced to a pop phenomenon.[3] According to this rather widely accepted idea, all that Žižek does is to borrow concepts from other thinkers (i.e., Lacan, Hegel, Marx, Schelling, etc.), distorting them through (re)placing them into different contexts, situations, and so on. The most problematic aspect of this is that these obliterations are being taken seriously. However, one should recall Adrian Johnston's warning: "Žižek's rhetorical flair and various features of his methodology are in danger of creating the same unfortunate sort of audience as today's mass media (with its reliance upon continual successions of rapid-fire, attention-grabbing sound bites), namely, consumers too easily driven to distraction."[4] In fact, to paraphrase Badiou apropos Deleuze (which Johnston uses in the same context for Žižek himself), Žižek's heterogeneous style often obscures/occludes him (or his readers) from the homogeneous content.

Taking all this into account, why a volume on Žižek, or why a book on his philosophical *system*? Or better still, why this book? In this regard, *Repeating Žižek* stands for an effective "betrayal" of Žižek through *repeating* his ultimate act. In *The Organs without Bodies*, Žižek writes:

> Becoming is thus strictly correlative to the concept of REPETITION: far from being opposed to the emergence of the New, the proper Deleuzian paradox is that something truly New can ONLY emerge through repetition. What repetition repeats is not the way the past "effectively was," but the virtually inherent to the past and betrayed by its past actualization. In this precise sense, the emergence of the New changes the past itself, that is, it retroactively changes (not the actual past—we are not in science fiction—but) the balance between actuality and virtuality in the past. Recall the old example provided by Walter Benjamin: the October Revolution repeated the French Revolution, redeeming its failure, unearthing and repeating the same impulse. Already for Kierkegaard, repetition is "inverted memory," a movement forward, the production of the New, and not the reproduction of the Old. "There is nothing new under the sun" is the strongest contrast to the movement of repetition. So, it is not only that repetition is (one of the modes of) the emergence of the New—the New can ONLY emerge through repetition.[5]

This should be understood in a Hegelian manner: Žižek's thesis is that although Hegel did think the repetition, his repetition is a repetition with sublation (*Aufhebung*), which is to say:

> through repetition, something is idealized, transformed from an immediate contingent reality to a notional universality (Caesar dies as a person and becomes a universal title); or, at least, through repetition, the necessity of an event is confirmed (Napoleon had to lose twice to get the message that his time was over, that his first defeat was not just an accident). The fact that Hegel misses the excess of purely mechanical repetition in no way implies that he is excessively focused on the New (the progress which takes place through idealizing Aufhebung)—on the contrary, bearing in mind that the radically New emerges only through pure repetition, we should say that Hegel's inability to think pure repetition is the obverse of his inability to think the radically New, that is, a New, which is not potentially already in the Old and has just to be brought out into the open through the work of dialectical deployment.[6]

Repetition of Žižek's work opens up another problematic, that of formalization of his thought. At the risk of going against Žižek's own position, I argue that the main task of philosophers who are Žižekians, and work on the premises of a Žižekian philosophy, is to formalize his thought. Žižek's system of thought can be said to function as a Borromean knot: philosophy, psychoanalysis, and politics.[7] According to Žižek, "the three theoretical circles are not, however, of the same weight: it is their middle term, the theory of Jacques Lacan, which is—as Marx would say—'the general illumination which bathes all the other colours and modifies their particularity,' 'the particular ether which determines the specific gravity of every being which has materialized within it.'"[8]

Herein resides the difficulty of its formalization. A problematic comparison is that with the philosophy of Alain Badiou. To put it in a very simplified manner, in an elementary level, it is not a difficult task to be a follower of Badiou, or a Badiousian in philosophy, due to his very well-structured system. This holds true for being a Badiousian in the exegesis level. However, the case with Žižek is different: not only the formalization of his philosophy but also being faithful to his thought is a much more complicated philosophical enterprise.[9] Although one shouldn't dismiss Žižek's own indifference toward the proper philosophical "system," I want to argue (in a rather bombastic fashion) that the *only* way for his philosophy to resist both its time and its (what is wrongly described as) interventionist character is to subject his system to a rigorous formalization.

Therefore, the paradigm of this book resides on the two problems that are at stake here: that is the problem of repetition qua betrayal and formalization. The two concepts are interlinked: repetition of the philosopher's thought is always-already realized in the form of betrayal.

This volume is structured bearing in mind the Borromean knot. It is divided in philosophy, psychoanalysis, and politics. The fourth additional ring to be added to the Borromean knot is religion, thus supplementing his system. In this regard, this volume relates precisely to the structure of Žižek's thought: philosophy, psychoanalysis, politics, religion, *and* related matters.

Notes

1   Slavoj Žižek, *Philosophy Is Not a Dialogue*, in Alain Badiou and Slavoj Žižek, *Philosophy in the Present* (Cambridge: Polity, 2009), 49.

2   Slavoj Žižek and John Milbank, *The Monstrosity of Christ: Paradox or Dialectic?*, ed. Creston Davis (Cambridge: MIT Press, 2009), 235.

3   Although it is interesting to note that there has been a shift in this regard: from being labeled the "Elvis of cultural theory," that is to say, he's an amusing and funny guy to listen to, Žižek's status has been switched to that of "the most dangerous philosopher in the West." These labels are forms of censorship that in the last instance, attempts to establish a distance from *really* taking his work seriously.

4   Adrian Johnston, *Žižek's Ontology: A Transcendental Materialist Theory of Subjectivity* (Evanston, IL: Northwestern University Press, 2008), xiv.

5   Slavoj Žižek, *Organs without Bodies: On Deleuze and Consequences* (New York: Routledge, 2012), 12–13.

6   Slavoj Žižek, *Less Than Nothing: Hegel and the Shadow of Dialectical Materialism* (London: Verso, 2012), 455–56.

7   Indeed, this is how he describes the structure of his *For They Know Not What They Do*: "As with *The Sublime Object of Ideology*, the theoretical space of the present book is moulded by three centres of gravity: Hegelian dialectics, Lacanian psychoanalytic theory, and contemporary criticism of ideology. These three circles form a Borromean knot: each of them connects the other two"; Slavoj Žižek, *For They Know Not What They Do: Enjoyment as a Political Factor* (London: Verso, 2008), 2.

8   Žižek, *For They Know Not What They Do*, 2.

9   There has been some remarkable work on what I want to call "formalization" of Žižek's work. See Johnston, *Žižek's Ontology*; Fabio Vighi, *On Žižek's Dialectics: Surplus, Subtraction, Sublimation* (New York: Continuum, 2010), and others.

PART I | **philosophy**

1

"Freedom or System? Yes, Please!": How to Read Slavoj Žižek's *Less Than Nothing* — Hegel and the Shadow of Dialectical Materialism

Adrian Johnston

Already eagerly awaited years in advance of its eventual appearance, the hulking 2012 tome *Less Than Nothing: Hegel and the Shadow of Dialectical Materialism* is a (if not the) leading candidate to date among Slavoj Žižek's many books for the title of his magnum opus. Apart from introducing a range of new material within the still-unfolding Žižekian corpus, *Less Than Nothing* also consolidates in a single volume numerous lines of thought running throughout Žižek's various prior texts. In particular, this 2012 work involves Žižek presenting his most thorough and detailed account thus far both of his interpretation of the full sweep of Kantian and post–Kantian German idealism as well as of how his own theoretical project carries forward these idealists' legacies in the contexts of the early twenty-first century.

My goal in this intervention is relatively modest: to establish the preliminary basis for an immanent critical assessment of *Less Than Nothing*. Given that Žižek grounds this book and his larger philosophical pursuits first and foremost in the history of German idealism, revisiting this history is one of the mandatory preconditions for properly evaluating Žižek's 2012 masterpiece. After putting this historical frame in place in what immediately follows, I then go on to spend time philosophically reexamining Immanuel Kant and G. W. F. Hegel especially (including the complexities of the Kant-Hegel relationship) in light of how Žižek comprehends and appropriates their ideas and arguments. To be more specific, I herein interpret Žižek's philosophy as fundamentally a creative extension (one drawing on such post-Hegelian resources as Marxism and psychoanalysis) of certain precise features of the post-Fichtean "Spinozism of freedom" already envisioned by Friedrich Hölderlin, F. W. J. Schelling, and Hegel starting in the 1790s. Interpreting Žižek thus, my intervention here builds, via its historical and philosophical traversals of German idealism, toward a conclusion pinpointing the exact questions and problems Žižek's materialism must address if his overall theoretical position is to be judged to be cogent, persuasive, and satisfying. In short, these questions and problems set the immanent critical criteria for determining what a successful realization of the philosophical program of *Less Than Nothing* would have to accomplish.

An extremely brief period between the end of the eighteenth and beginning of the nineteenth centuries sees an incredible explosion of intense philosophical activity in the German-speaking world, perhaps rivaled solely by the birth of Western philosophy itself in ancient Greece (although Alain Badiou passionately maintains that postwar France is philosophically comparable to these other two momentously important times and places).[1] Inaugurated by Kant and accompanied by the Romantics as cultural fellow travelers, the set of orientations that has come to be known by the label "German idealism"—this movement spans just a few decades—partly originates in the 1780s with the debates generated by F. H. Jacobi's challenges to modern secular rationality generally, as well as Kant's then-new critical transcendental idealism especially.[2] One of the most provocative moves Jacobi makes is to confront his contemporaries with a stark forced choice between either "system" or "freedom" (to use language that Schelling, a German idealist giant, employs to designate this Jacobian dilemma and its many permutations and variants).[3] In Jacobi's Pietist Protestant view, the systematization of the allegedly contradiction-ridden Kantian philosophy—the post-Kantian idealists at least agree with Jacobi that Kant indeed falls short of achieving thoroughly rigorous systematicity—inevitably must result, as with any rationally systematic philosophy on Jacobi's assessment, in the very loss of what arguably is most dear to this philosophy itself in its contemporaneity with both the Enlightenment and, later, the French Revolution: in a word, autonomy (in Kant's specific case, the transcendental subject's powers of spontaneous judgment and self-determination).[4] Suffice it to say, Jacobi is far from satisfied with the attempted resolution of the third of the "antinomies of pure reason" in the *Critique of Pure Reason*.[5] This dissatisfaction is supported by Jacobi's undermining of the Kantian noumenal-phenomenal distinction through his criticisms of the thing-in-itself (*das Ding an sich*),[6] criticisms subsequently broadened and deepened by the "big three" of post-Kantian German idealism: J. G. Fichte, Schelling, and Hegel.

With the unintended effect of igniting a burning fascination with Baruch Spinoza among a younger generation of intellectuals, Jacobi, as part of his anti-Enlightenment agenda, contentiously claims that Spinoza's monistic substance metaphysics is the one and only system inevitably arrived at by all unflinchingly consistent and consequent philosophical reasoning. Construing this metaphysics as materialistic and naturalistic, Jacobi equates Spinozist ontology with freedom-denying, subject-squelching determinism (i.e., "fatalism") and therefore also with atheistic "nihilism."[7] The "pantheism controversy" (*Pantheismusstreit*) triggered by Jacobi's polemicizing saddles Kant's idealist successors, insofar as they wish to systematize Kantian philosophy (with varying degrees of sympathy and fidelity), with the task of formulating a totally coherent metaphysics (qua a seamlessly integrated epistemology and ontology) nonetheless preserving space within itself for the spontaneity of self-determining subjectivity.[8]

Inspired by the failed efforts of K. L. Reinhold, the first (but far from foremost) post-Kantian German idealist, to ground Kant's critical-transcendental edifice on the firmer foundation of an apodictic first principle (i.e., an indubitable *Grundsatz* methodologically akin to René Descartes's Archimedean proposition "Cogito, ergo sum"),[9] Fichte opts for a radical "primacy of the practical" as the key to a systematized (post)-Kantianism. Skipping over numerous details here, Fichte's position, as per his 1794 *Wissenschaftslehre* rooted in nothing more than the free activity of spontaneous subjectivity, quickly is itself found to be wanting in turn by certain of his contemporaries and soon-to-be immediate successors. Hölderlin's 1795 fragment "Über Urtheil und Seyn" (On Judgment and Being), penned by someone fresh from hearing Fichte lecture on this "scientific teaching," lays down the initial sketches for myriad subsequent arguments of his Tübingen seminary classmates Schelling and Hegel against the allegedly excessive subjectivism of Fichte's (and Kant's) brand of idealism.[10] Hölderlin suggests the ultimate ontological unavoidability of presupposing or positing a non-/pre-subjective ground of being in relation to which the transcendental subject à la Kant and Fichte is a secondary outgrowth. His fragment heralds the final, post-Fichtean phase of classical German idealism (starting with Schelling's very public break with Fichte in 1801)[11] insofar as this phase is animated by, among other things, the pursuit of a "Spinozism of freedom," namely, a dialectical-speculative synthesis of Spinoza (qua a proper name for the system of substance) with Kant and Fichte (qua proper names for the freedom of the subject).[12] Hegel's insistence, in the deservedly celebrated preface to his 1807 *Phenomenology of Spirit*, on "grasping and expressing the True, not only as *Substance*, but equally as *Subject*" ("das Wahre nicht als *Substanz*, sondern ebensosehr als *Subjekt* aufzufassen und auszudrücken"),[13] is only the most famous slogan-like articulation of this far-reaching ambition kindled in him and Schelling by their dear old school friend the philosophically minded great poet.[14]

Dated a year later than "Über Urtheil und Seyn," the short "Earliest System-Program of German Idealism" can be read as resonating with Hölderlin's text. Although written in Hegel's handwriting, the authorship of this 1796 fragment remains a matter of dispute among specialists in German idealism, with Hölderlin, Schelling, and Hegel all being put forward as possibly responsible for it. Regardless of which member of the Tübinger Stift trio originally composed it — I happen to favor those scholars, such as Otto Pöggeler and H. S. Harris, who make the case for Hegel being its original author[15] — the "program" announced and outlined in it undeniably sets lasting key priorities for the subsequent philosophical agendas of both Schelling and Hegel.[16]

As regards the project of a post-Fichtean, Hölderlin-inspired Spinozism of freedom in particular, "The Earliest System-Program of German Idealism" gestures specifically at the project of reverse engineering a (quasi-)naturalistic fundamental ontology (dealing with substance as per a *Naturphilosophie*) out of an axiomatically postulated affirmation of the actual, factual existence of spontaneous, autonomous selves (i.e., the subjects of transcendental idealist reflections).[17] This fragment's author declares:

> Since the whole of metaphysics falls for the future within moral theory . . .
> this ethics will be nothing less than a complete system of all ideas or of all

practical postulates (which is the same thing). The first idea is, of course, the presentation of myself as an absolutely free entity. Along with the free, self-conscious essence, there stands forth—out of nothing—an entire world, the one true and thinkable creation out of nothing.—Here I shall descend into the realms of physics; the question is this: how must a world be constituted for a moral entity? I would like to give wings once more to our backward physics, that advances laboriously by experiments.[18]

The text continues:

Thus, if philosophy supplies the ideas, and experience the data, we may at last come to have in essentials the physics that I look forward to for later times. It does not appear that our present-day physics can satisfy a creative spirit such as ours is or ought to be.[19]

Hegel and Schelling, regardless of who originally composed these lines, both go on to carry out the endeavor called for in these quoted passages.[20] So, appropriately combining the two pairs of terms "substance" and "subject" (à la Hegel) and "system" and "freedom" (à la Schelling)—these terms refer in part to Hegel's and Schelling's subsequent fulfillments of this 1796 "program"—the "physics" (*Physik*)[21] demanded here would amount to nothing less than a philosophical/ontological system of natural substance as itself autodialectically self-denaturalizing ("a world . . . constituted for a moral entity") given that it has internally generated the freedom of autonomous subjectivity ("myself as an absolutely free entity") as a transcendence-in-immanence relative to it. In this context, the names "Spinoza" on the one hand and "Kant" and "Fichte" on the other stand for the monist-naturalist system of substance and transcendental idealist freedom of the subject, respectively.

Less Than Nothing requires for its proper evaluation being interpreted in relation to the background I have just summarized rather quickly in the preceding. (Incidentally, Badiou's sustained Lacan-inspired efforts to synthesize the existentialism of Jean-Paul Sartre and the structuralism of Louis Althusser likewise should be viewed as reengaging in the pursuit of a Spinozism of freedom—and this thanks to their avowed inheritance of Spinozism [Althusser] and transcendental idealism [Sartre].)[22] In the introduction to his 2012 magnum opus, Žižek clearly and explicitly situates this book with respect to the hypercompressed history of

German idealism in its full sweep. To begin with, he insists that the history of philosophy as philosophy proper only well and truly gets under way with Kant (an insistence he has voiced elsewhere too),[23] with this history rapidly gaining momentum through Kant's immediate successors.[24] Žižek speaks of "the unbearable density of thought . . . provided by the mother of all Gangs of Four: Kant, Fichte, Schelling, Hegel."[25]

Žižek's preliminary retelling of the story of German idealism as an introductory framing of *Less Than Nothing* focuses primarily on Kant's critical-transcendental turn as epitomized by the second half of the *Critique of Pure Reason*, namely, the "Transcendental Dialectic," wherein Kant purports to reveal the ultimate vanity of pure reason's pretensions to enjoy direct epistemological access to the independent ontological reality of such things-in-themselves as the soul, the cosmos, and God (i.e., the three "ideas of reason" generated by the "interest of reason" in achieving ultimate points of englobing synthesis: the "psychological," "cosmological," and "theological" ideas). Žižek, in his introduction, contrasts Kant's epistemological dialectics with the ontological dialectics of Schelling and Hegel, all the while acknowledging the profound indebtedness of the latter two to the former. As he lucidly spells out here, Kant's reactivation and redeployment of the ancient art of dialectics (paradigmatically on display in Plato's dialogue *Parmenides*, with which Žižek soon proceeds to engage)[26] begins by irreparably shattering pre-Kantian metaphysical worldviews, introducing corrosive antinomies, contradictions, and the like into them. And, in the hands of the post-Kantians Schelling and Hegel, this Kantian revival of dialectics ends up, as it were, destroying the world itself qua image of being as a monolithic, unified One, a harmonious, coherent All. In other words, the ontologization of Kantian critical epistemology as per the first *Critique*'s "Transcendental Dialectic" means that not only is the thinking of being inconsistent, but that being *an sich* is itself inconsistent too. Hegel achieves this breakthrough during his pre-*Phenomenology* Jena period when he finally drops the distinction between logic (as the thinking of epistemology) and metaphysics (as the being of ontology), with the consequence that the speculative dialectics of logic come to infect metaphysics/ontology.[27] As for Schelling, Žižek restricts his praise along these precise lines to Schelling's middle period running from 1809 (with the *Freiheitschrift*) to 1815 (with the third draft of the *Weltalter* manuscripts).[28] Furthermore, in the cases

of both the mature Hegel and the middle-period Schelling, Žižek per-
spicuously discerns a decisive advance over Hölderlin's pioneering 1795
vision in "Über Urtheil und Seyn": whereas the Spinozism of freedom
à la Hölderlin posits the ultimate substance of being as a seamless, un-
differentiated Absolute (in the style of a neo-Platonic One), the versions
of Hegel and Schelling beloved by Žižek radicalize this post-Fichtean
project by injecting antagonisms, conflicts, gaps, splits, and so on into
this Absolute itself[29] (although I think Žižek overlooks select moments
in the young Schelling's Naturphilosophie that already foreshadow, as
early as 1798, the theosophical framings of primordial negativity in his
subsequent 1809–1815 middle period).[30]

In my 2008 book *Žižek's Ontology: A Transcendental Materialist
Theory of Subjectivity*, I stress the importance for Žižek of construing the
transition from Kant to Hegel as one from epistemological to ontological
dialectics, with Hegel (and a specific Schelling) "ontologizing" the critical Kant.[31] (Given that I treat Žižek's philosophical apparatus as per his
earlier works at length in this book, I will focus here almost exclusively
on *Less Than Nothing*.) At multiple junctures in *Less Than Nothing*, Žižek
continues to characterize the Kant-Hegel rapport in these same terms.[32]
However, at other moments therein, he goes out of his way to correct
this (mis)characterization (a new gesture of his surfacing for the first
time in *Less Than Nothing*).[33] I suspect that, without him explicitly saying as much, this is both a self-critique of his earlier depictions of Kant
avec Hegel as well as a critique of my exegesis in this vein as per *Žižek's
Ontology*. Žižek's critical qualifications begin thusly:

> Kant . . . goes only half-way in his destruction of metaphysics, still main-
> taining the reference to the Thing-in-itself as an external inaccessible
> entity, and Hegel is merely a radicalized Kant, who moves from our nega-
> tive access to the Absolute to the Absolute itself as negativity. Or, to put
> it in terms of the Hegelian shift from epistemological obstacle to positive
> ontological condition (our incomplete knowledge of the thing becomes a
> positive feature of the thing which is in itself incomplete, inconsistent): it
> is not that Hegel "ontologizes" Kant; on the contrary, it is Kant who, in-
> sofar as he conceives the gap as merely epistemological, continues to pre-
> suppose a fully constituted noumenal realm existing out there, and it is
> Hegel who "deontologizes" Kant, introducing a gap into the very texture

of reality. In other words, Hegel's move is not to "overcome" the Kantian division, but, rather, to assert it "as such," to *remove the need for its "overcoming*," for the additional "reconciliation" of the opposites, that is, to gain the insight—through a purely formal parallax shift—into how positing the distinction "as such" already *is* the looked-for "reconciliation." Kant's limitation lies not in his remaining within the confines of finite oppositions, in his inability to reach the Infinite, but, on the contrary, in his very search for a transcendent domain beyond the realm of finite oppositions: Kant is not unable to reach the Infinite—what he is unable to see is how he *already has what he is looking for*.[34]

Kant might retort that it is not he who is invested in a "search for a transcendent domain" but, instead, the faculty of reason (*Vernunft*) itself whose operations he merely describes, including its interest-driven, illusion-generating "constitutive" abuses (rather than legitimate "regulative" uses) of its ideas (i.e., the ideas of the soul, the cosmos, and God).[35] He also perhaps would underscore that, on a couple of occasions in the second edition (B version) of the first *Critique* (and possibly in response to certain reactions to the first edition [A version]),[36] he deems his "Transcendental Analytic" of the understanding (*Verstand*) as well as transcendental philosophy *überhaupt* qua a specific treatment of the faculties of both understanding and reason to be replacements for traditional ontologies erroneously and vainly aiming at transcendent things-in-themselves.[37] (However, one readily could counter-argue that the subjective idealism of Kantian critique offers an "ontology" only on the basis of a glaringly equivocal use of this word.) Anyhow, Žižek soon proceeds to reiterate that "at its most elementary, Hegel's move is a reduction, not an enrichment, of Kant: a *subtractive* move, a gesture of taking away the metaphysical ballast and of analyzing notional determinations in their immanent nature."[38] Or, as he puts it again a little later,

> with his philosophical revolution, Kant made a breakthrough the radicality of which he was himself unaware; so, in a second move, he withdraws from this radicality and desperately tries to navigate into the safe waters of a more traditional ontology. Consequently, in order to pass "from Kant to Hegel," we have to move not "forward" but backward: back from the deceptive envelope to identify the true radicality of Kant's breakthrough—in this sense, Hegel was literally "more Kantian than Kant

himself." One of the points where we see this clearly is in the distinction between phenomena and noumena: Kant's explicit justification of why we need to introduce noumena remains well within the confines of traditional ontology with its distinction between appearance and true reality.[39]

As I indicated a short while ago, not only in his earlier writings, but even at other points in *Less Than Nothing*, Žižek still sometimes has recourse to the depiction of Hegel ontologizing Kant despite these just-quoted (seeming) inversions of this depiction. For now, I wish to take some time to show that the apparent contradiction between ontologizing and de-ontologizing in Žižek's 180-degree reversal is just an appearance. That is to say, my contention (perhaps with Žižek, perhaps against him) is that these are two sides of the same coin; rather than contradicting each other, they are of a piece, namely, the recto and verso of a single rendition of the transition from Kant to Hegel. How so?

The key to dispelling the semblance of incompatibility between talk of Hegel "ontologizing" and "deontologizing" Kant resides in appreciating the relation (or lack thereof) between epistemology and ontology in Kant's critical framework (particularly that of the *Critique of Pure Reason*). As Žižek observes elsewhere in *Less Than Nothing*, "one cannot avoid ontology."[40] This observation is directly relevant here because, on a certain reading, Kant indeed attempts to "avoid ontology" in his transcendental turn. To be more exact, the first *Critique* prohibits traditional ontological investigations insofar as it rules out as epistemologically invalid any robustly realist metaphysics purporting to address directly mind-independent objective (as asubjective) being(s) (i.e., the being qua being of things-in-themselves). Epistemology-obsessed critique bans and itself replaces every ontology ostensibly getting its hands on being over and above thinking. But, as with the John Locke of the inconsistency-riddled 1690 *An Essay Concerning Human Understanding*—this work intends to sidestep ontological issues in focusing exclusively on (empiricist) epistemological inquiries[41]—so too with Kant:

> no philosophy can avoid entirely certain foundational ontological commitments . . . even Kant's critical philosophy, which defensibly can be construed as an extremely careful and rigorous attempt to turn philosophizing away from speculations into the bedrock substantial reality of what is and toward primarily epistemological concerns, fails to refrain

from dogmatically endorsing select presuppositions about the fundamental nature of being apart from subjectively mediated knowledge of
it. Prior to Kant, the much more obvious and striking inconsistencies of
an important empiricist textual precursor of key aspects of Kant's first
Critique, John Locke's *An Essay Concerning Human Understanding*, arguably are symptomatic points of torsion and conflict within Kantian
transcendental idealism too. Therein, Locke basically seems to say such
self-contradictory things as "We can't intelligibly talk about substance in
itself, but only our mental ideas of it . . . Now, let's talk about substance in
itself." However, given Kant's significantly greater philosophical sophis-
tication and finesse as compared with Locke (at least at the level of theoretical, if not practical, philosophy), the inconsistencies glaringly manifest in the latter's 1690 text, inconsistencies resulting from the ontology
repressed in favor of epistemology intrusively and insistently returning in
a variety of ways, are less visible in the *Critique of Pure Reason*. Thanks to
his highly skillful and refined systematicity, Kant, whether purposefully
or not, is better at smoothly concealing what Locke, in his relative clum-
siness, stumbles into openly revealing—namely, than an epistemology of
the subjective mind cannot succeed at completely avoiding the violation
of its own self-imposed limits (such as the [in]famous Kantian "limits of
possible experience") by hypothesizing things about the ontology of the
objective world *an sich*.[42]

On such a construal of Kantian transcendental idealism, the critical
apparatus, inadvertently but inevitably contradicting itself, of necessity inconsistently presupposes and/or posits a spontaneous ontology in
tandem with its epistemology and vainly attempted ontological agnos-
ticism.[43] This ontology manifests itself primarily in the guise of the
notorious distinction between on one side subjective and intersubjective phenomenal objects-as-appearances and on another side asubjective
noumenal things-in-themselves. As is common knowledge, one of the
unifying features of post-Kantian German idealism is its pointed rejection of this very distinction, with it taking to heart Jacobi's quip about
das Ding an sich (as a "presupposition" in relation to the *Critique of Pure
Reason*) that, "*without* that presupposition I could not enter into the system, but *with* it I could not stay within it."[44] Fichte, Schelling, and Hegel,
in often overlapping manners, all launch multiple assaults against the

defensibility and coherence of *das Ding an sich*, itself a symptom of what they take to be a systematically untenable two-worlds metaphysics implicit in Kant's mature philosophy.[45] (The fact that legions of subsequent Kant scholars have strained mightily to exculpate Kant of any commitment whatsoever to a two-worlds metaphysics tacitly testifies to the devastating strength of the German idealists' criticisms of those aspects and moments of Kant's texts flirting with, if not outright embracing, such a metaphysics.) Hence, post-Kantian German idealism generally and Hegel specifically "deontologize" this Kant, namely, the one who, despite the breathtakingly inventive ingeniousness of his "Copernican" critical-transcendental revolution,[46] nonetheless continues to remain attached to a traditional mind-world image of the order of being(s) ultimately no more sophisticated than, for instance, that of Locke's vulgar, quotidian "common sense." In particular, Hegel's repeated demonstrations of the self-induced dialectics subversively sublating from within such load-bearing pillars of Kant's weltanschauung as the thing-in-itself and the *Verstand*-level dichotomies between subject and object as well as phenomena and noumena—Hegel's recurrent stress (echoed by Žižek)[47] on the self-undermining (il)logical nature of the figure of the "limit" relied on by Kant (with his central "limits of possible experience") attacks both dichotomies at their root,[48] in addition to the numerous separate criticisms of each dichotomy on its own—are immanent critiques of the spontaneous ontology of Kantian transcendentalism as "subjective idealism."

But one of the main aims of post-Fichtean idealism is precisely to (re)"ontologize" there where critique tried to deontologize (albeit arguably failed). Schelling's "objective idealism," as per his relatively youthful philosophies of nature and identity circa the late 1790s and early 1800s, and Hegel's "absolute idealism" are both efforts to overcome the alleged one-sided subjectivism of Kant's and Fichte's transcendental idealism (in line with Žižek's Hegelian partisanship—as Žižek remarks in *Less Than Nothing*, "for Hegel, the true ('concrete') universality is accessible only from an engaged 'partial' standpoint"[49]—I here obviously employ and endorse Hegel's tripartite distinction between subjective, objective, and absolute idealisms).[50] Schelling's and Hegel's talk of "the Absolute," "the Infinite," "Nature," "Substance," and so on, whatever differences there admittedly are both between these terms themselves as well as between

Schellingian and Hegelian senses of them, essentially involves reference to ontological dimensions repressed by Kantian and Fichtean transcendental idealisms—dimensions that Schelling and Hegel adamantly contend must return within a fully systematized postcritical philosophy (one violating the letter in the very name of the spirit of Kant's philosophy).

Schelling aside for now, Hegel's critiques of Kant result in a proper sublation *als Aufhebung* of transcendental idealism (as is to be entirely expected with Hegel). That is to say, these critiques are not mere indeterminate negations as one-sided cancellations or razings of Kant's philosophy from outside it, namely, simple annihilations or obliterations of this philosophy leading to nothing else specific in its place beyond this voiding destruction. Rather, as per the two-sidedness characteristic of Hegel's dialectical-speculative Aufhebung,[51] his Kant critiques are "determinate negations"[52] qua movements arguably immanent to the structures and dynamics of Kant's own position. As Jacques Lacan would put it, Hegel seeks to trace trajectories that are "extimate" (i.e., intimately and internally external, endogenously exogenous) with respect to Kant insofar as they are consequent extensions of Kantianisn "in Kantianism more than Kantianism itself."[53] Right before his death, in his 1831 Berlin course on the *Encyclopedia Logic*, Hegel himself observes that "what is most interesting are the points where Kant reaches beyond himself."[54] Put differently, in both senses of the prefix "post" (i.e., as the continuity of coming after and the discontinuity of moving beyond), Hegel is, with an ambivalence appropriate to dialectical speculation, a post-Kantian (rather than seeking to be a regressive pre-Kantian reacting against the critical Copernican revolution).[55]

More specifically, Hegel embraces and extends Kant's modern critical revivification of ancient dialectics (as per the latter half of the first *Critique*)[56] while nonetheless still jettisoning anything and everything in Kantian transcendental idealism even so much as hinting at a two-worlds metaphysics (such as *das Ding an sich*, the distinction between noumena and phenomena, and the figure of the limit à la the ostensible limits of possible experience). The implications of this composite, both-affirming-and-negating gesture vis-à-vis Kant bring me back to Žižek and the question of whether Hegel ontologizes or deontologizes Kant's critical-transcendental framework. As I underlined earlier, Žižek, in *Less Than Nothing*, both alternates between invoking ontologization and de-ontologization with respect to the Kant-Hegel transition and insists on the inevitability and necessity of ontological commitments even for philosophers (such as Locke and Kant) who wish to remain ontologically noncommittal. Remembering these features of Žižek's reflections in his 2012 book in conjunction with my immediately preceding glosses on Kantian and Hegelian philosophies, it now readily can be comprehended why I asserted above that Hegel's cancellation of the spontaneous ontology implicit in Kant's critical apparatus (i.e., Kant's subjective idealist two-worlds metaphysics) is, at one and the same time as a dialectical gesture, an elevation to a new ontology. Hegel's liquidation of Kantian two-worlds metaphysics is combined with his simultaneous retention of Kant's transcendental dialectics (with the latter being, for Kant himself, purely epistemological, ideational, and subjective, namely, de/non-ontological). If, as per both the post-Fichtean idealists and Žižek, ontology ultimately is unavoidable, then, after Hegel's negation of any noumenal Beyond as the transcendent subsistence of contradiction-free, self-consistent things-in-themselves, the contradiction-ridden, inconsistent realm of experience is all there is; with the unavoidability of the ontological, the antinomy-plagued not-All of multiple teeming phenomena must itself be treated as the very Real of being qua being. For Hegel, epistemology without ontology is impossible. This impossibility, were it possible, would be a nonmetaphysical theory of knowing and thinking subjectivity sans presuppositions or posits about asubjective being *an sich* (this would include Kant's subjectively idealist critical approach as non/post-metaphysical). With Hegel's post-Kantianism, this leaves the field of phenomena already dialecticized by the *Critique of Pure Reason* as the sole reality for the ontology of a one-world metaphysics devoid of any transcendent Elsewhere (i.e., as the Absolute in a certain Hegelian sense). As Žižek expresses this in the third chapter of *Less Than Nothing* ("Fichte's Choice"), *"the 'Absolute' beyond appearances coincides with an 'absolute appearance,' an appearance beneath which there is no substantial Being"* (I will refer to this line again later).[57]

A passage in a longish letter of October 23, 1812, from Hegel to his friend and professional protector Friedrich Immanuel Niethammer—by then Bavarian minister of education, on whom Hegel pins his hopes for a desperately desired university post—is especially revealing along these lines. Writing while he is in the midst of working on the *Science of*

Logic, Hegel explains (in connection with his pedagogy as a gymnasium teacher in Nuremberg):

> according to my view, metaphysics . . . falls entirely within logic. Here I can cite Kant as my predecessor and authority. His critique reduces metaphysics as it has existed until now to a consideration of the understanding and reason. Logic can thus in the Kantian sense be understood so that, beyond the usual content of so-called general logic, what he calls transcendental logic is bound up with it and set out prior to it. In point of content I mean the doctrine of the categories, or reflective concepts, and then of the concepts of reason: analytic and dialectic. These objective thought forms constitute an independent content [corresponding to] the role of the Aristotelian Categories [organon de categoriis] or the former ontology. Further, they are independent of one's metaphysical system. They occur in transcendental idealism as much as in dogmatism. The latter calls them determinations of being [Entium], while the former calls them determinations of the understanding. My objective logic will, I hope, purify this science once again, expositing it in its true worth, but until it is better known those Kantian distinctions already contain a makeshift or rough version of it.[58]

As I noted earlier, Hegel, already during his pre-*Phenomenology* Jena period, takes the crucial step of dissolving the distinction between ideational logic (as subjectivist and epistemological) and ontological metaphysics (as philosophically practiced by pre-Kantians ranging from Aristotle to the early modern rationalist substance metaphysicians [Descartes, Nicolas Malebranche, Spinoza, Gottfried Wilhelm Leibniz, and their ilk] and, even closer in time and place to the German idealists, Christian Wolff and his Leibnizian school). For the mature Hegel, logic properly conceived is the one and only possible metaphysics ("metaphysics . . . falls entirely within logic").[59] Furthermore, the quotation immediately above reveals that Kant's "transcendental logic"—Hegel here stipulates that by this phrase he means to encompass dimensions from both the "Transcendental Analytic" of the understanding and the "Transcendental Dialectic" of reason in the first Critique—furnishes the skeletal rudiments for the first two-thirds (i.e., the "Objective Logic" of "The Doctrine of Being" and "The Doctrine of Essence" in both the Science of Logic and Encyclopedia Logic) of Hegel's post–Jena system of speculative philosophical *Wissenschaft als Logik*.[60] As Hegel says in the quotation above, "those Kantian distinctions already contain a make-shift or rough version of it" ("it" being Hegel's "Objective Logic"). The beginning of the "Objective Logic," as the beginning of Hegel's logic überhaupt, starts with mere, sheer "Being" (Sein). This starting point is led up to by the 1807 *Phenomenology* as itself an "introduction" of a uniquely peculiar kind to the Hegelian system proper. This peculiarity is due to it being always-already immanently within the post-Spinozistic genuine (instead of bad/spurious) infinity of a system necessarily brooking no independent externalities as non/extra-systemic transcendences.[61] That is to say, if an introduction to something is external (as preceding) that which it introduces (as something else separate from and coming after it), then the *Phenomenology* is not an introduction since it is, from its inception and in its entirety, situated completely within what it nevertheless introduces in its own strange way(s).[62] In addition, the *Phenomenology* is defensibly describable as the (pre)history of self-sublating presuppositions (i.e., the Gestalten of consciousness [Bewußtsein] and/as Spirit [Geist]) leading up to what is presented as the "presuppositionless" initiation of the structured dynamics of more-than-phenomenological logic proper.[63]

In his prefacing of the *Encyclopedia Logic* (specifically, §§ 26–78 of the *Encyclopedia of the Philosophical Sciences* under the heading "Preliminary Conception"), Hegel employs a process-of-elimination argumentative strategy against alternate, non-Hegelian positions. One might feel licensed to reread the *Phenomenology*, with the benefit of this hindsight from the *Encyclopedia*, as a single, massive process-of-elimination argument—more precisely, this "elimination" is sublation als Aufhebung, rather than plain old negation as simple, straightforward elimination-without-remainder—executed by the figures/shapes of consciousness/Spirit bringing about their self-wrought ruin through "doing violence to themselves at their own hands."[64] The post-*Phenomenology* logical beginning of both the *Science of Logic* and the *Encyclopedia* therefore non-dogmatically presupposes, among other things, the (self-)sublation of Kant's two-worlds metaphysics and its accompanying supports. Dogmatism is avoided thanks to the positing of the immanent critical arguments thoroughly delineated by the *Phenomenology*; the arguments particularly relevant to Hegel's critiques of Kant's theoretical philosophy occur in, among other places in the *Phenomenology*, the second and third chapters on "Perception: Or the Thing and Deception" and "Force and the Understanding: Appearance and the Supersensible World."[65] Thus, the Being begun with at the logical start of the system as a whole, with this beginning being preserved (insofar as it is sublated [*als aufgehobene*]) throughout everything that follows thereafter,[66] is, contra the critical strictures of Kant's post-Lockean epistemological "limits of possible experience," something ontologically grounding a post-Kantian metaphysics (i.e., the "future metaphysics" Hegel maintains Kant did not realize he essentially already possessed in outline in the form of his transcendental logic[67]).

So, referring back to Žižek again, Hegel deontologizes Kant precisely through immanently critiquing his two-worlds metaphysics (a spontaneous metaphysics/ontology entailed by the limits of possible experience, themselves inextricably intertwined with the rigid dualism partitioning a subjective realm of phenomenal objects-as-appearances and an objective realm of noumenal things-in-themselves). However, Hegel affirms, extends, and intensifies Kant's analytics and, especially, dialectics of Verstand and Vernunft (particularly the dialectical antinomies of pure reason).[68] He is therefore compelled, by his own systematic rationality, to ontologize the explicit epistemology that these components of Kant's critical edifice constitute, since these are the only components left after the exorcism of any unknowable transcendent Beyond.

However, the Hegelianism of *Less Than Nothing* should not be misunderstood as categorically canceling out the notion of "appearance" à la Kantian transcendental idealism. In fact, a certain precise conception of appearances forms one of the (if not the) unifying motifs of the whole thousand-page course of Žižek's 2012 tour de force. Of course, as regards Hegel in this context, the first association likely to come to anyone's mind is a well-known passage from the third chapter of the *Phenomenology* ("Force and the Understanding"):

> the inner world [Das Innere], or supersensible beyond [übersinnliche Jenseits], has, however, *come into being*: it *comes from* the world of appearance, which has mediated it; in other words, appearance is its essence [die Erscheinung ist sein Wesen] and, in fact, its filling. The supersensible is the sensuous and the perceived [das Sinnliche und Wahrgenommenen] posited as it is *in truth*; but the *truth* of the sensuous and the perceived is

to be *appearance*. The supersensible is therefore *appearance qua appearance* [Erscheinung *als* Erscheinung]. We completely misunderstand [verkehrtes Verstehen] this if we think that the supersensible world is *therefore* the sensuous world, or the world as it exists for immediate sense-certainty and perception; for the world of appearance is, on the contrary, *not* the world of sense-knowledge and perception as a world that positively *is*, but this world posited as superseded [als aufgehobene], or as in truth an *inner world*. It is often said that the supersensible world is *not* appearance; but what is here understood by appearance is not appearance, but rather the *sensuous* world as itself the really actual [reelle Wirklichkeit].[69]

Just before these observations, Hegel vehemently insists on the null-and-void philosophical vacuity of Kantian-style subjective idealist versions of this "supersensible beyond" as an inaccessible realm of hidden, withdrawn noumenal presences.[70] (This reiterates some of Hegel's criticisms of Kant's thing-in-itself already advanced by the former prior to the *Phenomenology* itself in 1802's *Glauben und Wissen*.)[71] Now, the phenomenological genesis of the category of appearance in the *Phenomenology*'s third chapter is preceded and made possible by its first two chapters, namely, the sensuous immediacies and perceptual things (*das Sinnliche und Wahrgenommenen*) of "Sense-Certainty" (*sinnliche Gewißheit*) and "Perception" (*Wahrnehmung*), respectively. These prior two types of phenomenal objects of conscious experiences become appearances proper, in Hegel's precise sense of "appearance" here, if and when consciousness responds to the dialectics afflicting Sense-Certainty and Perception by morphing into "the Understanding" (Verstand) per se (i.e., the third figure/shape of consciousness after these first two). In other words, this metamorphosis occurs if and when the contradictions plaguing sensuous immediacies and perceptual things succeed at prompting an apperceptive shift in consciousness such that it proceeds to hypothesize the being of a non-phenomenal essence, ground, or substratum subsisting behind, beneath, or beyond the manifest façade of fragmentary, unstable phenomena.[72]

In transforming from Perception into the Understanding, phenomenological consciousness apperceptively transsubstantiates phenomena into appearances proper. But, what, for Hegel, is the difference between on the one hand a sensuous immediacy (à la Sense-Certainty) or perceptual thing (à la Perception) and on the other hand an appearance (à la the Understanding)? The former two categories of phenomena both treat their manifestations as direct disclosures of the objective being of the real world manifesting itself in and through such phenomena; the latter (i.e., appearance), by contrast, entails a doubling of reality whereby phenomena become, at best and most, indirect manifestations of nonmanifest entities and/or events. The very notion of appearance always-already brings with it by way of automatic implication the image of a veil of appearances, an image dear to the tradition of two-worlds metaphysics. That is to say, conceiving of a phenomenon as an appearance necessarily involves presupposing or positing a distinction between the appearing of the appearance itself and the underlying "what" of the nonappearing "x" presumably responsible for the appearance. Put differently, the Understanding divides the real world of Sense-Certainty and Perception into an "outer world" (i.e., the visible surface of the manifest phenomenon) and an "inner world" (i.e., the invisible depth of the nonmanifest noumenon or similar non-Kantian equivalent). Given the Hegelian phenomenological account, this inner world (*das Innere als übersinnliche Jenseits*) not only is a secondary effect rather than a primary cause—it "has . . . *come into being*" instead of, as per traditional two-worlds metaphysics (Kantian transcendental idealism as subjectivism included), the supersensible preexisting and producing the sensible—but also is generated specifically through the deployment by intentional consciousness of the category of appearance ("it *comes from* the world of appearance"). Hence, Hegel proclaims that "the supersensible is therefore *appearance qua appearance* (Erscheinung *als* Erscheinung)." That is to say, thinking of phenomena precisely as appearances in accordance with the strict meaning of "appearance" (i.e., as "*appearance* qua *appearance*" rather than as either appearance qua sensuous immediacy or appearance qua perceptual thing) is, at one and the same time, also to think of them as the sensible (mis)-representatives of supersensible beings. Subsequently, in various versions of his Logic, Hegel furnishes the logical scaffoldings of the dialectical-phenomenological dynamics of appearing in the earlier *Phenomenology*.[73]

Hegel retains the category of appearance despite his critical reflections regarding it (as is fitting in the process of sublation). In the block quotation from the *Phenomenology* above, he alerts readers to the fact that he is not here collapsing appearances back into phenomena as either sensuous immediacies or perceived things. ("We completely misunderstand [verkehrtes Verstehen] this if we think that the supersensible world is *therefore* the sensuous world, or the world as it exists for immediate sense-certainty and perception.") Only for a wrongheaded, upside-down understanding (as "verkehrtes Verstehen") is the denial of a supersensible beyond automatically tantamount to the (re)affirmation of a flat sensible here-and-now. This topsy-turvy Verstand, as still a figure/shape of Consciousness as per the first section of the *Phenomenology* (and, thus, still wedded, like Sense-Certainty and Perception before it, to asubjective objectivity as its self-imposed standard of the Whole Truth), lapses into this false dilemma between a supersensible beyond or a flat sensible here-and-now because, for it, *das Innere als übersinnliche Jenseits* can be only an external, objective inner world, namely, an outer inner, so to speak. In Hegel's eyes, the transition from sensed and perceived phenomena to apperceived appearances indeed counts as genuine dialectical progress.

In fact, at this stage in the *Phenomenology*, Hegel hails the emergence of the supersensible beyond in and through appearance as providing the first phenomenological glimpse of "Reason" (Vernunft) proper,[74] with the latter (as per the third section of the *Phenomenology* entitled "Reason") being already the initial incarnation of Hegel's own absolute idealism.[75] For Hegel, insofar as the Understanding's misunderstanding of its inner world as an objective interiority is an exact 180-degree inversion of the truth, it needs merely to be stood upright back on its own feet as, instead, a subjective interiority. In other words, phenomena actually are appearances insofar as there indeed is an inner world beyond them. ("The world of appearance is, on the contrary, *not* the world of sense-knowledge and perception as a world that positively *is*, but this world posited as superseded [als aufgehobene], or as in truth an *inner world*.") However, this inner world is nothing other than apperceiving subjectivity itself. Hence, as Hegel proposes at the end of the *Phenomenology*'s chapter "Force and the Understanding" (this being the conclusion of the entire first section on "Consciousness"), what Consciousness uncovers when it finally manages to tear aside the veil of appearances is just its own activity; behind this veil is, as it were, a mirror.[76] Consciousness becomes conscious of itself (i.e., Self-Consciousness, the subject of the next section of the *Phenomenology*) as a supersensible inner world to the extent that it now experiences itself as a beyond superseding the objective outer world of the sensible, the phenomenal, and the apparent.

All of the preceding apropos the topic of Hegel on appearances is immensely important to Žižek himself throughout various versions of the texts constituting his still-unfolding oeuvre.[77] The theme of appearance is especially central to *Less Than Nothing*. Already on its fourth page, Žižek asserts that "beyond the fiction of reality, there is the reality of the fiction."[78] This "reality of the fiction" is incarnated in a number of guises in the Žižekian theoretical universe, including "concrete universality" (as per Hegel), "real abstraction" (as per Karl Marx), and "structures that march in the streets" (as per Lacan).[79] Žižek and Alenka Zupančič also sometimes refer to this set of closely interrelated notions with the phrase "the Real of an illusion."[80]

With respect to German idealism generally and Hegel particularly, Žižek signals early in the introduction to *Less Than Nothing* that a major preoccupation throughout this gargantuan piece of work will be the topic of appearances. This topic is addressed by him along three precise lines of inquiry. First are the connected questions of how and why being appears to itself. (That is, how and why *Sein an sich* doubles itself in becoming self-reflective/reflexive by giving rise to appearances out of its own substantial, monistic flatness—neither Schelling nor Hegel consider their dear Spinoza as having asked and answered these ultimately unavoidable, mandatory queries,[81] and Žižek likewise indicts Badiou's materialism as guilty of the same failure.)[82] Second are the similar connected questions of how and why the internal genesis of appearance in and through being also generates subjectivity as a transcendence-in-immanence vis-à-vis its ontological ground *als Ur/Un-Grund*. (Žižek considers the above-glossed Hegel of the *Phenomenology*'s third chapter as largely having resolved this issue—however, Žižek's ambitions arguably go beyond Hegelian phenomenology strictly speaking to the extent that he aims to broaden and deepen Hegel's account of the emergence of self-conscious subjectivity in "Force and the Understanding" at the levels of Hegel's post-phenomenological Logic and corresponding *Realphilosophie* of *Natur und Geist*.) Third is the fundamental question of what sort of ontology results from, as per the contemporary reactivation of objective and absolute idealisms à la Schelling and Hegel, (re)inscribing the interlinked phenomena of appearances and subjects within the ontological field(s) from which these far-from-epiphenomenal phenomena originally arose. (Žižek, both in *Less Than Nothing* and throughout his corpus, relentlessly pursues investigations regarding how being qua being must be thoroughly reconceptualized in light of the facts both that it sunders itself into the parallax split between subjectivity and objectivity and that subjective reflectivity/reflexivity continues to remain immanent, although nonetheless irreducible, to it.) For Schelling's and Hegel's post-Fichtean idealisms alike (and in line with both Hölderlin's 1795 "On Judgment and Being" and the 1796 "Earliest System-Program of German Idealism" as discussed by me at the outset here under the heading of the Tübingen trio's "Spinozism of freedom" agenda), substance must be thought also as subject, and vice versa (to phrase this in Hegel's language from the preface to the *Phenomenology*). Particularly in *Less Than Nothing*, Žižek can fairly be depicted as focused primarily on this "vice versa," namely, on thinking subject also as substance (along with the requisite parallel, correlative rethinking of substance to the extent that it is now thought of as harboring transcendent[al]-while-immanent subjectivity within itself). As he puts it later in the book, "the real difficulty is to think the subjective perspective as inscribed in 'reality' itself."[83]

Tellingly, the first chapter ("'Vacillating the Semblances'") of *Less Than Nothing*, as the word "semblance" in its title hints at the get-go, already contains an extended ensemble of reflections on the matter of appearances. Žižek herein employs the Hegelian thesis according to which "the supersensible is *appearance* qua *appearance*" (supplemented with Lacan's variations on this theme)[84] so as to narrate a specific sequence running from Plato (more precisely, a heterodox Platonism inspired by Badiou)[85] through Hegel and up to Lacan and Gilles Deleuze.[86] At one point, he proposes that "essence is 'appearance as appearance' . . . essence appears in contrast to appearance within appearance . . . *the distinction between appearance and essence has to be inscribed into appearance itself*."[87] Žižek's proposition gestures at the complexity of Hegel's ontology as neither nominalism nor metaphysical realism:[88] on the one hand Hegel definitely is not a nominalist for a plethora of reasons, including his immanent dialectical critiques of both Sense-Certainty and Perception in the *Phenomenology* as well as of finite figurations of Being in "The Doctrine of Being" of his mature Logic;[89] on the other hand neither is Hegel a metaphysical realist since, within his triad of Universality (*Allgemeinheit*), Particularity (*Besonderheit*), and Individuality/Singularity (*Einzelheit*), not only are there actually no brute, raw particulars as imagined by nominalism, neither are there pure, transcendent universals as envisioned by metaphysical realism.[90] For Hegel, everything enjoying actuality (*Wirklichkeit*) is individual/singular qua a synthesizing sublation of universal and particular dimensions.[91] As regards Žižek's just-quoted remarks about appearance and essence, they emphasize, among other facets of Hegel on appearances, Hegel's immanentist conception of the more-than-apparent and more-than-particular (i.e., essences as supersensible universals).[92] Later in *Less Than Nothing*, Žižek underscores the absolutely immanent status of the transcendent(al) in Hegelian metaphysics, with this transcendent(al) mainly as "negativity" (such as the negativity involved, in the *Phenomenology*'s third chapter, in the inner world that becomes self-conscious subjectivity opening up simultaneously along with the surfacing of the category of appearance, with such subjects also superseding the appearances with which they are coemergent).[93]

While endorsing the Hegelian speculative handling of the dialectics of appearance and essence as a partial account of the genesis of transcendent(al)-while-immanent subjective negativity, Žižek nevertheless wants to push this line of speculation through to a more foundational ontological level. In a footnote to the second chapter of *Less Than Nothing*, he articulates, echoing some of his earlier work,[94] a revealing characterization of "Hegel's reversal of the classic metaphysical question" as a "shift" from querying "how can we see through false appearances to their underlying essential reality" to "how has appearance emerged out of reality?"[95] Subsequently, he likewise asks "how we pass from being to appearing, how and why does being start to appear to itself?"[96]

Other moments in *Less Than Nothing* testify to Žižek's insistence on orthodox Hegelian answers to these Hegelian questions. Very much faithful to the agenda set for German idealism during its rapidly shifting development in the mid-1790s,[97] Žižek maintains that "in appearing to the subject, the Absolute also appears *to itself* . . . the subjective reflection of the Absolute is the Absolute's self-reflection."[98] Two pages later, he asserts that "*the 'Absolute' beyond appearances coincides with an 'absolute appearance,' an appearance beneath which there is no substantial Being*" (as quoted earlier). This second assertion, in order to be interpreted correctly, requires recalling another aspect of the *Phenomenology*'s third chapter on "Force and the Understanding" related to the discussion therein of "appearance *qua* appearance." In particular, Hegel indicates that the positing of a supersensible beyond through the shift to treating phenomena as appearances (i.e., as outer [mis]representations of an underlying, veiled inner world) is motivated, at least in part, by a powerful impulse to calm and unify the fluctuating, fragmented field of phenomenal experience (perhaps akin to Kant's "interest of reason").[99] Whether as the Kantian domain of noumenal things-in-themselves or the Newtonian universe of mechanical laws of efficient causality (not to mention the Platonic realm of purely intelligible forms/ideas), the non-apparent beyond coemergent with and corresponding to the apparent *hic et nunc* provides minded subjectivity with "the *stable* image of unstable appearance."[100] Therefore, Žižek's "'*absolute appearance*' . . . *beneath which there is no substantial Being*" is not a subjective idealist reduction of everything to the phenomenal experience of consciousness. Rather, he is drawing attention to the Hegelian dialectical gesture of negating the picture of being as a serene invisible Elsewhere (i.e., the inner world of the supersensible beyond as the stable image of unstable appearance) while simultaneously retaining its evident discord, incoherence, and volatility at the surface level of appearances themselves. Combining this cancellation of being's transcendence with the sublation of subjective idealisms, this means that the remaining monistic ontology of lone immanence contains both being and appearing—and, hence, that appearing's conflicts, contradictions, and chaos are part of being itself, with the latter thereby undergoing desubstantialization through being permeated by antagonisms, inconsistencies, tensions, and the like (i.e., being deprived of its substantiality qua solid, indivisible oneness).

On the basis of the preceding, Žižek distinguishes between three different philosophical approaches. He states:

> We can . . . identify three positions: metaphysical, transcendental, and
> "speculative." In the first, reality is simply perceived as existing out there,
> and the task of philosophy is to analyze its basic structure. In the second,
> the philosopher investigates the subjective conditions of the possibility of
> objective reality, its transcendental genesis. In the third, subjectivity is re-
> inscribed into reality, but not simply reduced to a part of objective reality.
> While the subjective constitution of reality—the split that separates the
> subject from the In-itself—is fully admitted, this very split is transposed

back into reality as its kenotic self-emptying (to use the Christian theological term). Appearance is not reduced to reality; rather the very process of appearance is conceived from the standpoint of reality, so that the question is not "How, if at all, can we pass from appearance to reality?" but "How can something like appearance arise in the midst of reality? What are the conditions for reality appearing to itself?"[101]

This triad can be translated into that of transcendental realism (i.e., metaphysics), transcendental idealism (i.e., transcendentalism), and objective/absolute idealism (i.e., speculation). In this context, metaphysics as transcendental realism is perhaps best epitomized by the different substance ontologies of the early modern rationalists (such as Descartes, Spinoza, and Leibniz), all of them seeking to investigate the supposed mind-independent objective realities of such metaphysical objects as the soul, the cosmos, and God (i.e., Kant's three ideas of reason as the principle targets of precritical philosophical inquiry). Transcendentalism as transcendental idealism obviously is represented exclusively by the subjectivisms of Kant and Fichte. Finally, speculation as objective/absolute idealism is, of course, embodied by Schelling and Hegel. Throughout *Less Than Nothing*, Žižek is a fierce partisan on behalf of the speculative orientation as itself a sublation of the metaphysical and transcendental orientations.

Speculation, as Žižek defines it in the above quotation, involves several distinctive features. First of all, its reinscription of the appearance-subject couplet into the one and only plane of real being by no means entails a reduction or elimination of this couplet itself; subjectivity and the appearances it participates in (transcendentally) coconstituting in interaction with objectivity do not lose their effective independence in becoming sterile, illusory epiphenomena. Second, the divide between subject (as the for-itself) and substance (as the in-itself) is preserved despite the asserted becoming-immanent of subject to substance; that is to say, a gap persists between the substantial *an sich* and the subjective *für sich* (as itself substance *an und für sich*) entirely within the confines of the substantial *an sich*. Schelling and Hegel, in self-conscious adherence to Spinoza, rightly insist that the distinction between the infinite and the finite is a distinction internal to the infinite itself (and this contra a Verstand-type opposition between the finite on one side and the infinite on another, which results in the limitation and, hence, deinfinitization of infinity itself).[102] Likewise, as per the dialectical-speculative slogan of "the identity of identity and difference" shared between Schelling and Hegel (and inspired by Spinoza's insight into the true nature of the infinite as per authentic Vernunft),[103] the discrepancy between substance and subject is a discrepancy internal to substance itself. For Žižek, the orienting concern of speculation is therefore the enigma of how the negativity of this rift opens up out of being in the first place (as he says in the previous block quotation, "the question is not 'How, if at all, can we pass from appearance to reality?' but 'How can something like appearance arise in the midst of reality? What are the conditions for reality appearing to itself?'"). Relatedly, when all is said and done, Žižek also must explain how this split itself and its subjective side achieve and sustain self-determining autonomy/spontaneity vis-à-vis their ontological ground(s), thus being more than mere delusions, fantasies, fictions, hallucinations, unrealities, and so on (i.e., causally inefficacious epiphenomena).

Much later in *Less Than Nothing*, what earlier is called "speculation" is relabeled "transcendental materialism."[104] In the context of critiquing Quentin Meillassoux's "speculative materialism," Žižek puts forward a preliminary rendition of transcendental materialism:

> one can make out the contours of what can perhaps only be designated by the oxymoron "transcendental materialism" . . . : all reality is transcendentally constituted, "correlative" to a subjective position, and, to push this through to the end, the way out of this "correlationist" circle is not to try to directly reach the In-itself, but to inscribe this transcendental correlation *into the Thing itself*. The path to the In-itself leads through the subjective gap, since the gap between For-us and In-itself is immanent to the In-itself: appearance is itself "objective," therein resides the truth of the realist problem of "How can we pass from appearance For-us to reality In-itself?"[105]

It now readily can be appreciated that transcendental materialism involves, among other things, modifying and updating the dialectical-speculative objective/absolute idealisms of Schelling and Hegel within the circumstances of present-day conjunctures. In other words, as the latest system-program of German idealism (tracing its roots back to the earliest one of 1795–1796), Žižekian transcendental materialism strives to be what amounts to a new Spinozism of freedom. More precisely, as expressed in *Less Than Nothing*, it seeks to accomplish a systematic interfacing of on the one hand a materialist, quasi-naturalist ontology of substance and on the other hand a theory of more-than-material, denaturalized transcendent(al) subjectivity in its nonepiphenomenal autonomous spontaneity and self-determining. Put differently, Žižek intends to "repeat Hegel and Schelling," creatively reactivating in the context of the early twenty-first century their struggles of two centuries ago to combine the apparent opposites of the naturalistic monism of Johann Gottfried von Herder's Spinoza with Kant's antinaturalist dualism.[106] All the German idealists after Kant are animated by the pantheism/Spinozism controversy triggered by Jacobi's attempt, partly with respect to the Kantian critical edifice, to force an either/or choice between system (as allegedly always in the end deterministic/fatalistic and, thus, nihilistic) and freedom. (Apart from Jacobi, Salomon Maimon's and G. E. Schulze's neo-Humean skeptical challenges to Kantianism also further motivate the post-Kantian idealists to systematize Kant's thinking and thereby immunize it from such doubts.)[107] Starting with Reinhold, each post-Kantian idealist seeks to refute Jacobi through achieving the construction of a rigorously rational philosophical system that, in its very systematicity, does completely full justice to freedom as instantiated by human agency. (As I noted earlier, Reinhold, Fichte, Schelling, and Hegel at least agree with Jacobi that Kant himself fails to be thoroughly systematic within and between his three Critiques.) Žižek (and Badiou too) is a direct heir of this legacy, albeit with the Spinozism appropriated by Schelling and Hegel being replaced with the postidealist developments of the (seemingly) more deterministic dimensions presented by Marxist historical/dialectical materialism, Freudian-Lacanian psychoanalysis, and the natural sciences of the past century (in Žižek's case, both quantum physics and biology).[108] Just before introducing the phrase "transcendental materialism" in *Less Than Nothing*, Žižek poses a series of queries. He asks: ". . . how can one explain the rise of subjectivity out of the 'incomplete' ontology, how are these two dimensions (the abyss/void of subjectivity, the incompleteness of reality) to be thought together? We should apply here something like a weak anthropic principle: how should the Real be structured so that it allows for the emergence of subjectivity (in its autonomous efficacy, not as a mere 'user's illusion')?"

Putting aside for the time being the topic of ontological incompleteness, a version of this last question is similarly formulated by Ilya Prigogine and Isabelle Stengers—"we need an account of the material world in which it isn't absurd to claim that it produced us"[109] (with Terrence Deacon quoting this specific formulation quite recently).[110] That said, what arguably amounts to Žižek's decision to begin with/from this "weak anthropic principle" resonates with Fichte's starting point as per his primacy of the practical. (I consider it to be no coincidence that *Less Than Nothing* contains an important chapter devoted to Fichte, Žižek's most sustained engagement with this particular German idealist to date).[111] Moreover, it also audibly reverberates with "The Earliest System-Program of German Idealism," whose author (Hegel, Schelling, Hölderlin . . . ?) evidently pushes off from Fichte's chosen beginning and proceeds to the same basic question raised in slightly different terms by Prigogine, Stengers, Deacon, and Žižek himself—"the first idea is, of course, the presentation of myself as an absolutely free entity. . . . Here I shall descend into the realms of physics; the question is this: how must a world be constituted for a moral entity?" With the "I" as a "moral entity" qua "absolutely free entity" (i.e., transcendental subjectivity à la Kant and Fichte) and Physik ("physics") as the empirical, experimental natural sciences of modernity, it appears that this two-hundred-year-old mystery setting the agenda for post-Fichtean German idealism (as objective/absolute) remains a pressing theoretical motivator to this very day. In this vein, both dialectical and transcendental materialism can be construed as materialist inheritors of this venerable program, one whose fulfillment, if ever attained by Hegel and/or Schelling over the course of their intellectual itineraries, seems to have been undone by developments intervening between then and now. To be faithful to this project, its contemporary defenders must alter it in heterodox fashions.

I wholeheartedly agree with Žižek's Hegelian insistence that only immanent critiques are worthwhile, with merely external ones being unproductive and ineffective.[112] The whole of my preceding commentary is intended primarily for the initial establishment of the historical and philosophical background against which a thorough immanent critical assessment of *Less Than Nothing* can and should be conducted. In light of this stage-setting by me, a verdict on the cogency of Žižek's transcendental materialist endeavors in his 2012 magnum opus must be reached on the basis of whether he satisfactorily speaks to the following six (if not more) interrelated, overlapping issues: one, a strictly materialist establishment and explanation, at least compatible with if not based on the sciences of nature, of the purported incompleteness of being in and of itself; two, a detailed account of the exact nature of the relationship between an incomplete ontology (as the being of substance) and a theory of self-relating spontaneity (as the thinking and appearances of the subject); three, a narrative of the emergence of appearing out of being that does not surreptitiously presuppose apperceiving subjectivity as always-already there and phenomenologically operative beforehand; four, the sufficient conditions for the immanent genesis of transcendent(al) actors out of the sole baseless base of natural, material objects and processes over and above the necessary conditions for this; five, the possibility and actuality of strongly emergent subjects reciprocally coming to exert so-called downward causation on the substances from which they originally arose; and six, the priceless bridges, if any there are, between both matter and mind as well as mere indeterminism and robust freedom (i.e., solutions to everything ranging from Kant's third antinomy to David Chalmers's "hard problem").[113] The degree to which Žižek succeeds at synthesizing German idealism with post-idealist materialisms and naturalisms depends on the extent to which he resolves these difficulties just enumerated. What is more, transcendental materialism enjoying a viable, enduring future hinges on it getting firmly to grips with such demanding philosophical challenges.

Notes

1   Alain Badiou, *The Adventure of French Philosophy*, ed. and trans. Bruno Bosteels (London: Verso, 2012), li–lxiii.

2   Paul Franks, *All or Nothing: Systematicity, Transcendental Arguments, and Skepticism in German Idealism* (Cambridge, MA: Harvard University Press, 2005), 10–11.

3   F. W. J. Schelling, *Philosophical Inquiries into the Nature of Human Freedom and Matters Connected Therewith*, trans. James Gutmann (Chicago: Open Court, 1936), 7, 9–11.

4   Dieter Henrich, *Between Kant and Hegel: Lectures on German Idealism*, ed. David S. Pacini (Cambridge, MA: Harvard University Press, 2003), 116–17.

5   Immanuel Kant, *Critique of Pure Reason*, trans. Paul Guyer and Allen Wood (Cambridge: Cambridge University Press, 1998), A444–51/B472–79, pp. 484–89; A538–58/B566–86, pp. 535–46.

6   F. H. Jacobi, "David Hume on Faith, or Idealism and Realism: A Dialogue (1787)," in *The Main Philosophical Writings and the Novel "Allwill,"* trans. George di Giovanni (Montreal: McGill-Queen's University Press, 1994), 336; Henrich, *Between Kant and Hegel*, 119.

7   F. H. Jacobi, *Concerning the Doctrine of Spinoza in Letters to Herr Moses Mendelssohn*, in Jacobi, *Main Philosophical Writings*, 234; F. H. Jacobi, "Jacobi to Fichte," in *Main Philosophical Writings*, 519; Jacobi, "David Hume on Faith, or Idealism and Realism, A Dialogue: Preface and also Introduction to the Author's Collected Philosophical Works (1815)," in Jacobi, *Main Philosophical Writings*, 583, 586–87.

8   Jean-Marie Vaysse, *Totalité et subjectivité: Spinoza dans l'idéalisme allemande* (Paris: Vrin, 1994), 18–19, 63.

9   René Descartes, *Meditations on First Philosophy*, trans. Donald A. Cress (Indianapolis: Hackett, 1993), 17. K. L. Reinhold, *Über das Fundament des philosophischen Wissens* (Hamburg: Felix Meiner, 1978), 27, 47, 68–69, 78, 89, 110–11, 114, 136–38; K. L. Reinhold, *Letters on the Kantian Philosophy*, ed. Karl Ameriks, trans. James Hebbeler (Cambridge: Cambridge University Press, 2005), 42; J. G. Fichte, *Concerning the Concept of the Wissenschaftslehre or, of So-called "Philosophy,"* in *Fichte: Early Philosophical Writings*, ed. and trans. Daniel Breazeale (Ithaca: Cornell University Press, 1988), 96; J. G. Fichte, *Selected Correspondence, 1790–1799*, in *Fichte*, 376–77, 384, 390, 400, 406; Henrich, *Between Kant and Hegel*, 125, 127–29, 157; Frederick C. Beiser, *The Fate of Reason: German Philosophy from Kant to Fichte* (Cambridge, MA: Harvard University Press, 1987), 226–27.

10 Friedrich Hölderlin, *Über Urtheil und Seyn*, trans. H. S. Harris, in H. S. Harris, *Hegel's Development: Toward the Sunlight, 1770–1801* (Oxford: Oxford University Press, 1972), 515–16; Vaysse, *Totalité et subjectivité*, 138; Terry Pinkard, *German Philosophy, 1760–1860: The Legacy of Idealism* (Cambridge: Cambridge University Press, 2002), 141–42; Eckart Förster, *The Twenty-Five Years of Philosophy: A Systematic Reconstruction*, trans. Brady Bowman (Cambridge, MA: Harvard University Press, 2012), 279.

11 F. W. J. Schelling, *Presentation of My System of Philosophy (1801), The Philosophical Rupture between Fichte and Schelling*, ed. and trans. Michael G. Vater and David W. Wood (Albany: State University of New York Press, 2012), 141–43.

12 Henrich, *Between Kant and Hegel*, 80–81, 93–98, 100–101, 240, 273, 286, 292, 295, 304–5; Frederick C. Beiser, *German Idealism: The Struggle against Subjectivism, 1781–1801* (Cambridge, MA: Harvard University Press, 2002), 350, 352–53, 355–63, 368–72.

13 G. W. F. Hegel, *Phänomenologie des Geistes*, *Werke in zwanzig Bänden*, vol. 3, ed. Eva Moldenhauer and Karl Markus Michel (Frankfurt am Main: Suhrkamp, 1970), 23; G. W. F. Hegel, *Phenomenology of Spirit*, trans. A. V. Miller (Oxford: Oxford University Press, 1977), 10.

14 Adrian Johnston, *Adventures in Transcendental Materialism: Dialogues with Contemporary Thinkers* (Edinburgh: Edinburgh University Press, 2014).

15 Otto Pöggeler, "Hölderlin, Hegel und das älteste Systemprogramm," in *Das älteste*

Systemprogramm, Hegel-Studien, no. 9, ed. Rüdiger Bubner (Bonn: Bouvier, 1982), 239–43, 245–46, 258; Otto Pöggeler, *Hegel, der Verfasser des ältesten Systemprogramms des deutschen Idealismus, Mythologie der Vernunft: Hegels "ältestes Systemprogramm" des deutschen Idealismus*, ed. Christoph Jamme and Helmut Schneider (Frankfurt am Main: Suhrkamp, 1984), 126–43; H. S. Harris, *Hegel's Development: Toward the Sunlight, 1770–1801* (Oxford: Oxford University Press, 1972), 249–57.

16 Vaysse, *Totalité et subjectivité*, 126–27.

17 Johnston, *Adventures in Transcendental Materialism*.

18 G. W. F. Hegel, *The Earliest System-Program of German Idealism*, trans. H. S. Harris; *Miscellaneous Writings of G. W. F. Hegel*, ed. Jon Stewart (Evanston: Northwestern University Press, 2002), 110.

19 Hegel, *The Earliest System–Program of German Idealism*, 110.

20 Heinz Kimmerle, *Das Problem der Abgeschlossenheit des Denkens: Hegels "System der Philosophie" in den Jahren 1800–1804, Hegel-Studien*, no. 8 (Bonn: Bouvier, 1970), 18; Johnston, *Adventures in Transcendental Materialism*.

21 G. W. F. Hegel, *Das älteste Systemprogramm des deutschen Idealismus*, in *Werke in zwanzig Bänden*, vol. 1, *Frühe Schriften*, ed. Eva Moldenhauer and Karl Markus Michel (Frankfurt am Main: Suhrkamp, 1971), 234.

22 Alain Badiou, *Beckett: L'increvable désir* (Paris: Hachette, 1995), 7; Alain Badiou, *Can Change Be Thought?: A Dialogue with Alain Badiou* (with Bruno Bosteels), in *Alain Badiou: Philosophy and Its Conditions*, ed. Gabriel Riera (Albany: State University of New York Press, 2005), 242; Adrian Johnston, *Badiou, Žižek, and Political Transformations: The Cadence of Change* (Evanston: Northwestern University Press, 2009), 62–63; Adrian Johnston, *Prolegomena to Any Future Materialism: Vol. 1, The Outcome of Contemporary French Philosophy* (Evanston: Northwestern University Press, 2013), 108–9.

23 Slavoj Žižek, *On Belief* (New York: Routledge, 2001), 160; Adrian Johnston, *Žižek's Ontology: A Transcendental Materialist Theory of Subjectivity* (Evanston: Northwestern University Press, 2008), 12–16.

24 Slavoj Žižek, *Less Than Nothing: Hegel and the Shadow of Dialectical Materialism* (London: Verso, 2012), 7–9.

25 Žižek, *Less Than Nothing*, 8.

26 Žižek, *Less Than Nothing*, 50–52.

27 G. W. F. Hegel, *Science of Logic*, trans. A. V. Miller (London: Allen and Unwin, 1969), 63–64; G. W. F. Hegel, *The Encyclopedia Logic: Part I of the Encyclopedia of the Philosophical Sciences with the Zusätze*, trans. T. F. Geraets, W. A. Suchting, and H. S. Harris (Indianapolis: Hackett, 1991), § 9, p. 33, § 24, p. 56; G. W. F. Hegel, *Lectures on Logic: Berlin, 1831*, trans. Clark Butler (Bloomington: Indiana University Press, 2008), § 19, p. 3; G. W. F. Hegel, *Hegel to von Raumer: Nuremberg, August 2, 1816*, in *Hegel: The Letters*, trans. Clark Butler and Christiane Seiler (Bloomington: Indiana University Press, 1984), 341; Žižek, *Less Than Nothing*, 49; H. S. Harris, *Hegel's Development: Night Thoughts (Jena, 1801–1806)* (Oxford: Oxford University Press, 1983), 178, 410–18; Jean Hyppolite, *Logic and Existence*, trans. Leonard Lawlor and

Amit Sen (Albany: State University of New York Press, 1997), 34–35, 51, 122, 154–58, 166; Gérard Lebrun, *La patience du Concept: Essai sur le Discours hégélien* (Paris: Gallimard, 1972), 395–412; André Doz, *La logique de Hegel et les problèmes traditionnels de l'ontologie* (Paris: Vrin, 1987), 15–16, 18–19, 23, 298; Rolf-Peter Horstmann, *Die Grenzen der Vernunft: Eine Untersuchung zu Zielen und Motiven des Deutschen Idealismus* (Frankfurt am Main: Vittorio Klostermann, 2004), 133–34, 138–41; Frederick Beiser, *Hegel* (New York: Routledge, 2005), 53; Stephen Houlgate, *An Introduction to Hegel: Freedom, Truth and History* (Oxford: Blackwell, 2005), 43–46; Stephen Houlgate, *The Opening of Hegel's Logic: From Being to Infinity* (West Lafayette, IN: Purdue University Press, 2006), 115–19, 436–38; Förster, *The Twenty-Five Years of Philosophy*, 301–2.

28 Žižek, *Less Than Nothing*, 11–13.

29 Žižek, *Less Than Nothing*, 12–13, 15–16; Dieter Henrich, "Hegel und Hölderlin," in *Hegel im Kontext: Mit einem Nachwort zur Neuauflage* (Frankfurt am Main: Suhrkamp, 2010), 37–38; Henrich, *Between Kant and Hegel*, 293, 309; Vaysse, *Totalité et subjectivité*, 200, 205.

30 F. W. J. Schelling, *On the World-Soul*, trans. Iain Hamilton Grant, in *Collapse: Philosophical Research and Development*, vol. 6, January 2010, 73–74, 85–86, 92–95; F. W. J. Schelling, *First Outline of a System of the Philosophy of Nature*, trans. Keith R. Peterson (Albany: State University of New York Press, 2004), 17, 39, 48, 87, 106–8, 113, 116–17, 122–23, 204–5, 213, 216, 218–20, 232.

31 Johnston, *Žižek's Ontology*, 12–15, 69–70, 128–44, 148, 161–66, 172, 187, 200–201, 207–8, 265–67.

32 Žižek, *Less Than Nothing*, 149, 536–39, 706–7, 740, 907, 924–26.

33 Žižek, *Less Than Nothing*, 268–69.

34 Žižek, *Less Than Nothing*, 267.

35 Kant, *Critique of Pure Reason*, A297–98/B353–55, pp. 386–87; A302/B359, p. 389; A305–6/B362–63, pp. 390–91; A671–74/B699–702, pp. 606–8; Immanuel Kant, *Prolegomena to Any Future Metaphysics*, trans. Paul Carus; rev. James W. Ellington (Indianapolis: Hackett, 1977), § 40–44, pp. 69–73, § 56, p. 90.

36 Beiser, *German Idealism*, 88–131.

37 Kant, *Critique of Pure Reason*, B303, pp. 358–59; A845–47/B873–75, pp. 698–99.

38 Žižek, *Less Than Nothing*, 269.

39 Žižek, *Less Than Nothing*, 280–81.

40 Žižek, *Less Than Nothing*, 195.

41 John Locke, *An Essay Concerning Human Understanding in Two Volumes: Volume One*, ed. Alexander Campbell Fraser (New York: Dover, 1959), 25–33.

42 Adrian Johnston, "Repeating Engels: Renewing the Cause of the Materialist Wager for the Twenty-First Century," *Theory @ Buffalo* 15: *animal.machine.sovereign* (2011): 155–56.

43 Adrian Johnston, *Prolegomena to Any Future Materialism*, vol. 2, *A Weak Nature Alone* (Evanston: Northwestern University Press, forthcoming).

44 Jacobi, "David Hume on Faith," 336.

45 Johnston, *Žižek's Ontology*, 133–42, 152–63; Pinkard, *German Philosophy, 1760–1860*, 92; Horstmann, *Die Grenzen der Vernunft*, 55.

46 Kant, *Critique of Pure Reason*, Bxvi–xvii, pp. 110–11; Bxxii, p. 113.

47 Žižek, *Less Than Nothing*, 282–84.

48 Hegel, *Science of Logic*, 132, 134–35; Hegel, *The Encyclopedia Logic*, § 60, pp. 105–6; § 92, p. 148; Hegel, *Lectures on Logic*, § 93, p. 104; G. W. F. Hegel, *Philosophy of Mind: Part Three of the Encyclopedia of the Philosophical Sciences with the Zusätze*, trans. William Wallace and A. V. Miller (Oxford: Oxford University Press, 1971), § 386, pp. 23–24.

49 Žižek, *Less Than Nothing*, 226.

50 G. W. F. Hegel and F. W. J. Schelling, "Introduction for the *Critical Journal of Philosophy*: On the Essence of Philosophical Criticism Generally, and Its Relationship to the Present State of Philosophy in Particular," in *Miscellaneous Writings of G. W. F. Hegel*, 211–12; G. W. F. Hegel, *Faith and Knowledge*, trans. Walter Cerf and H. S. Harris (Albany: State University of New York Press, 1977), 75–77; G. W. F. Hegel, *How the Ordinary Human Understanding Takes Philosophy (as Displayed in the Works of Mr. Krug)*, in *Miscellaneous Writings of G. W. F. Hegel*, 229; Hegel, *Science of Logic*, 45–47, 489; Hegel, *The Encyclopedia Logic*, § 24, pp. 56–57; § 41, p. 81; § 42, p. 86; § 45, pp. 88–89; Hegel, *Lectures on Logic*, § 43, p. 36; G. W. F. Hegel, *Lectures on the History of Philosophy: Volume Three*, trans. E. S. Haldane and Frances H. Simson (New York: Humanities Press, 1955), 535–36, 541–42, 551–53.

51 Hegel, *Phenomenology of Spirit*, 13–14, 55; Hegel, *Science of Logic*, 32, 106–8.

52 Hegel, *Phenomenology of Spirit*, 36; Hegel, *Science of Logic*, 28, 54–56, 832–33; Hegel, *The Encyclopedia Logic*, § 82, pp. 131–32; § 91, p. 147.

53 Jacques Lacan, *The Seminar of Jacques Lacan, Book VII: The Ethics of Psychoanalysis, 1959–1960*, ed. Jacques-Alain Miller, trans. Dennis Porter (New York: Norton, 1992), 139; Jacques Lacan, *The Seminar of Jacques Lacan, Book XI: The Four Fundamental Concepts of Psychoanalysis, 1964*, ed. Jacques-Alain Miller, trans. Alan Sheridan (New York: Norton, 1977), 268; Jacques Lacan, *Le Séminaire de Jacques Lacan, Livre XVI: D'un Autre à l'autre, 1968–1969*, ed. Jacques-Alain Miller (Paris: Éditions du Seuil, 2006), 224–25, 249.

54 Hegel, *Lectures on Logic*, § 60, p. 59.

55 Béatrice Longuenesse, *Hegel et la critique de la métaphysique* (Paris: Vrin, 1981), 17, 19–21, 188; Robert B. Pippin, *Hegel's Idealism: The Satisfactions of Self-Consciousness* (Cambridge: Cambridge University Press, 1989), 6–7, 9, 16–17, 28–31, 79, 120–21, 132, 176, 225, 230, 248; Slavoj Žižek, *Tarrying with the Negative: Kant, Hegel, and the Critique of Ideology* (Durham, NC: Duke University Press, 1993), 265–66; Slavoj Žižek, *The Metastases of Enjoyment: Six Essays on Woman and Causality* (London: Verso, 1994), 187; Slavoj Žižek, *The Ticklish Subject: The Absent Centre of Political Ontology* (London: Verso, 1999), 55, 60; Slavoj Žižek, *Organs without Bodies: On Deleuze and Consequences* (New York: Routledge, 2004), 58.

56 Hegel, *Science of Logic*, 55–56, 190–92, 197–98, 831–33; Hegel, *The Encyclopedia Logic*, § 48, pp. 91–93; § 81, pp. 128–31; Hegel, *Lectures on Logic*, § 48, pp. 41–44;

§ 81, pp. 73–74; G. W. F. Hegel, "Logic [For the Middle Class]," in *The Philosophical Propaedeutic*, ed. Michael George and Andrew Vincent; trans. A. V. Miller (Oxford: Blackwell, 1986), § 78, p. 90; G. W. F. Hegel, "Hegel to Niethammer: Nuremberg, October 23, 1812," in *Hegel: The Letters*, 281.

57 Žižek, *Less Than Nothing*, 143.

58 Hegel, "Hegel to Niethammer: Nuremberg, October 23, 1812," 277.

59 Hegel, *Science of Logic*, 51; Hegel, *The Encyclopedia Logic*, § 24, p. 56.

60 Hegel, *Science of Logic*, 61–64.

61 Schelling and Hegel, "Introduction for the *Critical Journal of Philosophy*," 214–16; Hegel, "How the Ordinary Human Understanding Takes Philosophy, 231; G. W. F. Hegel, *The Difference between Fichte's and Schelling's System of Philosophy*, trans. H. S. Harris and Walter Cerf (Albany: State University of New York Press, 1977), 90, 95–96, 158–59; Hegel, *Faith and Knowledge*, 107–8, 112–13; G. W. F. Hegel, *The Jena System, 1804–5: Logic and Metaphysics*, ed. John W. Burbidge and George di Giovanni (Montreal: McGill–Queen's University Press, 1986), 35; Hegel, *Science of Logic*, 137–40, 142–43; Hegel, *The Encyclopedia Logic*, § 93–95, pp. 149–52; § 104, p. 165; Johnston, *Adventures in Transcendental Materialism*.

62 Hegel, *Phenomenology of Spirit*, 1–3.

63 Hegel, *Science of Logic*, 48–49, 68–69, 72–75, 78; Hegel, *Lectures on Logic*, § 87, p. 93; Houlgate, *The Opening of Hegel's Logic*, 29–71.

64 Hegel, *Phenomenology of Spirit*, 9, 15–17, 28, 31–33, 35–36, 49–56.

65 Hegel, *Phenomenology of Spirit*, 68–70, 72–77, 87–91.

66 Hegel, *Science of Logic*, 71–72.

67 Žižek, *The Ticklish Subject*, 84–85; Johnston, *Žižek's Ontology*, 128–33.

68 Žižek, *Less Than Nothing*, 950.

69 Hegel, *Phänomenologie des Geistes*, 118–19; Hegel, *Phenomenology of Spirit*, 89.

70 Hegel, *Phenomenology of Spirit*, 88–89.

71 Hegel, *Faith and Knowledge*, 76–77.

72 Hegel, *Phenomenology of Spirit*, 87–88.

73 Hegel, *Science of Logic*, 489, 499, 507; Hegel, *The Encyclopedia Logic*, § 131, pp. 199–200; Hegel, *Lectures on Logic*, § 135, pp. 149–50; G. W. F. Hegel, *Encyclopedia of the Philosophical Sciences in Outline*, trans. Steven A. Taubeneck, in *Encyclopedia of the Philosophical Sciences in Outline and Critical Writings*, ed. Ernst Behler (New York: Continuum, 1990), § 81, p. 89; § 89, p. 93.

74 Hegel, *Phenomenology of Spirit*, 87–88.

75 Hegel, *Phenomenology of Spirit*, 151.

76 Hegel, *Phenomenology of Spirit*, 100–103.

77 Slavoj Žižek, *The Sublime Object of Ideology* (London: Verso, 1989), 193, 195; Slavoj Žižek, *Enjoy Your Symptom!: Jacques Lacan in Hollywood and Out* (New York: Routledge, 1992), 53, 137; Žižek, *Tarrying with the Negative*, 36–37, 39, 241, 245–46; Slavoj Žižek, *Postface: Georg Lukács as the Philosopher of Leninism*, in Georg Lukács, *A Defense of History and Class Consciousness: Tailism and the Dialectic*, trans. Esther Leslie (London: Verso, 2000), 181; Žižek, *Organs without Bodies*, 60–61, 65; Slavoj Žižek,

The Parallax View: Toward a New Reading of Kant, Epoché, vol. 8, no. 2 (Spring 2004), 259–60; Slavoj Žižek, The Parallax View (Cambridge, MA: MIT Press, 2006), 29–30, 106; Johnston, Žižek's Ontology, 136–44, 162.

78   Žižek, Less Than Nothing, 4.

79   Žižek, Less Than Nothing, 244–45, 252–53, 361–64; Johnston, Adventures in Transcendental Materialism.

80   Alenka Zupančič, Das Reale einer Illusion: Kant und Lacan, trans. Reiner Ansén (Frankfurt am Main: Suhrkamp, 2001), 141–42; Alenka Zupančič, The Odd One In: On Comedy (Cambridge: MIT Press, 2008), 17; Žižek, Less Than Nothing, 721–22; Johnston, Žižek's Ontology, 43–44, 281–83.

81   Schelling, Philosophical Inquiries into the Nature of Human Freedom, 10–11, 13–14, 16–19, 23–24; F. W. J. Schelling, "Stuttgart Seminars," in Idealism and the Endgame of Theory: Three Essays by F. W. J. Schelling, trans. Thomas Pfau (Albany: State University of New York Press, 1994), 214; F. W. J. Schelling, The Ages of the World: Third Version (c. 1815), trans. Jason M. Wirth (Albany: State University of New York Press, 2000), 104–5; F. W. J. Schelling, On the History of Modern Philosophy, trans. Andrew Bowie (Cambridge: Cambridge University Press, 1994), 64–75; F. W. J. Schelling, The Grounding of the Positive Philosophy, trans. Bruce Matthews (Albany: State University of New York Press, 2007), 126; Hegel, Phenomenology of Spirit, 10–13; Hegel, The Encyclopedia Logic, § 151, pp. 226–27; G. W. F. Hegel, Philosophy of Nature: Part Two of the Encyclopedia of the Philosophical Sciences, trans. A. V. Miller (Oxford: Oxford University Press, 1970), § 359, pp. 385–86; Hegel, Philosophy of Mind, § 415, p. 156; Hegel, Lectures on the History of Philosophy: Volume Three, 257–61, 263–64, 268–69, 280, 287–89; Johnston, Adventures in Transcendental Materialism.

82   Žižek, Less Than Nothing, 807–9.

83   Žižek, Less Than Nothing, 907.

84   Lacan, The Seminar of Jacques Lacan, Book XI, 103, 111–12; Johnston, Žižek's Ontology, 138–40.

85   Žižek, Less Than Nothing, 40–42; Alain Badiou, La République de Platon (Paris: Fayard, 2012), 9, 165, 169, 380, 383, 400–401, 526–27, 571–72, 590.

86   Žižek, Less Than Nothing, 31–39.

87   Žižek, Less Than Nothing, 37.

88   Žižek, Less Than Nothing, 96–97.

89   Hegel, Phenomenology of Spirit, 58–79; Hegel, Science of Logic, 109–56.

90   G. W. F. Hegel, "Who Thinks Abstractly?," trans. Walter Kaufmann, in Miscellaneous Writings of G. W. F. Hegel, 284–85; Johnston, Adventures in Transcendental Materialism.

91   Hegel, Phenomenology of Spirit, 1, 27–28, 60; Hegel, Science of Logic, 600–622; Hegel, The Encyclopedia Logic, § 6, pp. 29–30; § 20, pp. 50–51; § 24, pp. 56–57; § 70, pp. 117–18; § 142, pp. 213–15; § 164, pp. 241–42; § 212, p. 286.

92   Žižek, Less Than Nothing, 235.

93   Žižek, Less Than Nothing, 197, 740–41.

94 Žižek, *The Parallax View*, 29; Johnston, *Žižek's Ontology*, 162–65.

95 Žižek, *Less Than Nothing*, 131.

96 Žižek, *Less Than Nothing*, 808.

97 Žižek, *Less Than Nothing*, 144.

98 Žižek, *Less Than Nothing*, 141.

99 Hegel, *Encyclopedia of the Philosophical Sciences in Outline*, § 75, p. 87; Žižek, *Tarrying with the Negative*, 38; Slavoj Žižek, *The Indivisible Remainder: An Essay on Schelling and Related Matters* (London: Verso, 1996), 139; Slavoj Žižek, "Foreword to the Second Edition: Enjoyment within the Limits of Reason Alone," in *For They Know Not What They Do: Enjoyment as a Political Factor* (London: Verso, 2002), xlix–1; Slavoj Žižek, *The Puppet and the Dwarf: The Perverse Core of Christianity* (Cambridge, MA: MIT Press, 2003), 66; Johnston, *Žižek's Ontology*, 140–42, 160.

100 Hegel, *Phenomenology of Spirit*, 90.

101 Žižek, *Less Than Nothing*, 144–45.

102 G. W. F. Hegel, *Natural Law: The Scientific Ways of Treating Natural Law, Its Place in Moral Philosophy, and Its Relation to the Positive Sciences of Law*, trans. T. M. Knox (Philadelphia: University of Pennsylvania Press, 1975), 71, 111–12; Hegel, *The Jena System, 1804–5*, 35–36; Johnston, *Adventures in Transcendental Materialism*.

103 G. W. F. Hegel, *Fragment of a System*, trans. Richard Kroner, in *Miscellaneous Writings of G. W. F. Hegel*, 154; Hegel, *The Difference Between Fichte's and Schelling's System of Philosophy*, 156; F. W. J. Schelling, *Bruno, or On the Natural and the Divine Principle of Things*, trans. Michael G. Vater (Albany: State University of New York Press, 1984), 136, 143.

104 Žižek, *Less Than Nothing*, 906–9; Johnston, *Adventures in Transcendental Materialism*.

105 Žižek, *Less Than Nothing*, 906.

106 Johann Gottfried Herder, "Gott," in *Schriften: Eine Auswahl aus dem Gesamtwerk*, ed. Walter Flemmer (Munich: Wilhelm Goldmann, 1960), 209–10; Johann Gottfried von Herder, *On the Cognition and Sensation of the Human Soul* (1778), in *Philosophical Writings*, ed. and trans. Michael N. Forster (Cambridge: Cambridge University Press, 2002), 216–17; Harris, *Hegel's Development: Toward the Sunlight*, 295; Beiser, *The Fate of Reason*, 159–61.

107 Salomon Maimon, *Essay on Transcendental Philosophy*, trans. Nick Midgley, Henry Somers-Hall, Alistair Welchman, and Merten Reglitz (London: Continuum, 2010), 37–38, 42–43; G. E. Schulze, *Aenesidemus*, trans. George di Giovanni, in *Between Kant and Hegel: Texts in the Development of Post-Kantian Idealism*, ed. George di Giovanni and H. S. Harris (Indianapolis: Hackett, 2000), 104–35; Beiser, *German Idealism*, 240–59.

108 Johnston, *Žižek's Ontology*, 269–87; Johnston, *Adventures in Transcendental Materialism*.

109 Ilya Prigogine and Isabelle Stengers, *La nouvelle alliance: Métamorphose de la science* (Paris: Éditions Gallimard, 1979), 278.

110   Terrence W. Deacon, *Incomplete Nature: How Mind Emerged From Matter* (New York: Norton, 2012), 143; Adrian Johnston, "Lacking Causes: Privative Causality from Locke and Kant to Lacan and Deacon," *Speculations: A Journal of Speculative Realism*, 2014; Johnston, *Prolegomena to Any Future Materialism*, vol. 2.

111   Žižek, *Less Than Nothing*, 137–89.

112   Žižek, *Less Than Nothing*, 104–5.

113   David J. Chalmers, *The Conscious Mind: In Search of a Fundamental Theory* (Oxford: Oxford University Press, 1997), xii–xiii.

2

How to Repeat Plato?

For a Platonism of

Frank Ruda | **the Non-All**

Eppur Egli Si Muove

Many people love to hate Slavoj Žižek. This became again abundantly clear after the publication of his 2012 book on Hegel. Here a best-of: John Gray: "in a stupendous feat of intellectual overproduction Žižek has created . . . a critique that claims to repudiate practically everything that currently exists and in some sense actually does, but that at the same time reproduces the compulsive, purposeless dynamism that he perceives in the operations of capitalism. Achieving a deceptive substance by endlessly reiterating an essentially empty vision, Žižek's work . . . amounts in the end to less than nothing."[1] Žižek's work is for John Gray, the author of these lines, nothing but an intellectual symptom of capitalism. If one is an anticapitalist (and against appearances, one may assume that Gray considers himself to be one) one is anti-Žižek. Even more so, for Žižek is a deceiver, a fake, without intellectual substance; someone "engaged—wittingly or otherwise—in a kind of auto-parody," which is also why "the Hegel that emerges in Žižek's writings thus bears little resemblance to the idealist philosopher who features in standard histories of thought." Ultimately his position cannot be taken seriously. Yet, one cannot but seriously declare that he cannot be taken seriously. Since "interpreting Žižek on this or any issue is not without difficulties. There is his inordinate prolixity, the stream of texts that no one could read in their entirety, if only because the torrent never ceases flowing."[2] No one could read his texts in their entirety and why should one, for one would constantly encounter difficulties in interpretation, and for Gray this cannot be what philosophy is about. Peter Osborne: "for all the variety of these materials, there is something machinic about the way in which Žižek processes them by subjecting them to the hermeneutical structure of Hegel-Lacan. . . . In this respect, there is a danger of him remaking 'Hegel, the Difference-Obliterating Dialectical Machine' . . . His own script is re-enacted so repeatedly that it appears as a new standardized formula. This is the point at which knowing cannot save Žižek from his own doing."[3] Žižek for Peter Osborne may know what he is doing, but against his own will it turns against him, becomes machinic and brings about the very idealist philosophy that features in standard histories of thought: a Hegelianism obliterating all differences. He does "render all social forms indifferent, reduced to a single structural model," performs a "reduction of the social to a single figure," and although Žižek proposes a multiheaded philosophical bastard, a "Hegel-Lacan (or Hegel-Lacan-Schelling-Badiou . . .)," this bastard "has become: HLSB, he is after all by now a kind of philosophical bank."[4] Žižek's Hegel is so monstrous, he is a philosophical home loan state bank (HSLB) that swallows everything in disregard of its content. His proposal is capitalism in philosophy—that ultimately lets "history go hang itself." This is not an attack of an empty vision that even exits philosophy, but an attack on a vision that is repetitive, all-devouring, and reductive and relies on its own "signature move," namely "demonstrating a philosophical identity of"[5] anything with anything. Either Žižek is not to be taken seriously, his work is not philosophy, even Hegel is not recognizable, Žižek is too difficult, and he is ultimately expelled from the circle of philosophers and can only be attacked on another (declarative, or simply: personal) level. Or Žižek is too much of a philosopher (even too many philosophers) for whom everything is based on a single structural model, which makes him into too much of a traditional reductive, identitarian Hegel, in which all relevant things, real "historically determinate social forms,"[6] are evaporated into philosophical abstraction. Žižek then is not expelled but taken as the paradigmatic figure of a too abstract and idealist (old-school Hegelian) philosophy. Once he is attacked for not being a philosopher, generating an unrecognizable Hegel and mimicking the excessive dynamic of capitalism, once for being too much of a traditional idealist Hegelian

philosopher whose will to consumption mirrors the operation of capitalist banks. Once he is outside philosophy, once he is a Hegelian banker
inside philosophy trying to cash in the real world. It is noteworthy that
Žižek is attacked from two different perspectives precisely for the opposite wrongdoing.

There is another response to Žižek's book, written by a self-
proclaimed Hegelian idealist who at least pretends to treat Žižek as a
philosopher and hence avoids taking him as symptom of contemporary
capitalism in or outside philosophy. Robert Pippin[7] seems to share with
Žižek that Hegel is neither a hyperrationalist, who hypostatizes reason
(this is Osborne's reproach to Žižek) nor the great philosopher of reconciliation (Gray's image of Hegel). Both interpretations consider his
thought to be invalidated by what happened after 1831 (Hegel's death)
in history (a version of Osborne): Nazism, Stalinist terror, and "a communist China full of billionaires" (a version of Gray).[8] These developments smashed all dreams of reconciliation and totalizable reason, the
proof of which is that "no one has succeeded in writing a *Phenomenology
of Spirit. Part Two*"[9]—for the time after Hegel. Pippin agrees with Žižek:
one needs to reanimate Hegel. But Pippin believes that the Hegel to be
revamped can only be the thinker of self-consciousness, who praised
Kant's "I think" as the highest philosophical insight. Hegel can help to
develop a comprehension of the idea that self-consciousness does not
imply any split. Pippin's Hegel therefore argues that when I have a conviction, me having it and me being conscious of it is one and the same act
(this is the "I think" accompanying all my representations). His Hegel is
a non-Napoleonic Hegel, since Napoleon's famous "On s'engage, puis
on voit" does not hold for self-consciousness. Acting implies being conscious of one's actions. To act implies to be an "I" that "think(s)." Self-
consciousness is in this sense performative, and I am (in all) my actions.
Self-consciousness does not imply a two-step model, but a one-step performative (the mode of how the "I think" is accompanying my representations is performativity). Acting (being conscious) is like playing bridge:
I do not need to know why people do it, I just do it but I have reasons I
could make explicit. One is always already (and completely) in what Pippin and others call the (one) space of reasons, a space I cannot leave. But
it is a comfortable prison space, because when I act within it, I am ready
to give reasons and ask for them. I am therefore always already related to

other agents (as much as to myself) who also rely on the reasons provided by the collective of agents who vivify the space of reasons in a historically specific sense. (Self-)relation is not a problem.

From such a perspective "no gaps in being need apply; any more than the possibility of people playing bridge, following the norms of bridge, and exploring strategies for winning need commit us to any unusual gappy ontology."[10] Pippin (in a Gray-like manner) states that "I do not fully understand the claims about holes in the fabric of being . . . we do not need the claim if we go in the direction I am suggesting . . . all without a gappy ontology."[11] His criticism thus can be resumed in a one-liner: one simply does not need Žižek. He gives the wrong answers to already solved problems, problems that are not real problems any more. He argues that Žižek can only make such a fuss about his gappy ontology because he simply does not get that we are always already in the space of reasons, no gaps needed (and thinkable). But why is Žižek so disoriented? "The way Žižek poses the question itself, then, reveals a deeply Schellingian orientation at the beginning and throughout the whole book." This is why he is led into asking the wrong questions, providing the wrong answers, which even force him into "the original Eleatic problems of non-being . . . hence Žižek's sustained attention to the second half of Plato's *Parmenides*." Pippin on the contrary contends that "the German version has a unique, different dimension and that dimension is the beginning of my deepest disagreement with Žižek."[12] This disagreement resides in the fact that the whole obsession with nonbeing (gaps in being), has nothing to do with Hegel's rational account of self-conscious agency. Žižek is too old-fashioned and occupied with problems that have been solved hundreds of years ago. He is drawn away from Hegel via Schelling back to the obsolete problems of Plato's *Parmenides*.

What does one do with these criticisms? I will take up some of their points but without endorsing any of them. I will show how Žižek *is* a philosopher, at the same time immanently related to something outside philosophy; that this is the very systematic locus of his "gappy ontology," an ontology needed to overcome the insuperable givenness of the one space of reasons (and account for how one can get into it in the first place). This comes with the need to return to some of the oldest problems of philosophy (problems of the one, of the many, of being and nonbeing) that are by no means obsolete and stand at the heart of Plato's *Parmenides* dialogue. I thereby want to demonstrate that Žižek's project may indeed be called an idealism, but as a renewed, an incomplete idealism—what I call an *idealism without idealism*.[13] Hence Žižek contends following Alain Badiou, and I agree, that one needs "a *repetition* of Plato's founding gesture." For this "is our basic philosophico-political choice (decision) today: either repeat in a materialist vein Plato's assertion of the meta-physical dimension of 'eternal Ideas,' or continue to dwell in the postmodern universe of 'democratic-materialist' historicist relativism, caught in the vicious cycle of the eternal struggle with 'premodern' fundamentalisms. How is this gesture possible, thinkable even?"[14] This is the question I will address in what follows. Pippin is hence correct in one respect: Žižek is led back to a specific kind of old problem, namely Platonism. But what is, if there were, a Žižekian Platonism? I will begin to answer this question, but will limit the scope of my investigation to Žižek's recent book on Hegel and to the reading of Plato's *Parmenides* therein. Yet, before turning to Žižek, a detour to delineate what is at stake will prove instructive.[15] This detour leads to a reading of *Parmenides* proposed by Badiou.[16]

For Today: Plato's Being and Event

A reading of Plato's *Parmenides*, rarely commented on, is presented in meditation 2 of Badiou's *Being and Event*. He demonstrates in meditation 1 that any ontology, since its "Parmenidean disposition,"[17] constitutively has to rely on a decision. Ontology is a truth procedure, that is to say: it is something relying on something undecidable (an event), which necessitates a decision that then produces consequences brought about by a faithful subject.[18] The present created in this ontological procedure is for Badiou a theory.[19] The *Parmenides* offers an account of how to conceive of theory (i.e., the present in ontology), since "the revolving doors of Plato's *Parmenides* introduce us to the singular joy of never seeing the moment of conclusion arrive."[20] There is no logical—no objective—manner in which one may be able to infer if being is one or multiple. It remains undecidable, and thereby it depicts the necessity of a decision constitutive of any ontology. *Parmenides* is a metaontological treatise, a philosophical treatise on ontology.

Clearly, one can conceive of (present) being by means of the multiple. But if what is conceived of (presented) is also inherently one, the multiple (presentation) is not. This generates a contradiction. But if the multiple (presentation) is, being is not one. This also generates a contradiction, since any presentation of being can only be *this* presentation of being if it is *one* presentation.[21] The two options (either the one is *or* the multiple is) cannot be logically reconciled. This impossibility necessitates a decision. This is the outcome of the exercise in undecidability,"[22] that is, the *Parmenides*. This very reading thus proves the fact that ontology cannot but be dependent on an event, or in other words: ontology is a subjective truth procedure grounded on undecidable events. There is no and never will be any objective ontology. The decision is thus as much logically impossible as it is necessary. It indicates the real of (any) ontology. The decision decides that the *presentation of being is multiple*. This is to say that being as such is not identical to its presentation. Hence it is subtracted from the one and from the multiple. But it also decides that the one is not. How can this be made consistent? Being is presented as multiple, but being is not multiple. The very consistency of any presentation relies on counting being as *this* multiple, yet it is not one, for the one is not. This is to say: being as such escapes the dialectic of one/multiple, for "there is no structure of being . . . we declare it heterogeneous to the opposition of the one and the multiple."[23] Being stands as that which is unpresentable on one side, presentation (that is, the one and the multiple) stands on the other, yet *what* is presented is being. This is where the proponent of a proclaimed "*Platonism of the multiple*"[24] turns to Plato's *Parmenides*.

In this dialogue Plato elaborates—depending on the count[25]—eight, nine, or even ten hypotheses concerning the relation between the one, the multiple, being, non/not-being. Although this logical exercise has been read as "mythical sacred text,"[26] as foundation of negative theology, as "humorous polemic, designed to reduce the Eleatic doctrine of a One Being to absurdity,"[27] or as mere logical sophism, Badiou takes it absolutely seriously and thereby follows Cornford's contention that it "is an extremely subtle and masterly analysis, dealing with the problems of the sort we call logical,"[28] even onto-logical. What the dialogue investigates is what follows from the assumptions that "the One is" or that "the One is not." In meditation 2 of *Being and Event*, Badiou investigates only what follows from the assumption that the one is not. The decision has already been taken.[29] One can only start with the second part of the dialogue, since it is precisely the relation between the first assumption (the one is) and the second one (the one is not) where the decision is located. This is a decided reading. Initially Badiou diagnoses that "there is fundamental asymmetry between the analytic of the multiple and the analytic of the one itself" concerning the consequences of the assumption that the one is not. This is because "the non-being of the one is solely analyzed as non-being" and nothing is conceptually derivable about the one itself, "whilst for the other-than one . . . it is a matter of being."[30] If the one is not, one at the same time cannot but ascribe a being to it, the being-not-to-be. "If we assert that something is not, we yet name it in the same breath."[31] But there is thus no positive conceptualization of one-ness in itself.[32]

On the other side, there are logically derivable consequences for that which is not the (not-being-)one: First one can claim that the others are not simply others-to-the-one because the one is not. One may say that "the others are Others."[33] If the others are others (to) themselves because the one is not, the others are but pure and inconsistent multiplicity. This is to say that one assumes the purest form of presentation of being (a presentation without one), that is, presentability as such, which logically precedes any-one. But if any presentation implies (a count as) one and thought itself needs a presentation, for without a "mediation of the one"[34] it would not be consistent, what Badiou finds in *Parmenides* is the idea that thought is logically grounded on something that is "actually unthinkable as such."[35] Thinking being is grounded in the nonbeing of the one; the presentation of being qua being is pure multiplicity—pure multiplicity, which as such, at least for Plato, cannot be thought, as any thought would transpose it into consistent multiplicities. Pure presentation is indistinguishable from unpresentation.

What can ultimately be said about the others? This is precisely where the end of Plato's dialogue becomes significant. Plato there states "without the one, it is impossible to conceive of many."[36] "If none of them is one thing [if multiplicity is inherently multiple], all of them are no thing."[37] For Badiou the whole question amounts to the status of this no-thing. He states that "if the one is not, what occurs in the place of the 'many' is the pure name of the void, insofar as it alone subsists *as being*."[38] This is to say, that being is neither multiple (pure multiplicity is only the mode of presentation of being) nor one (as the one is a necessary operator of any consistent presentation).[39] Being can only be named as that which is unpresentable and can only be thought by thinking what cannot be thought—the name emerges as an index of the paradox. This name presents being as being-unpresentable. The void—"no thing"—as that which indexes this singular place is the name of being. Only by thinking what one cannot think can one arrive at naming being. Thinking being therefore relies on the unthinkable becoming thinkable (as unthinkable) and this is precisely why *Parmenides* is a treatise on eventality—for only events generate a new thinkability of the unthinkable. Only against this background is one also able to turn to the first part of the dialogue (investigating the assumption that the one is), for the one is that which emerges as an effect of a paradoxical (self-belonging) multiplicity (event) and cannot sustain itself other than by being formed into one (name).[40]

The negative consequence that there is no-thing if there is no-one leaves for Badiou only one solution: to contend that the one in ontology is an operation that generates structure(d presentation), which itself emerges due to an event, that is, due to the appearance of a rupture in ontology. One has to be absolutely clear here: an event is never an event of being. The being of an event is multiple (it is a paradoxical multiplicity), but being is itself not eventral. Also there is not a first (ur-)event. Being simply can be (re)named if there are historically specific events in ontology (i.e., in the discourse on being), that is, an event "opens a new access to the Real as such."[41] This is why the latter part of *Parmenides* for Badiou precedes the first; first it is that which cannot come first, the thought of an event that then retroactively generates the nameability of the real of ontology. Only from the assumption that the one is not, one can derive that there is being, event, and then an operation of the count (since there is no action of being, being is unpresentable). Badiou's twist is to argue that conceiving of the one as counting and structuring operation makes it possible to state that (1) thought needs presentation, that (2) any presentation relies on the one, and that (3) thereby one can think of that which is counted as one retroactively as that which will have been logically prior to the count. (The name of being as result of the count is posterior to and constitutive of an event.) This means, if pure multiplicity is pure presentation and being is unpresentable, being is that which can only be thought as subtracted from multiplicity, as multiple of no-thing that can only be named and thereby decided to be.[42] It is necessary to think being, yet impossible. Being is—this is the ultimate consequence of *Parmenides*—the real of ontology. *Parmenides* is Plato's

Being and Event—Badiou's work is thus repetition of Plato. How does Žižek repeat?

For Today: Plato's Less Than Nothing

Plato's *Parmenides* is the first text extendedly commented on by Žižek in some dense passages in his *Less Than Nothing*. He takes it as "the first exercise in dialectics proper."[43] With Parmenides one is dealing with the origin of (the thought of) dialectics. It shall be clear that dialectics is here reserved for materialist thought proper, hence one is dealing with a thinker reading the origin of dialectical thought itself as the emergence of dialectical materialism—hence any contemporary materialist has to repeat Plato's gesture. So, what to do with a text "heavily commented upon for 2.500 years"?[44] The first gesture is—like Plato's—to break with anything that seems self-evident. How to do this? By simply asking the question: "What if it is *Parmenides* that delivers Plato's true teaching—not as something hidden but in plain view?"[45] The "dialectical gymnastics"[46] of *Parmenides* do not amount to any positive doctrine, but this is their very peculiar result: "the only result is that there is no consistent totality, no 'big Other.'"[47] The true result is a nonresult. This means that the contradictions throughout the whole dialogue belong "to the 'thing itself.'"[48] Žižek does not relate this to any necessity of an impossible decision. Rather he indicates the necessity of the impossibility of consistency (hence the place of decision). Yet, this implies that there is always the impossible possibility of a decision and this is what the *Parmenides* presents. Its logical inconsistency thus presents an ontological truth. Where does this truth lie?

It is precisely situated in the *relation* between the first and the second part of the dialogue. The question of how to repeat Plato is thus translated into the question of how to read the first part, where Plato discusses the contradictions that arise from attributing opposite predicates to the same entity (under the assumption that the one is), in relation to the second, where he starts from the assumption that the one is not. The problem one confronts when seeking to repeat his founding gesture is hence a *problem of relation*. Žižek distinguishes four ways of reading the relation of the Parmenides: (1) The first part presents a theory of ideas that is supposed to account for why one thing can be one and multiple at the same time (say Socrates is idea-wise one, yet he has multiple attributes), whereas the second introduces this contradiction "into the real of Ideas themselves."[49] That is to say that even though it seems that "contradictory attributes can be described to things, but not to ideas"[50]—what Dolar beautifully calls "Plato's immense heroism"[51] consists in delineating subsequently that the ideas (in opposition to what most readers of Plato assume) are themselves not consistently constituted. (2) The relation between the parts of the dialogue can thus be conceived of in similar terms as the relation between Hegel's *Phenomenology* and his *Logic*. In the first part someone pretends to know and is questioned, similar to Plato's early dialogues; the second part presents a "logical self-deployment of notional determinations." But this time it is Socrates who pretends to know (he presents his theory of Ideas) and is questioned. The whole Platonic procedure has here become self-reflexive, self-critical. Plato's *Parmenides* is Hegel. (3) This is why any reading that sees in the second part a resolution of the logical impasses of the first has to be dismissed in a further step, since one would end with a reconciliatory version of Plato(-Hegel)—with one that although endorsing progression via contradiction ultimately presents a final sublation. Against this Žižek argues for taking the dialogue immediately in its totality, whereby the different hypotheses of the Parmenides can be read as presenting "a formal matrix of eight possible worlds"[52]—Plato explodes any consistent transcendental structure and rather depicts a multiplicity of transcendentals that structure completely different worlds, in Badiou's sense of the term. The *Parmenides* is "Plato's 'logics of worlds.'"[53] (4) It follows from this that the first part presents a critique of any dualist account of the doctrine of Ideas (ideas on one level, appearances on the other), whereas the second spells out the ultimate consequence of the assumption that the ideas themselves are inconsistent, namely that "nothing fully exists, reality is a confused mess about which nothing consistent can be said."[54] Yet, this is not merely a negative result but needs to be given its full ontological weight. In Žižek's words: "Is this not the most succinct, minimal definition of dialectical materialism?"[55]

One can clearly see that the totality of these four accounts of the inner relation of the *Parmenides* presents precisely what Žižek calls dialectical materialism (not as something hidden, but in plain view). One starts with a too external, abstract account of the dualism of appearances and ideas that accounts for the relation between one and the multiplicity (of attributes ascribable) and inscribes this duality into the realm of ideas itself (1). Yet, this is a move which is analogous to moving from the logic of phenomena to the logic of the logic (2), whereby one generates a supplement, that is, the self-reflexivity that does away with the dualism between ideas and appearances still assumed in the first immediate transition from phenomena to ideas. A shift of perspective changes everything. Thereby one can also account for the fact that there is not one stable consistent world, not even the otherworldly world of the ideas. One hence moves back to the logic of phenomena (as in a movement constitutive of anamorphosis) into which the inconsistency is inscribed again. This means that the inconsistency of ideas generates the insight that there are many worlds; no particular world as such is (transcendentally or phenomenally) consistent (3). This is to say, that there is no consistent (meta)transcendental standpoint from which the relation between logical and phenomenal inconsistency could be accounted for—there is only the shift of perspective. Ultimately, this leads to the proper dialectical (materialist) outcome that one has to account for the inconsistency of all three elements involved: the ideas, the phenomena, and the relation between the two. It is not only that the phenomena are inconsistent and one finds stability on the level of ideas, but it is also not the case that in addition ideas are inconsistent and therefore there is some collateral damage done for the phenomena it can be seen that ultimately even their relation is inconsistent. This is why this very relation can only be presented in a series of progressive impasses, higher-level nonresolutions and inconsistencies. It is as if "each time we get a very specific negative result not to be confused with the others."

This *is* Žižek repeating Plato's gesture:[56] a reading of the *Parmenides* that demonstrates its persistent actuality by depicting how the dialogue itself is non-all, incomplete. Žižek's repetition of Plato in reading *Parmenides* presents it as putting forward the idea of an idea, since an idea is "appearance as appearance. . . . Ideas are nothing but the very form of appearance."[57] The form of the *Parmenides* is hence the very form of appearance (in its progression to higher nonresolutions). Its ultimate outcome is "that there is not ultimate Ground guaranteeing the consistent unity of reality, i.e. that the ultimate reality is the Void itself."[58] Plato's *Parmenides* presents his doctrine of Ideas in plain view, namely as systematic unfolding of the very inconsistent form of appearance as such—this is why the form of the dialogue *is* the form of appearance and hence *is* an Idea. Yet, to see it, one needs a repetition of Plato: Žižek's reading of the *Parmenides* such that it enables a proper shift of perspective by itself performing one. There is thus no idea without repetition.

An idea is located in the very inconsistency of appearances, appearing only through repetition. This is why it is, literally repeating, *appearance as appearance*. One may even contend that repetition precedes the idea—for it is only through Žižek's incompleting reading that Plato becomes a Hegelian, a Badiousian, a dialectical materialist, and ultimately Plato. Žižek here also repeats a gesture he takes from Lacan.[59] The statement "in Plato, idealism is all there is" can be negated either by saying that "in Plato, idealism is not all there is" and then attempting to detect another stratum of his thought that could properly be called materialist (yet Plato opposes this very option himself); or it can be negated by stating "in Plato, idealism is non-all." Whereas the first negation points to an exception with regard to the first statement (there is all this idealism in Plato, with the exception of his for example theory of the state), the second negation does not rely on any exception with regard to Plato. It rather asserts that there is nothing that is not idealist in Plato and idealism is non-all. Thereby Žižek's Platonism is idealist—but of a specific kind. It is an *idealism without idealism*, an incomplete idealism. Plato turns out to be the first Hegelian, Badiousian, dialectical materialist, and Žižekian.[60]

To conclude: What one can learn from Žižek's reading of Plato is that only through his repetition emerges something that may prove to be a point of orientation for materialist thought today, of a materialism that finally overcomes any myth of the given. And one can learn that only through repetition can one delineate the consequences for any contemporary dialectical stance within philosophy. One needs to open philosophy to that which can only be thought of as that which cannot be thought. For Žižek as much for Badiou this means: there is a Platonism of the Non-All. One can additionally learn from Badiou that repeating Plato implies a decision. If this also forces one to decide between Badiou and Žižek, or if one has to read them together, as an inconsistent couple, for the answer of this question it may here suffice to recall that for Freud repetition is only the second step. First there is remembering, then there is a repetition of that which cannot be repeated. Then there is working through. The latter takes time (and transforms it). The good news one gets from Badiou and Žižek is: the second step has been undertaken.

Notes

1 John Gray, "The Violent Vision of Slavoj Žižek," review of *Less Than Nothing: Hegel and the Shadow of Dialectical Materialism* and *Living in the End Times*, by Slavoj Žižek, *New York Review of Books*, July 12, 2012, www.nybooks.com/articles/archives/2012/jul/12/violent-visions-slavoj-zizek/?pagination=false.

2 Gray, "Violent Vision of Slavoj Žižek."

3 Peter Osborne, "More Than Everything: Žižek's Badiouian Hegel," review of *Less Than Nothing: Hegel and the Shadow of Dialectical Materialism*, by Slavoj Žižek, *Radical Philosophy* 177 (January/February 2013), 25.

4 Osborne, "More Than Everything," 24.

5 Osborne, "More Than Everything," 20.

6 Osborne, "More Than Everything," 25.

7 Robert Pippin, "Back to Hegel?," review of *Less Than Nothing: Hegel and the Shadow of Dialectical Materialism*, by Slavoj Žižek, *Mediations: Journal of Marxist Literary Group* 26, 1–2 (Fall 2012–Spring 2013), 7–29.

8 Pippin, "Back to Hegel?," 8.

9 Pippin, "Back to Hegel?," 8. Yet this is not true. See Andrew Cutrofello, *The Owl at Dawn: A Sequel to Hegel's Phenomenology of Spirit* (Albany: State University of New York Press, 1995).

10 Cutrofello, *Owl at Dawn*, 12.

11 Cutrofello, *Owl at Dawn*, 12.

12 Cutrofello, *Owl at Dawn*, 10.

13 See Frank Ruda, *For Badiou: Idealism without Idealism* (Evanston: Northwestern University Press, forthcoming).

14 Slavoj Žižek, *Less Than Nothing: Hegel and the Shadow of Dialectical Materialism* (London: Verso, 2012), 42.

15 For a brief account of the different traditions of reading the *Parmenides*, see Francis Macdonald Cornford, *Plato and Parmenides* (London: Routledge and Kegan Paul, 1939).

16 I refer to Badiou not only because Žižek does but also because it seems undisputed (maybe this is the only undisputed fact about Badiou) that he is a philosopher.

17 Alain Badiou, *Being and Event* (London: Continuum, 2005), 23, translation altered.

18 For a more detailed reconstruction, see Frank Ruda, "Subtraction," in *The Badiou Dictionary*, ed. Steve Corcoran (Edinburgh: Edinburgh University Press, 2015).

19 See Alain Badiou, *Logics of Worlds: Being and Event, 2* (New York: Continuum, 2009), 77.

20 Badiou, *Being and Event*, 23.

21 As Dolar resumes the fifth hypothesis of the Parmenides, which appears here: "there is

no multitude without counting, and there is no counting without one." Mladen Dolar, "In *Parmenidem* Parvi Commentarii," *HELIOS* 31, 1–2 (2004), 82.

22   Alain Badiou, *Le Poème de Parménide: Séminaire d'Alain Badiou (1985–1986)*, www .entretemps.asso.fr/Badiou/85–86.htm, accessed July 25, 2014.

23   Badiou, *Being and Event*, 26.

24   Alain Badiou, *Manifesto for Philosophy* (Albany: State University of New York Press, 1999), 103.

25   For the question of how to count: Francois Regnault, "Dialectic of Epistemologies," in *Concept and Form: Key Texts from the* Cahiers pour l'Analyse, vol. 1, ed. Peter Hallward and Know Peden (London: Verso, 2012), 119–50.

26   Dolar, "In *Parmenidem* Parvi Commentarii," 64.

27   Cornford, *Plato and Parmenides*, vii.

28   Cornford, *Plato and Parmenides*, ix.

29   And this "impossible choice leads to another impossible choice—which traces a pattern of impossibility"; Dolar, "In *Parmenidem* Parvi Commentarii," 78.

30   Badiou, *Being and Event*, 32.

31   Dolar, "In *Parmenidem* Parvi Commentarii," 87.

32   This is a result of Plato's first hypothesis, namely to consider the one solely in itself, the result of which is nothing can be said about the one, it remains ineffable. See Dolar, "In *Parmenidem* Parvi Commentarii," 73.

33   Badiou, *Being and Event*, 33.

34   Badiou, *Being and Event*, 34. On this also: Adam J. Bartlett, *Badiou and Plato: An Education by Truths* (Edinburgh: Edinburgh University Press, 2011), 150.

35   Badiou, *Being and Event*, 34. This is for Badiou the reason why Plato uses the "image of a dream."

36   Plato, *Parmenides*, trans. with commentary R. E. Allen (New Haven: Yale University Press, 1997), 166b, 64, translation modified.

37   Plato, *Parmenides*, 165e, 64.

38   Badiou, *Being and Event*, 35.

39   Badiou dialecticizes this point by demonstrating that within set theory it is possible to count as one without having any definite criteria to determine the one of the count. Set theory counts as one without counting as one and is able to present that which is counted, namely multiplicity in its purest form, as multiplicity of multiplicities (without one)—yet it still has to rely on the name of the void (the empty set). Although Plato "is Pre-Cantorian" (Badiou, *Being and Event*, 34), his systematic endeavor has to be sustained, even today. *This is how to repeat Plato's founding gesture.*

40   For the concept of forming into one, which depicts the act of naming that "is not really distinct from the count-as-one," see Badiou, *Being and Event*, 91.

41   Alain Badiou, "The Critique of Critique," Simon Gros website, http://simongros.com /audio/recordings/alain-badiou/introductory-lecture-notion-critique/, accessed July 25, 2014.

42   In Badiou's metaontology, his account of set theory, it is easy to see how he reformulates this Platonic point, when he claims: "the one is what counts the void as existence,

nominal existence of the unpresentable, a count that is an event, not a being" (Badiou, *Le Poème de Parménide*). This offers what some readers of Badiou contended he does not offer, an account of the count itself. That there is the unpresentable indexed by a name (which is what constitutes ontology proper—and in difference from philosophy) cannot but mean that it originated in an event. This is to say, ontology, i.e., mathematics as condition of philosophy, cannot but be understood as truth procedure. This is Badiou's tenth hypothesis.

43 Žižek, *Less Than Nothing*, 6.

44 Dolar, "In *Parmenidem* Parvi Commentarii," 63.

45 Žižek, *Less Than Nothing*, 49.

46 Žižek, *Less Than Nothing*, 48.

47 Žižek, *Less Than Nothing*, 49. A similar argument has been made with regard to other dialogues by Koyré. See Alexandre Koyré, *Introduction à la lecture de Platon/Entretiens sur Descartes* (Paris: Gallimard, 1991).

48 Koyré, *Introduction*, 51.

49 Koyré, *Introduction*. Plato is here a fierce critique of himself; it is, as Dolar remarked, as if he already formulates all of Aristotle's criticisms before Aristotle. (See Dolar, "In *Parmenidem* Parvi Commentarii," 64.) Žižek parallelizes the couple Plato-Aristotle with the couple one-being. See Žižek, *Less Than Nothing*, 52.

50 Dolar, "In *Parmenidem* Parvi Commentarii," 67.

51 Dolar, "In *Parmenidem* Parvi Commentarii," 73.

52 Žižek, *Less Than Nothing*, 52.

53 Žižek, *Less Than Nothing*, 51.

54 Žižek, *Less Than Nothing*, 53.

55 Žižek, *Less Than Nothing*, 67.

56 Obviously, I am consciously vulgarizing Žižek's far more elaborate reading of the particular hypotheses, and I also leave out his criticism of Plato. For the latter see Žižek, *Less Than Nothing*, 56. Nonetheless I contend that this vulgarization does offer an adequate dialectical account of Žižek's take.

57 Žižek, *Less Than Nothing*, 31.

58 Žižek, *Less Than Nothing*, 207.

59 Žižek, *Less Than Nothing*, 742.

60 If it once has been contended that the whole history of philosophy is nothing but a series of footnotes to Plato, one can here witness a proper Hegelian reversal. Yes, the complete history of philosophy is nothing but a series of footnotes to Plato until Hegel—after Hegel even Plato will have been a footnote to Hegel.

3

Materialism between

Samo Tomšič   **Critique and Speculation**

Contemporary philosophy is marked by a double turn, which is both materialist and speculative. There is a proliferation of new materialisms, which is already a sufficient reason for reserve. In this situation, Slavoj Žižek's work makes a double exception in regard to the speculative and critical tradition in philosophy. In what follows I would like to situate this exception by returning to the continuity between Hegel, Marx, and Freud, the three key "partners" of Žižek's work. In doing so I want to circumscribe the kernel of the encounter of Hegel's "absolute idealism" with what remain the most radical and politically subversive materialist projects, psychoanalysis and critique of political economy, to which Žižek's work provides an original contribution precisely by stubbornly insisting on the necessity of a materialist return to Hegel (just as Lacan, in his turn, accomplished a materialist return to Freud).

Let me enter the materialist debate by departing from the most discussed representative of today's speculative-materialist turn, Quentin Meillassoux. One of the propositions of Meillassoux's manifesto for a renewal of speculative-materialist thinking is the affirmation of speculation against critique, a systematic rejection of tradition inaugurated by Kant, whose critical project strived to restrict "groundless" speculation. Today, however, critique and speculation are both banalized. The omnipresence of critical thinking lost its "sharp razor," making critique indistinguishable from cynicism. This course is undoubtedly due to the renouncement of speculation and dialectics. Speculation on the other hand is often presented as the paradigm of thinking, which lost its connection to empiric reality and resides most often in humanities and in financial economy. In addition, did not Kant show that speculative thinking could easily turn into *Schwärmerei*, a combination of apparent reasoning and affection through enthusiasm, which pushes thinking toward delirium and madness? A step back might be in order here.

Kant's notion of critique responded to the epistemological crisis produced by scientific modernity. The radical shift of philosophical coordinates demanded a rethinking of the role of metaphysics. Kant was already in his precritical writings aware of the new tasks that awaited philosophy in the universe of modern science. *Dreams of a Spirit-Seer Explained through Dreams of Metaphysics*, where Kant expressed his philosophical crisis in his confrontation with the Swedish mystic Emmanuel Swedenborg, situated the new role of metaphysics in the following way: "metaphysics is science of the *limits of human reason*."[1] Kant's emphasis on the limits of thinking is, of course, the main target of Meillassoux's rejection of critique and of its accent on finitude.[2] However, the main lesson of Kant's writing concerns the uncanny closeness of dogmatic metaphysics and Schwärmerei, in which speculation becomes inseparable from illusions, dreams, and hallucinations.

How should we understand "science" and "limit" in Kant's rather ambiguous formulation? In other words, does science necessarily restrict thinking? Not necessarily. An alternative reading of Kant's formulation would be to focus on the deadlock of thinking in the encounter of its limits. Such deadlocks would then have to be turned into an object of science of thinking. Now, metaphysics is science of thinking as thinking already from Plato and Aristotle onward. However, in the universe of modern science thinking as thinking is understood differently from in the premodern *episteme*. It is no longer embedded in a harmonious relation of the macrocosmos and the microcosmos but instead manifests precisely in the encounter of the limits of thinking, the disruptions, breakdowns, and decentralizations of thinking. Kant's critical project may have distinguished critique of speculation, but the subsequent history of critique, notably in Hegel, Marx, and Freud, demonstrated that the discussion of the limits of thinking necessitates the critical *and* the speculative aspect, inseparability and even equivocity of speculation and critique. This is the kernel of the materialist current that, also according to Žižek, unites the three thinkers.

A "science of the limits of reason" is necessary because positive science does not conceptualize the breakdowns and the decentralizations it produces in thinking. Philosophy, on the other hand, always comprised the thinking of thinking. However, the modern scientific revolution subverted precisely the *space* of thinking. We can here recall the main theses of Koyré's epistemology.[3] Scientific modernity produced two groundbreaking effects: the abolition of the ancient division of the superlunary sphere, the seat of eternal mathematical truths and of cosmic harmony, and the sublunary sphere of generation and corruption, the seat of contingency, where the use of formalization made little sense for the classics. In modern science, on the contrary, mathematics no longer "saves the phenomena,"[4] that is, explains the appearances and the observable, but instead formalizes the contingent, thereby abolishing the three cornerstones of ancient episteme: totality, harmony, regularity. The immediate result of this formalization is not so much the "necessity of contingency," as Meillassoux would want it, but the demonstration of the contingency of necessity, or to put it with Žižek, the incomplete ontological constitution of reality, through which reality no less consists, albeit as nonall. This is the kernel of Hume's problem, which awoke Kant from his "dogmatic sleep." The second consequence of modern scientific revolution consisted in the abolition of the soul. Here dogmatic metaphysics for the first time encounters the limits of thinking, the immanent split of thinking, which will finally become the object of rigorous examination in Hegel, Marx, and Freud.

In this constellation the task of materialism is to explain the link between the discourse and the "limits of reason," that is, the breakdowns of thinking. In his book on Lacan, Jean-Claude Milner proposed the following definition of materialism: "the greatness of all authentic materialisms is that they are not totalizing. The fact that *De rerum natura* and *Capital* are unachieved is due to chance and, for this very reason, it follows from a systematic necessity."[5] The sign of materialism, which is not simply a (precritical) materialism of matter or (antispeculative) empiricism, lies in the departure from the non-all. Milner calls this materialist orientation "discursive materialism," which he introduces in the following way: "Lacan said that, in order to hit the walls, it is not necessary to know the plan of the mansion. Better put: in order to meet the walls where they are it is better not to know the plan, or if we happen to know it, it is better not to stick to it."[6] Discursive materialism discusses its object in relation to other objects, outlining the space that situates them. It thereby constructs the space of thinking. This thinking is again marked by limits, which manifest through the encounter of deadlocks or obstacles that resist thinking within the space of thinking and demonstrate its decentralization. Milner's formulation suggests that a materialist orientation implies a new understanding of the subject: not the subject of cognition but the subject implied by the encounter of the limits of thinking. Should metaphysics become a *materialist* science of the limits of reason it has to substitute the subject of cognition with what Lacan called the subject of modern science, the subject of decentralized thinking, explicitly addressed by both Marx and Freud.

The term "discursive materialism" is not without negative connotations. Žižek articulated its systematic critique, linking it with what Badiou in *Logics of Worlds* calls "democratic materialism," which attributes positive existence exclusively to bodies and language.[7] The *Materialismusstreit* in contemporary philosophy concerns the rejection of vulgar materialism and naïve empiricism, which systematically discredit dialectical speculation, and the "weak" postmodern version of discursive materialism:

> The basic premise of discursive materialism was to conceive language itself as a mode of production, and to apply to it Marx's logic of commodity fetishism. So, in the same way that, for Marx, the sphere of exchange obliterates (renders invisible) its process of production, the linguistic exchange also obliterates the textual process that engenders meaning: in a spontaneous fetishistic mis-perception, we experience the meaning of a word or act as something that is a direct property of the designated thing or process; that is, we overlook the complex field of discursive practices which produces this meaning.[8]

This fetishistic relation to language contains an ambiguity. On the one hand it seems to rely on the distinction between the things themselves and the human projection of meaning onto them; on the other hand it can also claim that our "symbolic activity ontologically constitutes the very reality to which it 'refers.'"[9] The first version still presupposes a distinction between words and things, situating linguistic production as an excess of meaning over objective qualities. The second one relativizes the externality of reality by reducing it to a performative linguistic effect.

However, the suggested homology of Marx and Freud misses their materialist point. Already Marx's introductory chapter to *Capital* leaves no doubt that the main discussion does not concern either the "adequate relation" between values and commodities or the projection of fetishist illusions on commodities themselves, or the constitution of the market as an enclosed and autonomous reality through the relations between values.[10] The true question that occupies Marx is how can the autonomy of value and the transformation of labor into labor-power, which can be correctly understood only through this autonomy, explain the production of surplus value, which is neither objective nor subjective: it can neither be found in things themselves nor can it be reduced to pure subjective illusion or performative effect of exchange. Marx departs from the autonomy of exchange, which constitutes a system of differences. His first thesis is that surplus value can be correctly situated only under the condition that we abstract from use values. However, this abstraction also transforms different forms of concrete labor into "abstract" labor-power, the exceptional commodity, which possesses the capacity to produce other commodities. Marx thereby situates two discursive consequences of the autonomy of exchange value, which are material but not empirical; they are both produced through abstraction from use values but are more real than performative effects of symbolic structures.

The difference between the Marxian and the postmodern understanding of discursive materiality implies two concurrent interpretations of the autonomy of value, in which Lacan famously recognized the anticipation of the structuralist discovery of the autonomy of the signifier. The postmodern discursive materialism reads this autonomy in a transcendental sense: the performative effects and production of meaning remain *inside* the symbolic. Surplus value and labor-power, however, go *beyond* the symbolic, or better, they highlight the flip side of the autonomy of the symbolic, its encounter with the real within discursive production. Lacan's homology between Marx and Freud claims something else than postmodern discursive materialism: "*Mehrwert* is *Marxlust*, Marx's surplus jouissance."[11] The inverse is also true: *Lustgewinn* (surplus jouissance) is Freud's surplus value; and the subject of the signifier is Lacan's labor-power. The psychoanalytic discussion of jouissance correctly situates the problem of discursive production: behind production of meaning and performative effects there is another production and another satisfaction, just as for Marx production of use values masks production of surplus value, and the satisfaction of needs, whether bodily or mental, masks an "other satisfaction" (Lacan), which aims at surplus value and surplus jouissance. This internal doubling of discursive production remains unaddressed in postmodern linguistic fetishisms.

Freud's *Interpretation of Dreams* repeats the logical steps of Marx's analysis of production.[12] On the one hand *Traumarbeit*, the dreamwork, produces narrated formations, which can be interpreted by ways of meaning. However, as long as we stick to this hermeneutic aspect of the unconscious, we cannot account for the satisfaction of unconscious desire and of repressed drive that takes place in the same production. Only surplus jouissance, Lustgewinn, as Freud puts it, explains why the unconscious labor in dreams, jokes, and slips of the tongue takes long and complex detours of condensation, displacement, and repression. These processes produce a "pleasure, which cannot be felt as such [Lust die nicht als solche empfunden werden kann]."[13] Freud thereby proposed the best description of what Lacan calls jouissance: a pleasure that cannot be experienced as pleasure, pleasure produced in radical discrepancy with meaning. Production of jouissance remains irreducible to meaning, even if it parasites on it, as Lacan's neologism *joui-sens* (enjoyed meaning) suggests. Freud's analysis of unconscious production, too, amounted to the discovery of the autonomy of the signifier.

What is matter according to Marx's and Freud's materialist orientation? Lacan provided the appropriate answer, nothing other than the signifier: "the signifier is matter that transcends itself into language."[14] Lacan thereby reformulates the basic and nowadays banal-sounding lesson of structuralism and of critique of political economy: the autonomy of the system of differences. That the system of exchange values is the same as the system of signifiers is explicitly indicated in Marx's idea of commodity language, which is, in addition, inseparable from the language of political economists, as Marx's prosopopoeia of commodities suggests. In his discussion of commodity fetishism, Marx imagines what commodities would say, could they speak, and then surprises the reader by quoting a political economist (Simon Bailey), who repeats, to the letter, the potential speech of commodities. But again, the main critical and dialectical point is that the act of transcendence (of the signifier into language and of exchange value into commodity language) is productive in the sense that it causes, in the living body that it affects in the process of labor and speech, two effects that need to be envisaged as real consequences of the signifier.

For Marx and Freud speech and labor are two privileged processes that reveal the constitution of the subject through alienation. Here, however, their common predecessor turns out to be none other than Hegel. In *Phenomenology of Spirit* we read the following discussion: "This outer, in the first place, makes only as an *organ* the inner visible or, in general, a being-for-another; for the inner, in so far as it is in the organ, is the *activity* itself. The speaking mouth, the working hand, and, if you like, the legs too are the organs of performance and actualization which have within them the action *qua action*, or the inner as such; but the externality which the inner obtains through them is the act as a reality separated from the individual."[15]

The chapter on physiognomy and phrenology contains an entire "philosophy of organs," in which Hegel goes well beyond the Aristotelian "linguistics," which still echoes in antispeculative thinkers like Wittgenstein and Chomsky, and according to which language is *organon*, an organ and a tool of communication and of social relation. Hegel rejects this linguistic Aristotelianism and develops probably the first *modern* theory of language, in accordance with the radical implications of scientific modernity, the latter departing precisely from the autonomy of (mathematical) language, detaching it from its communicative and meaningful dimension. Hegel's discussion of organs thus unveils a more complex reality behind the apparent relationality and utility of language.

In the organs of speech and labor the interior and the exterior intersect. Unlike other bodily organs, these two perform actions in which the self becomes a being-for-another. Better put, the two organs contain both the difference between the inner and the outer and establish the topological continuity between them. The move beyond the pragmatic discussion of organs is most apparent in the claim that the organs of speech and labor contain action qua action, which means that speech and labor are privileged actions, not aiming exclusively at an external goal but containing an autonomous goal in itself. Thereby they abolish the classical teleological context of action, for instance communication in the case of speech or production of use values in the case of labor. We can already observe in which respect Hegel's philosophy of organs anticipates the essence of Marx's and Freud's discussion of labor and speech through the autonomy of the system of differences. Action qua action contains a distortion, a minimal shift that splits the action from within. Through externalization, the interior is separated from the individual: it turns into an otherness that stands opposite to the individual self. To put it with Žižek, the mouth and the hand are "organs without a body"—autonomous organs, which serve other purposes than mere communication and production of use values. In them the movement of actualization assumes the form of alienation.

Hegel then continues:

> Language and labour are expressions [Äußerungen] in which the individual no longer keeps and possesses himself within himself, but lets the inner get completely outside of him, disclosing it to the other. For that reason we can equally say that these expressions express the inner too much, as that they do so too little: *too much*, because the inner itself breaks out in them and there remains no antithesis between them and it; they give not merely an *expression* of the inner, but are directly the inner itself; *too little*, because in language and action the inner turns itself into the other, thus disclosing itself to the element of metamorphosis [Verwandlung], which twists the spoken word and the accomplished act and makes of them something other than they are in and for themselves, as actions of this particular individual.[16]

Language and labor reveal the imaginary status of consciousness and individuality, for the action qua action implies a subject that is heterogeneous to consciousness and to the subject of cognition. The topological continuity between the interior and the exterior cannot be located. It is everywhere and nowhere in language and labor. In speech and labor a deindividuation of the body takes place, and for this reason they become, already for Hegel, the privileged processes of subjectivation. Hegel situates alienation in the equivocity of expression and externalization. The continuity between the self and the other indicates that for Hegel the self is not self-enclosed. This would still be a precritical understanding of the self. Because embedded in relation immanent to action, the self is constitutively split.

The actualization of the inner in the outer through speech and labor contains a discrepancy. This is what Hegel envisages when he writes that the externalization expresses simultaneously *too little* and *too much*, without there being a right measure or adequate relation between the expression and the expressed. The externalization produces a lack and a surplus, which makes alienation a productive operation, within which it is necessary to recognize a production of *subjective* lack and a production of *objective* surplus. Production is thus marked by a parallax structure. From the position of the self, externalization through speech and labor produces a loss because the translation of the inner in the outer cannot faithfully reproduce the self—precisely because the self does not preexist externalization but is constituted through its reflection in the Other. Because the self is constitutively split, this split assumes the form of incompleteness and loss that necessarily accompanies the metamorphosis of the inner into the outer.

The metamorphosis introduces a topological *torsion*—a twist, as Hegel puts it—into words and actions, highlighting that speech and labor necessarily cause nonidentity and too-much-ness. In and for itself they might appear as actions of particular individuals, but they are also autonomous: the in-and-for-itself is contained in the organs of action, which makes it actual for others. Hegel very precisely formulates that in the same action the inner breaks out of itself, it becomes more than it is when considered as retreated in itself. The action of speech and labor only retroactively makes the self and the other appear in opposition and external difference. Such differentiation makes no sense in the organ, where the action qua action is precisely the torsion of the inner in the outer and the alienation of the subject in the Other. Language and labor are continuously marked by productive errors rather than adequate reproductions.

The discussion of speech and labor concludes in the following way:

> The action, then, as a completed work, has the double and opposite meaning of being either the *inner* individuality and *not* its *expression*, or, qua external, a reality *free* from the inner, a reality which is something wholly other from the inner. On account of this ambiguity, we must look around

for the inner as it *still is on the individual himself*, but visible or external. In the organ, however, it is only as the immediate *activity* itself, which attains its externality in the act, which either does, or again does not represent the inner. The organ, regarded in the light of this antithesis, does not therefore provide the expression, which is sought.[17]

The completed work is actual opposition, entirely intertwined with the inner and entirely autonomous from it, indifference of the self and the Other. However the focus on the organ reveals more than the product. It shows that every action involves a constitutive inadequacy. The act does and does not represent the inner: it represents the inner for another, for instance for another signifier, in the case of language, or for another value, in the case of labor. The action qua action is concretization of the autonomous system differences. This concretization, of course, also implies adequacy: who would seriously claim that there is absolutely no communication in language, or that values and words do not designate things? But this relationality is not essential because the same concretization also implies inadequacy, which produces the loss and the surplus. The latter have no equivalent or adequate reference in the order of things and are grounded in the minimal gap between thinking and being: alienation. Because of this "antithesis," as Hegel says, aiming at the simultaneity and inseparability of adequacy and inadequacy, representation and misrepresentation of the inner in the outer, of the self in the Other, the organ does not provide the wanted or the sought expression. To return to the ambiguity of the German *Äußerung*: the organ does not merely express but externalizes; it does not merely constitute an imaginary relation but a symbolic nonrelation. Language and labor are both actualizations and movements of this nonrelation and contradictory tension between expression and externalization. Expression would be a faithful reproduction of the inner in the outer, while externalization is an unfaithful production, which introduces into reality more than it contains.

The question of the subject and of the mode of production that brought it into existence is the privileged *Kampfplatz* of materialism and idealism. This is no less true for contemporary discussions, where the question of the subject can serve as a test of the new materialisms. In a way, Hegel's philosophy of organs already anticipates the materialist turn accomplished by Marx's labor theory of value and Freud's labor theory of the unconscious. In his *Theses on Feuerbach*, Marx criticized the old and new materialisms of his time for remaining stuck in the idealist frames of philosophical theories of cognition, referring to consciousness, human essence, sensuality, and so on.[18] Marx detects the lack of precritical materialism (and of his own early humanism) in the fact that it failed to articulate a materialist theory of the subject. For this reason, he concludes that (materialist) philosophers have merely interpreted the world. This seemingly antiphilosophical thesis contains a legitimate point: (materialist) philosophers have approached the ontological and the social reality through the lenses of cognition, whereas a theory of action and change would necessitate a different theory of the subject, a sharp distinction between the idealist subject of cognition, which replaced the premodern metaphysical soul, and the subject of alienation, produced by the autonomy of the system of differences, which determines speech and labor. The subject of cognition is precisely *not* the subject of politics. Marx claims this in his *Theses* when he writes that the subject should be thought of as an *effect of the ensemble of social relations*: not as substance, which would be unaffected by the symbolic relations that constitute the self and the Other, to put it with Hegel, but as their real consequence. Alienation now becomes the privileged name of production process, which results in a subjectivity that is heterogeneous to consciousness. As production of subjectivity, alienation should not be considered as secondary (something that would alienate some preexisting human essence) but as primary (something that precedes the division on the self and the Other). In other words, alienation should be thought of not only as constituted alienation but also as constitutive alienation. In this respect, Marx's critical project strives to overcome the ambiguity that can still be detected in Hegel's discussion of alienation through externalization, thereby providing the radicalization of Hegel on the terrain of labor.

Lacan's structural psychoanalysis accomplished the same radicalization on the terrain of language. Saussure's isolation of the autonomy of the signifier and Freud's analysis of the unconscious detect the set of formal operations that stand for constitutive alienation and that produce the subject as the materialization of loss and the object as the materialization of surplus. Saussure, however, failed to make the materialist move that would amount to a materialist theory of the subject. Only Freud's linguistic and labor theory of the unconscious explored the aspect of the autonomy of the signifier that Saussure neglected, precisely its productive dimension actualized in speech. In this precise sense, Freud unknowingly resolved in Hegel the same ambiguity as Marx.

There is thus a deep continuity between critique of political economy and psychoanalysis: they both anticipate the linguistic isolation of the signifier, but they also both already make a move beyond the structuralist discovery by focusing on the productive side of the autonomy of the system of differences. In this way they restrict the transcendentalism of the symbolic, pursuing the Hegelian line of discussing labor and speech as the privileged processes of constitutive alienation. The anticipation of the autonomy of the signifier in both critical projects helps to expose the materialist kernel of Hegel's philosophy and shows that this autonomy is more generally the critical-speculative core of authentic materialism. The main task of materialism consists in isolating the subject *caused* by the autonomy of the system of differences. In this way, Marx and Freud appropriated and mobilized the subject of modern science.

At the critical point of the subject the epistemological aspect of Materialismusstreit intertwines with politics. This intertwining can be approached through Milner's rather provocative thesis that there is no politics that would be entirely synchronic to the modern universe.[19] We could claim that the term "communism" strives to account for this political gap and envisages a politics that *would* be entirely synchronic to the modern universe, meaning that it would abolish the ongoing division on the "superlunary" sphere of capitalist abstractions and the "sublunary" sphere of the proletariat. Communism would then stand for a repetition of modern epistemological revolution in the social and the subjective sphere. This also suggests that the capitalist "permanent revolution" is essentially a reactionary formation, an attempt to neutralize the emancipatory potential of modern science. Marx addressed this reaction in his well-known claim that, rather than freeing laborer from labor, modern science, in its capitalist appropriation, ended up freeing labor from its content, transforming labor into commodity labor-power. One of the challenges of politics that wants to reclaim the communist idea, is to detect and to mobilize the emancipatory potential of science, as far as scientific modernity has produced a new form of subjectivity, which is irreducible to the capitalist and the democratic segregation. Capitalism managed to mobilize scientific knowledge in order to produce the subject qua commodity (labor-power). By turning the subject of modern science (which would also be the subject of modern politics) into an object, capitalism revealed itself to be essentially Ptolemaic, constituting the closed world of universal commodification, where the market, as we are repeatedly told, is endowed with the power of self-regulation and harmonious movement. In this closed world, labor-power may be the only universal subjective position but it is equipped with a commodity soul. All this suggests that capitalist modernity is actually pseudomodernity.

The intertwining of human language and commodity language, highlighted by Marx's critique of political economy, and the neutralization of language of emancipatory politics through commodification, which is precisely a form of language, shows that the absence of politics, which would be synchronic to the modern universe, is expressed also as the absence of an autonomous language of political emancipation, a language that would detach the subject from commodity language and from commodity soul. The communist politics would then need to produce a discursive shift, as Lacan would put it, an inversion within language: not in order to construct some sort of political metalanguage but to force a tension in commodity language that would amount to decommodification of the subject rather than to the construction of new particular social identities, which reassume the commodity form, or to some fantasmatic abolition of alienation, something that Freudo-Marxism used to argue.

Notes

1   Immanuel Kant, "Träume eines Geistersehers erläutert durch Träume der Metaphysik," in *Werkausgabe*, vol. 2 (Frankfurt: Suhrkamp, 1972), 983.

2   Quentin Meillassoux, *After Finitude*, trans. Ray Brassier (London: Continuum, 2008).

3   See Alexandre Koyré, *Études d'histoire de la pensée scientifique* (Paris: Gallimard, 1973), 170, 197.

4   Koyré, *Études d'histoire de la pensée scientifique*, 89.

5   Jean-Claude Milner, *L'oeuvre claire: Lacan, la science, la vérité* (Paris: Seuil, 1995), 10.

6   Milner, *L'oeuvre claire*, 9.

7   Alain Badiou, *Logics of Worlds*, trans. Alberto Toscano (London: Continuum, 2009).

8   Slavoj Žižek, *Less Than Nothing: Hegel and the Shadow of Dialectical Materialism* (London: Verso, 2012), 7.

9   Žižek, *Less Than Nothing*, 7.

10 Karl Marx, *Capital*, vol. 1, trans. Ben Fowkes (New York: Vintage Books, 1977).

11 Jacques Lacan, *Autres écrits* (Paris: Seuil, 2001), 434.

12 Sigmund Freud, *Die Traumdeutung, in Studienausgabe*, vol. 2 (Frankfurt: Fischer, 2000).

13 Sigmund Freud, "Jenseits des Lustprinzips," in *Studienausgabe*, vol. 3, 220.

14 Lacan, *Autres écrits*, 209.

15 G. W. F. Hegel, *Phenomenology of Spirit*, trans. A. V. Miller (Oxford: Oxford University Press, 2004), 187, translation modified. See also G. W. F. Hegel, *Theorie Werkausgabe*, vol. 3 (Frankfurt: Suhrkamp, 1970), 235.

16 Hegel, *Phenomenology of Spirit*, 187–88, translation modified; *Theorie Werkausgabe*, 235–36.

17 Hegel, *Phenomenology of Spirit*, 188, translation modified.

18 Karl Marx, "Thesen über Feuerbach," in *Werke*, vol. 3 (Berlin: Dietz, 1969).

19 See Milner, *L'oeuvre claire*, 151.

4

Benjamin Noys | **Žižek's Reading Machine**

In an interview Alain Badiou makes a comment on Žižek's practice of interpretation: "you can ask him, 'What do you think about this horrible movie?' And he will have a brilliant interpretation that is much better than the actual movie because his conceptual matrix is very strong and very convincing." Badiou continues: "Žižek offers us something like a general psychoanalysis, a psychoanalysis that exceeds the question of clinics and becomes an absolutely general psychoanalysis. This is the first time that anyone has proposed to psychoanalyze our whole world."[1] It is the aim or claim to psychoanalyze our whole world that is often regarded as the problem with Žižek. Even Badiou seems to register some anxiety about the omnivorous quality of Žižek's psychoanalytic reading of the world. In another interview from the same period Badiou gives a rather different take on Žižek's "matrix": "I say to him often, because he is really a friend, 'you have a matrix, a terrible matrix, and you apply your matrix to everything.'"[2] This "terrible matrix" is terrible because it encompasses everything, in a hyperbolic gesture that plays on the worst fears of psychoanalytic reductionism.

For those less sympathetic to Žižek the matrix is more terrible in the literal sense. The threat is that Žižek is not only an omnivorous reader but also a *bad* reader. Žižek is sloppy, inaccurate, overly dependent on secondary sources, repetitive, and too rapid—to summarize the usual reader's report critics like to give Žižek. In Geoffrey Galt Harpham's characterization, Žižek's method is antithetical to academic and democratic norms, presenting a "closed universe" or "a virtually totalitarian world."[3] Like some nightmarish postmodern incarnation of Hegel, Žižek not only subsumes the world under his matrix but if the world should not fit the matrix then too bad for the world.[4]

This would seem to be the final antinomy for readers of Žižek: either dazzling conceptual capacity or totalitarian reduction. Badiou, however, makes another comment concerning Žižek's "matrix": "that is, in my opinion, why Žižek is not exactly in the field of philosophy, but in the field of a new topology, a new topology for the interpretation of concrete facts in a situation, political events and so on."[5] This "not exactly in the field of philosophy" suggests that while Žižek has more and more stridently insisted that he is a philosopher, and a "dialectical materialist philosopher" at that, there may be something to this turn or twist of Žižek's matrix. This thread of a "new topology" suggested by Badiou offers a means to think against the antinomy of sophist versus philosopher by which philosophy demarcates its own limit.

My initial claim, to follow this thread, is that Žižek is *more* of a philosopher when he strains *less* to claim the title of philosopher. This involves taking seriously Badiou's claim that Žižek is "not exactly in the field of philosophy" as the means to neither dismiss or celebrate Žižek but to grasp the provocation of his work. In an ironic fashion this provocation can be grasped in that rather unpopular genre of philosophy: method. Žižek has a method of reading, and this method of reading can also help us grasp how we should read Žižek. To test this claim at the most extreme point of tension I will examine Žižek as a reader of philosophy. It is here that we can find the articulation of a "new topology" that neither fully inhabits philosophy nor simply claims to exit from philosophy.

How Žižek Reads

In Žižek's preface to *The Žižek Reader* he remarks: "I always perceived myself as the author of books whose excessively and compulsively 'witty' texture serves as the envelope of a fundamental *coldness*, of a 'machinic' deployment of the line of thought which follows its path with utter indifference towards the pathology of so-called human considerations."[6] Contrary to the constant stress on the singular nature of Žižek, with the focus on his mannerisms, clothing, speech, and physical appearance, Žižek "himself" suggests that he is a "reading machine." It is this "coldness" and, echoing Deleuze's essay on Sacher-Masoch, "cruelty," that reveals Žižek's method of reading. There is no such thing as "Žižek." There is no Žižek reading, except as the deployment of a conceptual machine that has as its bearer the empirical person named "Žižek."

This initial provocation is the key to grasping how Žižek reads, and especially how he reads philosophy. Against all the claims for Žižek as a strong reader, who bends and distorts the meaning of texts to serve his purpose, we have Žižek surrounding the cold core of conceptual articulation with a series of effects to allow us to read. To use a term deployed by Žižek, all the obscene jokes, gestures, and repetitions are merely ways to "gentrify" this machinic core that processes the world. This abdication of the self, in the guise of inflation, makes Žižek's reading machine operate in what Lacan calls the "discourse of the analyst."[7]

Žižek, drawing on Lacan's account of the four discourses (Master, Hysteric, University, and Analyst) refuses the encrypted mastery at work in the "discourse of the University." In that discourse the transmission of knowledge is passed off as neutral, while beneath the position of enunciation we find the function of mastery. For example, the opening of this chapter, which invokes Badiou, could be characterized as a typical example of this discourse—encrypting my authority in the voice of another. The analyst does not disavow authority in this fashion; in Lacan's famously scandalous pronouncement: "I always speak the truth."[8] And yet, unlike the Master, who simply makes an injunction, the Analyst speaks from the position of the loss or excess of the object a. Lacan goes on to say: "not the whole truth, because there's no way to say it all. Saying it all is materially impossible: words fail. Yet it is through this very impossibility that the truth holds to the real."[9] In this way the analyst mimics but also subverts the position of Master in the act of interpretation.

Žižek is not an analyst, and his method of reading does not seem even to correspond to the usual procedures of psychoanalytic criticism. Serge Doubrovsky argues that "psychocriticism" can be distinguished from all other forms of criticism by beginning where they stop, at the "production of an insignificant textual detail."[10] This kind of procedure, perhaps ironically, is closer to that of Derrida, who "produces" an insignificant textual detail (*supplément* in the case of Rousseau, *pharmakon* in the case of Plato) that forms the quasi-transcendental condition of the text. Žižek proceeds more like Heidegger in aiming at the ontological core of the text, as in Heidegger's reading of Kant.[11] Žižek objects to the historicizing procedure of cultural studies that operates "without even asking the naive, but none the less necessary, question: OK, but what *is* the structure of the universe? How *does* the human psyche 'really' work?"[12] What matters is the ontological question.

Žižek's method is to read philosophy as the site of ontological questioning, but a site that can only be understood through Lacanian psychoanalysis. Jacques Alain-Miller famously asked Lacan: "what is your ontology?"[13] Žižek's answer to this question is that Lacan's ontology is an ontology of the Real, but that such an ontology can only be grasped by the detour through philosophy or, more precisely, German idealism. In this double-reading, philosophical mastery is disrupted by the turn to psychoanalysis, but then as the condition of a return to philosophy. In this detour and return we avoid the reduction of psychoanalysis to what Jacques-Alain Miller calls a "pious hermeneutic."[14] Against meaning, although always in close proximity to meaning, the reading machine needs to operate at the "ontological" point of the objet a, which disrupts the function of meaning.

This procedure is best demonstrated in Žižek's readings of Schelling.[15] In topological terms the turn to Schelling is not simply a turn to philosophy but a torsion of philosophy. Žižek addresses through Schelling a political question: "How does an Order emerge out of disorder in the first place?"[16] If we find, as Žižek argues, that power depends on an obscene supplement of "subversion," and if, therefore, resistance can be absorbed by power, then the true path to the inconsistency of power is through the probing of "ordering" and the constitution of order in a new form. The second topological twist is that the turn to Schelling is due to the fact that Schelling is "out of joint." Schelling is in between—between the moment of German idealism, which he embodies at its highest point, and the moment of a post-Hegelianism of finitude, temporality, and contingency, which Schelling predicts. What Žižek extracts from this is a moment irreducible to both: a brief moment in which a new myth could form, a new relation to philosophy, which has since been ignored—the thinking of the absolute.[17] The third twist is that it is only through Lacanian psychoanalysis that we can grasp the *Grundoperation* of German idealism.[18]

The essential intervention of Schelling is to inscribe a necessary incompletion that overlaps with the thinking of the absolute. It is the audacity to think the absolute as the moment or process of decision and interruption that generates out of itself the vortex of the drives.[19] This inscribes incompletion in the absolute, and this is visible in Schelling's failure to complete any of the drafts of the *Weltater* project. This attests, for Žižek, to a materialist way of thinking that operates with and through incompletion.

Contrary to numerous criticisms of Žižek, and Žižek's occasional equivocations, the Real has to be read *in* the moment of appearing. It is, if we like, a constant companion to "reality." The Real is, therefore, not the simple province of the subject, as in Sartre's confining of nothingness to the act of the subject, but the Real is what that links, in inconsistency, the subject and "reality."[20] Inconsistency is inscribed in reality, for example in the famous scene from *Nausea* (1938), with Roquentin's encounter with the "knotty, inert, nameless" tree root.[21] Roquentin experiences the disintegration of reality: the "veneer had melted, leaving soft, monstrous masses in disorder—naked, with a frightening, obscene nakedness."[22] It is not that for Roquentin "words had disappeared,"[23] as Sartre suggests, and an overcrowded world of existence revealed. Instead, the Schellingian Ground or Lacanian Real emerges in the signifying order's lack and excess, which inscribes a remainder. "Nausea" belongs to reality; in Schelling's words, quoted by Žižek: "if we were able to penetrate the exterior of things, we would see that the true stuff of all life and existence is the horrible."[24]

This inscription of the Real is not a universal "key to all mythologies," à la poor Edward Casaubon in George Eliot's *Middlemarch*, that scholar who does not know German. Rather, it is a fleeting insight into a topological distortion that can only be tracked through the effects of that distortion. We cannot dwell in the nausea of the Real. This is evident through Žižek's procedure of reading through the "formal envelope of error," which consists of not only the errors of Schelling and Hegel but also our errors and the errors of Žižek. The "incompletion" of Žižek's own text lies in its constant return to Schelling's beginning as a beginning that always goes awry, and that we are always tempted to misunderstand. Schelling is a vanishing mediator of what will not vanish, of the indivisible remainder, that is thrown-up and then reingested, but at the cost of error. These errors include the Deleuzian positivation of the material, which is coupled with the Kantian tendency to posit the Real as merely negative vanishing point. The solution is to pass through these errors to reveal that the Real is "not a kind of external kernel" but "the 'irrationality,' the unaccountable 'madness,' of the very founding gesture of idealization/symbolization."[25] The Real is deduced "from the paradoxes of the negative self-relating of the Ideal."[26]

This proceeding through error is, at the same time, the most and the least philosophical procedure. It is the most philosophical as it tracks philosophy at its most exorbitant claim to the absolute. It is the least philosophical as this moment inscribes an incompletion that does not simply signal a negative limit to philosophy but places philosophy in constant relation to its own incompletion as a site of thinking. The gamble of Žižek's method of reading is to traverse philosophy by traversing its fantasy of mastery, which does not simply abandon philosophy but constantly returns to it as a necessary beginning.

How to Read Žižek

Žižek often announces his distaste, even horror, for debate, using the example of Gilles Deleuze.[27] It then might seem another instance of Žižek's "inconsistency" that he constantly engages in debate, replying to his critics at length. The accusation of "performative contradiction" is, as Derrida once noted, a "puerile weapon."[28] In this case it refuses to grasp how Žižek responds to his critics and what his method of response is. To read Žižek reading Žižek, or responding to the readings of his work, is one way to grasp how to read Žižek.

In his responses Žižek usually begins with the claim that he will not dialogue or debate and instead will repeat what he actually said. Žižek's insistence is that we need to read Žižek again; we need to read carefully, to the letter. In doing so we should bear in mind Lacan's invocation of the "letter" as the asignifying function that, borrowing from James Joyce, "litters" the "letter." To read to the letter is to read litter—to read the trash of the objet a. It is another return to the beginning, to the "madness" of that moment that cannot be reduced but that insists that it be read, all the while turning reading into rubbish.

Žižek's demand to be read in this fashion is to counter the fantasmatic construction of "Žižek" that he often faces. The reason for this method is that critics who accuse Žižek of the usual sins of inaccuracy, sloppiness, using bad taste jokes, and being offensive go on to commit all those sins themselves. It is as if once Žižek has been found to be breaking academic standards those standards themselves are no longer in play. In fact (without intending the hyperbole attached to the concept), we can say that Žižek finds himself in the position of "inclusive exclusion" in relation to these norms, as in the logical structure that Giorgio Agamben uses to analyze the operation of sovereign power on "bare life."[29] Žižek is included within the academic field, but in the mode of an excluded object, which marks the exception to academic norms. Geoffrey Galt Harpham offers perhaps the most hyperbolic instance of this argument when he suggests that Žižek's violation, in his eyes, of academic norms will lead not only to the extinction of knowledge but also of life itself "as we know it."[30] Harpham then violates those norms himself by constructing a bizarre fantasy scene of intellectual café life in Yugoslavia as what can only be called the "primal scene" of Žižek's practice.[31] This is even one of the more mild examples, considering the level of personal insult, patronizing or racist characterization, and political smearing to which critics, and often academic critics, of Žižek have stooped. Perhaps even worse, for the reader, is when such critics attempt to "outjoke" Žižek. That many of these gestures lack even the remotest shred of proof, whether they would be acceptable in academic discourse at all, merely adds to the (vicious) irony.

We can draw an analogy with the treatment of Jacques Derrida. The claim that Derrida violated reason was used to abandon any actual reading of his work and so to engage in gross accusations and criticisms that bore only tangential relation to reality. Žižek, like Derrida, in response simply suggests that we *read* the work. This might be considered the baseline for any academic practice, and certainly in the humanities it is difficult not to find an academic who does not complain about lack of reading in students. What Žižek suggests, in effect, is that this complaint be returned to sender. If, in the scandalous Lacanian aphorism, a letter always arrives at its destination, in this case the critics of Žižek send a letter that arrives at the correct destination: themselves. In this way Žižek's response is always the same for a reason; the reason being that the dismissal of his work has already prevented any actual reading taking place.

What, however, might it mean to read to the letter? In a discussion of Kafka, Žižek offers some reading advice: "Reading Kafka demands a great effort of abstraction—not of learning more (the proper interpretive horizon of understanding his work), but of *unlearning* the standard interpretive references, so that we become able to open up to the raw force of Kafka's writing."[32] This advice might be taken as a model for reading Žižek. Žižek engages with three discourses usually treated as the standard of "strong reading": psychoanalysis, Marxism, and Hegelian philosophy. The effort of abstraction to be made with reading Žižek would be one of "unlearning" our received images of these discourses, abstracting from the historical and hermeneutic reconstructions, to "open up to the raw force."

The "raw force" in question cannot be accessed as such. To return to the use of error as method, to try to recover or dwell in the "raw force" of the Real outside of discourse would be an error incited from within discourse. Instead, to "unlearn" requires the immense learning of a discourse. In parallel with the procedure of reading Schelling, to read Žižek requires close attention to his text, to its constant correction of its own errors, to its sudden breaks, to its interruptions, as necessary forms of incompletion that return us to the Real. The "Real" appears in these textual fractures, not as an insurgent force but as a logical and conceptual result of the machine of reading.

Žižek remarks that his critics constantly accuse him of oscillation.[33] This oscillation is, Žižek suggests, actually the result of three "errors": missing the actual shifts in Žižek's own position, a bad reading of what Žižek is saying, or an oscillation actually in the "thing itself." This last suggestion is, as Žižek notes, the crucial one. Oscillation or ambiguity belongs to the very nature of appearing and, especially, to the appearing of the Real. We are bound to commit an error of description as we try to align the Real within the usual coordinates. In this way we "frame" the Real. The difficulty is to keep thinking through the error, to follow the path to the oscillation.

If incompletion forms the horizon of Žižek's method of reading then the method of reading Žižek involves attention to oscillation. These moments converge. If we are to read Žižek then we must attend to the paradox of incompletion emerging through a thinking of the absolute. The sign of this emergence is the paradoxical moment of oscillation that refuses stabilization or resolution. This, however, is the moment of beginning. We cannot simply remain with oscillation, but have to trace this as a moment or effect internal to the gesture of beginning.

The method to read Žižek would therefore require an effort to trace how Žižek is a writer of beginnings. The sense of completion or saturation that sometimes seems to surround his work is the lure par excellence. Saturation, the ability to digest everything in the "terrible matrix," is a sign of the stretching of the matrix to its own internal and fractured constitution. Far from being a sign of completion, the textual production does not saturate the world but tracks into it to trace the beginning, the moment of "madness," that is constitutive of the "world."

Conclusion: Truth and Method

In his review of Žižek's *Less Than Nothing* (2012) Robert Pippin chides Žižek for being insufficiently Hegelian. This is due to the fact that Žižek is "deeply Schellingian."[34] For Pippin, Žižek tacks onto Hegel a "gappy ontology" that Hegel does not require.[35] Antagonism is not constitutive of reality but rather a feature of psychic or social reality.[36] This clarifies the stakes involved in Žižek's reading of philosophy. The tension of the moment of beginning remains, for Žižek, but it remains "internal" to reality as its moment of constitution. The beginning can never be gotten over, and it is not simply the beginning because in the moment of beginning it posits what came before: the vortex of the drives. Žižek's "materialism" is one that transits through idealism to suggest the indivisible remainder that is the trace of the beginning and also the result of the "negative self-relating of the Ideal."[37]

The difficulty remains, and this is one way to grasp Žižek's textual productivity, in clarifying this moment. The return of the beginning means we must begin again, and again, and again. In the repetition we constantly risk either treating negativity as a vanishing mediator that vanishes to reveal some positive materiality as such. This is the error of Deleuze and, we could add, many others. Here the moment of affirmation rests with an opening that exhibits a hypernegativity that is indistinguishable from a hyperaffirmation. The second error is to contemplate the negative moment of the beginning as an eternal limit, which returns us to a Kantian thematics of finitude and restraint. Again such a position is not uncommon today. It often returns to a political claim of the virtue of restrained action, which would ward off instantiating the negative.

Žižek's method is to constantly court, if not inhabit, these errors. It is only by constantly proceeding through these errors, which recur again and again, that we can think of the absolute as a thinking of the Real. What happens at this moment is not some magical solution in which we finally behold the truth of the Real. Instead, to borrow from what we could call Žižek's "best fiend" (after Werner Herzog) Deleuze, this moment is the moment of the posing of the problem. The problem, at this point, does not simply belong to the discourse of philosophy. At this moment a displacement takes place that generates a torsion in the field of philosophy and that places it within a "new topology" of the world. This beginning is the beginning that puts philosophy outside of itself, into intimate contact with all those cultural forms and practices that provide some of Žižek's best readings and that attract the most critical attention.

The point, to return to the metaphor of Žižek as reading machine, is that these moments of reading are lures that can disguise the machinic conceptual operation at work. In the same way Žižek's "personality" gentrifies the actual operation of his thought, the turns to culture, often in the mode of obscenity, ironically gentrify the reading machine as a delightful machine of insightful or provocative meaning. The truth of the method, instead, lies in the scandal that these are mere effects of meaning that disappear. The very excess of such readings, their digressive and interruptive character, places us in relation to a lack or absence. To find the same meaning is to find an empty meaning. This is not to place culture as secondary to philosophy, as mere "window dressing." Rather, the incompletion of philosophy requires the constant supplement of culture, which itself requires philosophy to dignify its own operations. We only have to attend to the constant use of theoretical tropes and resources by contemporary writers, musicians, and artists to see that the problem of the present does not lie in the fact that theory is detached from reality, which it then imposes itself on. The reverse is true. Reality is saturated with the theoretical.

Žižek's response is to proceed through philosophy at its most "abstract" to grasp this effect of saturation, especially in its ideological and political effects. This accounts for the centrality of Deleuze. Deleuze is not only an ideological symptom of the very success of theory. The fact that reality is Deleuzian, the Deleuze of vitalism and desiring-production, requires attention to the other Deleuze: the Deleuze of the sterile sense-event.[38] The fissuring of Deleuze from within creates the possibility of a new beginning, a new problem that results from the disruption of the smooth transition from philosophy to reality. It is the short circuit, to use a favorite Žižek trope, that opens the field of philosophy again. This is the point at which Žižek is a philosopher. This is also the moment of negativity.

The "truth" is the foundering on that moment, which requires the interruptive "gappy ontology" that Pippin rejects. If we sanitize Hegel as moving within the field of reality absorbing everything in his path, we cannot access the scandal of the absolute as the interruptive beginning and moment of madness. The topology of the world is the topology of the "night of the world," the empty interiority of the human subject, which we gaze into and in which we glimpse the Real.[39] This is the moment of negativity, the rending of the subject, that also emerges "in" the world and that prevents the closure of either the subject or reality.

Notes

1   Adam S. Miller, "An Interview with Alain Badiou: 'Universal Truths and the Question of Religion,'" *Journal of Philosophy and Scripture* 3, 1 (2005), 41.

2   Max Blechman, Anita Chari, and Rafeeq Hasan, "Human Rights Are the Rights of the Infinite: An Interview with Alain Badiou" (2005), *Historical Materialism* 20, 4 (2012), 184.

3   Geoffrey Galt Harpham, "Doing the Impossible: Slavoj Žižek and the End of Knowledge," *Critical Inquiry* 29, 3 (Spring 2003), 459.

4   Oxana Timofeeva has sympathetically reconstructed Hegel's logic of the notion; see Oxana Timofeeva, *History of Animals: An Essay on Negativity, Immanence and Freedom* (Maastricht: Jan Van Eyck Academie, 2013), 71–73.

5   Badiou in Miller, *Historical Materialism*, 41.

6   Slavoj Žižek, "Preface: Burning the Bridges," in *The Žižek Reader*, ed. Elizabeth Wright and Edmond Wright (Oxford: Blackwell, 1999), viii.

7   Jacques Lacan, *The Other Side of Psychoanalysis, The Seminar of Jacques Lacan, Book XVII*, trans. Russell Grigg (New York: Norton, 2007), 54.

8   Jacques Lacan, *Television*, ed. Joan Copjec (New York: Norton, 1990), 3.

9   Lacan, *Television*, 3.

10   Serge Doubrovsky, "'The Nine of Hearts': Fragment of a Psychoreading of *La Nausée*," in *Literature and Psychoanalysis*, ed. Edith Kurzweil and William Phillips (New York: Columbia University Press, 1983), 379.

11   Martin Heidegger, *Kant and the Problem of Metaphysics*, translated with an introduction by James S. Churchill (Bloomington: Indiana University Press, 1962).

12   Slavoj Žižek, *Did Somebody Say Totalitarianism? Five Interventions in the (Mis)use of a Notion* (London: Verso, 2001), 218.

13   Jacques Lacan, *The Four Fundamental Concepts of Psycho-Analysis*, trans. Alan Sheridan (Harmondsworth, UK: Penguin, 1977), 72.

14   Jacques-Alain Miller quoted in Bruno Bosteels, translator's introduction to Alain Badiou, *Wittgenstein's Antiphilosophy* (London: Verso, 2011), 1.

15   Slavoj Žižek, *The Indivisible Remainder: On Schelling and Related Matters* (New York: Verso, 2007).

16   Žižek, *The Indivisible Remainder*, 3.

17   Žižek, *The Indivisible Remainder*, 8.

18   Žižek, *The Indivisible Remainder*, 92.

19   Žižek, *The Indivisible Remainder*, 42.

20   Žižek, *The Indivisible Remainder*, 218.

21   Jean-Paul Sartre, *Nausea*, trans. Robert Baldick (London: Penguin, 1965), 186.

22   Sartre, *Nausea*, 183.

23   Sartre, *Nausea*, 182.

24   Žižek, *The Indivisible Remainder*, 24.

25   Žižek, *The Indivisible Remainder*, 52.

26   Žižek, *The Indivisible Remainder*, 110.

27   Slavoj Žižek, *Organs without Bodies: On Deleuze and Consequences* (New York: Routledge, 2004), ix.

28   Jacques Derrida, *Monolingualism of the Other*, trans. Patrick Menash (Stanford: Stanford University Press, 1998), 4.

29   Giorgio Agamben, *Homo Sacer: Bare Life and Sovereign Power*, trans. Daniel Heller Roazen (Stanford: Stanford University Press, 1998).

30   Geoffrey Galt Harpham, "Doing the Impossible," 468.

31   Harpham, "Doing the Impossible."

32   Slavoj Žižek, *The Parallax View* (Cambridge, MA: MIT Press, 2006), 144.

33   Slavoj Žižek, "*Concesso non dato*," in *Traversing the Fantasy: Critical Responses to Slavoj Žižek*, ed. Gregg Boucher et al. (Aldershot, England: Ashgate, 2005), 219.

34   Robert Pippin, "Back to Hegel?," *Mediations* 26, 1–2 (Fall 2012–Spring 2013), 10.

35   Pippin, "Back to Hegel?," 12.

36   Pippin, "Back to Hegel?," 24n11.

37   Žižek, *The Indivisible Remainder*, 110.

38   Žižek, *Organs without Bodies*, 21.

39   Slavoj Žižek, "The Abyss of Freedom," in *The Abyss of Freedom/The Ages of the World* (Ann Arbor: University of Michigan Press, 1997), 8.

The phenomena of anamorphism and the subversive effects, which results from the shift or switch of perspectives, is indeed much present and in my view also important for the work of Slavoj Žižek. It is closely connected to the question of the visual, the gaze, namely object a as the Real of late Lacan. This is used mostly in Žižek's analysis of cultural and aesthetic phenomena, and most frequently in his analysis of film art. It is no coincidence therefore that one of the best-known collections of his essays that tackle this problematic carries the title *Looking Awry*. There Žižek introduces the gaze and the voice as objects in the following way:

> for Lacan, these objects are not on the side of the subject but on the side of the object. The gaze marks the point in the object (in the picture) from which the subject viewing it is already gazed at, i.e., it is the object that is gazing at me. Far from assuring the self-presence of the subject and his vision, the gaze functions thus as a stain, a spot in the picture disturbing its transparent visibility and introducing an irreducible split in my relation to the picture: I can never see the picture at the point from which it is gazing at me, i.e., the eye and the gaze are constitutively asymmetrical. The gaze as object is a stain preventing me from looking at the picture from a safe, "objective" distance, from enframing it as something that is at my grasping view's disposal. The gaze is, so to speak, a point at which the very frame (of my view) is already inscribed in the "content" of the picture viewed.[1]

My leading task here however will not be to display Žižek's use of this Lacanian concept in the field of the visual arts but to focus on the locus and the function of the gaze as the object within Žižek's philosophy, within his philosophical writing. By now I have already introduced Lacan's idea of the gaze as the object; but why is Žižek particularly interested in the question of the awry look? A good way to begin with the adjective awry is by using the following quote from the Merriam Webster dictionary. The following anecdote, which is an illustration of the definition of the word *awry* in this particular English dictionary, may perhaps become useful for us.

> In his 1942 story "Runaround," Isaac Asimov offered his now-famous Three Laws of Robotics: A robot may not injure a human being or, through inaction, allow a human being to come to harm; a robot must obey orders given to it by human beings except where such orders would conflict with the First Law; and a robot must protect its own existence as long as such protection does not conflict with the First or Second Law. Most of Asimov's stories deal with things going *awry* because these laws don't equip robots to tackle real-world situations. — Robert J. Sawyer, *Science*, 16 Nov. 2007[2]

This anecdote relates the question of things "going awry" with the question of the functionning of robots as the symbol of science and human rationality, which are in Lacanese comprised in the term "the Symbolic." And Žižek as a Lacanian is theoretically interested precisely in those moments, when things go awry, when laws collapse and when things don't run the way they are supposed to. The question regarding Asimov's robotics is thus, do things go awry themselves or do we perceive them as such, and to whom does this awry nature, this askewness, belong? This leads us back to the reversal of perspectives in Hegel's motto that the Evil resides in the very gaze. And, if we paraphrase this thought of Hegel, we could say that the askewness (the awry character) resides in the very gaze that perceives askewness all around itself. Therefore, whose gaze captures that things go awry? To whom does the awry look belong?

Žižek's philosophical work as such resides in and functions through the specific transcendentality of the awry gaze, that is, to the Kantian transcendentalism with yet another Hegelian twist. This in a Hegelian way overturns Kant's own stake here. Namely, this evilness or awry character of the look (gaze) is transposed back into ontology, into being itself. What interests Žižek philosophically in recent works is the ontological structure of this gaze. He is interested in a kind of switch (shift) of the gaze, which determines the coordinates of our very being as such. According to Žižek, this gaze is the fundamental feature of the Lacanian concept of fantasy, but also the basis of the "objectively necessary appearance" of Marx's fiction of commodities in commodity fetishism. What I would like to underscore here is that for Žižek the meaning of philosophical dialectic resides precisely in this gaze as the reversal of perspective.

If the question of the gaze as the Real is at stake, then we could say that one of the most distinguished features of Žižek's theoretical work in general is his particular interest in the Real as the shifting movement of perspectives: "the Real is simultaneously the Thing to which direct access is not possible and the obstacle which prevents this direct access; the Thing which eludes our grasp, and the distorted screen which makes us miss the Thing; More precisely, the Real is ultimately the shift of perspective from the first to the second standpoint."[3]

Apart from Žižek's emphasis of the Hegelian subject in the *Phenomenology of the Spirit* as the bare act of looking behind the curtain of phenomena, behind the appearance, where one can find nothing, it is not coincidental that he is constantly following and giving special attention to particular shifts also in Lacan's thought.[4] As Žižek claims, Lacan in his later teachings (after *Seminar XI*) struggled to overcome the Kantian horizon in his rearticulaton of the concept of drive, and to move from "symbolic castration" to the "beyond castration" via Hegel: "there are thus three phases in the relationship of Lacan toward the tension between Kant and Hegel: from universal—Hegelian self-mediation in the totality of the Symbolic, he passes to the Kantian notion of the transcendent Thing that resists this mediation, and then, in an additional twist, he transposes the gap that separates all signifying traces from Otherness into the immanence itself, as its inherent cut."[5] Thus not only is Žižek interested in following the shifts (reversing) of perspectives (a Hegelian move) in his most important authors, Hegel, Lacan, and Marx, but also the shift determines the nature of his thought as such as well.

Let us first shift our attention to the question of Žižek's philosophical work on the materialist dialectic. We could say that his basic philosophical endeavor is to provide for a new materialist dialectic by, as Adrian Johnston puts it, "buggering" Hegel with Lacan and by reading Freudian death drive (*Todestrieb*) against the notion of subjectivity as self-relating negativity in German idealism. Žižek's philosophical acme thus lies in his unique materialist rendering of Hegel's dialectic through the Lacanian reading of the logic of the signifier, accompanied with the question of the difference and repetition. However, in terms of understanding the materialist dialectic based on the Lacanian logic of not-all, Žižek in *Less Than Nothing: Hegel and the Shadow of Dialectical Materialism* himself admits that there are some unsurpassable limits in Hegel. Nevertheless, two unique characteristics of Žižek's undertaking within the realm of contemporary philosophy are first, his insistence on the philosophical autonomous subject as the always already anterior gap (void) of negativity as the pure difference (based on his insight into the question of the subject in the philosophy of German idealism), in contrast to the project of the positive subjectivation after the Event (typical for the French thought of Althusser, Badiou, and Rancière, as he has largely shown in *Ticklish Subject: Absent Centre of Political Ontology*),[6] and second, the structure of the negativity of the drive as the Real as jouissance in later Lacan. Both of these are tightly connected to Žižek's relocation of the subject, as the negativity back into the substance, or into Being, if you will. As Johnston emphasizes in his *Žižek's Ontology: A Transcendental Materialist Theory of Subjectivity*, in Žižek there must always already exist the immanent transcendental conditions of possibility for the constitution of the free subject as an utterly ephemeral event of the transcendence, within the immanent materiality of Being, as the Hegelian "appearance qua appearance." It appears only when the normal historical, psychological, biological run of things breaks down and retroactively changes the coordinates of this being itself. However, in order for the ideological misrecognition, the failure of the interpellation into the Imaginary-Symbolic to happen as the true name for the subjectification, there must always already be a cleft, the negativity of the Real within the realm of Being, within the materiality itself. Adrian Johnston is here pointing to the idea of the subject as the result of the overlapping of two lacks, of the Symbolic and of the Real:

> the process Žižek describes in the passage quoted immediately above, a process in which the subject-as-$ arises out of signifiers as a medium of

subjectification, relies on the lack of a unifying closure in the symbolic order, namely, the fact that the big Other is barred because its own internal constituents and their laws create, one could say, a chaotic, broken-up hall of mirrors in which reflexive regressions potentially stretch out to infinity. And prior to this entrance into the defiles of the symbolic order's signifying batteries (an entrance creating both subjectification and the subject), a barred Real (as the anxiety-laden, conflict-perturbed corpo-Real) propels the human organism into the arms of this barred big Other. The subject-as-$ is a by-product of both the barred Real and the barred Symbolic.[7]

According to Žižek's understanding of the "Phallus" as the quasi-cause of the Sense, Johnston claims that Žižek's subject is transcendental, albeit in a strictly immanent way. The Lacanian understanding of the Symbolic castration, the Master-Signifier as the signifier of castration, is also the fundamental category of Žižek's understanding of dialectical materialism. Namely, the logic of the phallus enables the emergence of the pure surface of the autonomous Sense-Event, the emergence of the mind on the surface of the body, without the establishment of some material dual connection between the body and the mind: "its transcendental status means that there is nothing 'substantial' about it: phallus is the semblance par excellence . . . the transcendental constitutive power is a pseudo power representing the flipside of the subject's blindness concerning true bodily causes. Phallus qua cause is a pure semblance of a cause."[8] The spectral or transcendental nature of the phallus as the cause is, according to Johnston, crucial for understanding Žižek's idea of materialism, and moreover his take on the dialectical materialism. It is the question of this part of the Real as semblance that is constitutive of the materiality. However, this spectrality is the product of the overlapping of two lacks, which causes a particular homology.

It was Lacan who in his later teaching stopped talking about the Real of the symbolic fiction and the "lack of being" and introduced a particular ontology of the Real as *objet a*, as the "being of lack." The partial objects, the voice and the gaze, are part of Lacan's later focusing on the Real as *objet a* as the realm beyond castration, which actually entails a peculiar homology with the Subject as the Real of the quilting point (Symbolic castration):

While all this is well known, what is usually left out of consideration is the formal homology (as well as substantial difference) between this reflexive logic of the Master-Signifier—the signifier of the lack of the signifier, the signifier which functions as a stand-in (filler) of a lack—and the logic of the objet petit which is also repeatedly defined by Lacan as the filler of a lack: an object whose status is purely virtual, with no positive consistency of its own, only a positivization of a lack in the symbolic order. Something escapes the symbolic order, and this X is positivized as the *objet a*, the *je ne sais quoi* which makes me desire a certain thing or person. . . . However, this formal parallel between the Master-Signifier and the *objet petit a* should not deceive us: although, in both cases, we seem to be dealing with an entity which fills in the lack, what differentiates the objet a from the Master-Signifier is that, in the case of the former, the lack is redoubled, that is, the objet a is the result of the overlapping of the two lacks, the lack in the Other (the symbolic order) and *the lack in the object—in the visual field, say, the objet a is what we cannot see, our blind spot in relation to the picture.* Each of the two lacks can operate independently of the other: we can have the lack of the signifier, as when we have a rich experience for which "words are missing": or we can have the lack in the visible for which, precisely, there is a signifier, namely the Master-Signifier, the mysterious signifier which seems to recapture the invisible dimension of the object. *Therein resides the illusion of the Master-Signifier: it coalesces with the objet a, so that it appears that the subject's Other/Master possesses what the subject lacks.* This is what Lacan calls alienation: the confrontation of the subject with a figure of the Other possessing what the subject lacks.

However, even more important here is the second part, the part dealing with the subject's separation. What Žižek claims, that *objet a* as the Real (in this case the gaze), does not belong to the lower side of the bar, as the signified part of the Master-Signifier, but actually is part of the upper side of the bar; it appears within the chain of signifiers:

in separation, which follows alienation, the *objet a* is separated also from the Other, from the Master-Signifier; that is, the subject discovers that the Other also does not have what he is lacking. The axiom Lacan follows is "no I without a": "wherever an I (unitary feature, signifying mark that represents the subject) emerges, it is followed by an a, the stand-in for what was lost in the signification of the real. . . . Is, then, the *objet a* the signified of the S of the Master-Signifier? It may appear so, since the Master-Signifier signifies precisely that imponderable X which eludes the series of positive properties signified by the chain of "ordinary" signifiers (S). But, upon a closer look, we see that the relationship is exactly the inverse: with regard to the division between signifier and signified, the *objet a* is on the side of the signifier, it fills in the lack in/of the signifier, while the Master-Signifier is the "quilting point" between the signifier and the signified, the point at which the Signifier falls into the signified.[9]

This strange homology between the Master-Signifier and *objet a*, which is the gaze as the reversal of perspectives "from outside to within," namely, "the lack in the object-in the visual field, say, the objet a is what we cannot see, our blind spot in relation to the picture,"[10] is something that Žižek is not using only as regards his interpretation of the aesthetic phenomena, because it is not pertaining to the Realm of the Imaginary, but also and above all to the Symbolic, since it is located within the chain of signifiers.

Therefore, according to Žižek, the devaluation of the Symbolic in later Lacan does not involve the shift toward some fetishised "Real in itself," since there is always the question of the redoubleness and intervoweness of the three registers, the Symbolic, the Imaginary and the Real in question. The phenomena of repetition and redoubleness make the core of Žižek's subject of the material dialectic, for the latter is inscribed in the very gap of this minimal difference between the two lacks. Johnston describes this as the peculiar homology of the lack in later Lacan, as the constitution of the subject in the following way:

> In the same seminar in which the lamella is invoked (the eleventh seminar), Lacan also sketches a logic of two intersecting lacks, a Real lack (introduced by the fact of sexual reproduction) and a Symbolic lack (introduced by the subject's alienation via its mediated status within the defiles of the signifying big Other). The Real lack is nothing other than the individual's "loss" of immortality due to its sexual-material nature as a living being subjected to the cycles of generation and corruption, albeit as a loss of something never possessed except in primary narcissism and/or unconscious fantasy. Symbolic lack serves, in a way, as a defensive displacement of this more foundational lack in the Real. Not only are psychoanalytic

psychopathologies painful struggles with both of these lacks, but "it is this double lack that determines the ever-insistent gap between the real and the symbolico-imaginary, and thus the constitution of the subject."[11]

Recall Badiou's differentiation between two versions of the "passion of the Real," in the twentieth century, as the destruction and the subtraction. There are actually two kinds of the Real involved, the Real Real and the Imaginary Real of the minimal difference as the subtle appearance. If Badiou is to overcome the Scylla and Charybdis of the disastrous Naming of the event on one side and the Kantian dualism between Being and Event, the latter functioning only as the Regulative idea in order to render a proper materialist philosophy, he should, according to Žižek, deal with the "ontology of the Event,"[12] as the result of this reduplication of the void as the Real, alias the gap, the cleft within Being, that is the true locus of the subject. The phenomenon of redoubleness as the crucial dialectical feature is present also in Žižek's understanding of Lacan's Borromean knot, that is, the internal interwovenness of the realms of the Real, the Symbolic, and the Imaginary.[13] If one starts from the realm of the Real, one can distinguish between the Real Real, the Symbolic Real, and the Imaginary Real, which are always already intervowen and thus redoubled. And this is valid for the other two Registers as well.

This gap of the pure Difference between the phenomenon and noumenon, between Being and Event, is already located within Being as such, for the subject is only "knowable" through the shift or reversal of the perspective known as the parallax view. However, what is most important to point out is that this knowledge of the unconscious is not on the side of the transcendental subject but part of the object as gaze within the constituted empirical reality, part of Being as such. It is perhaps something Lacan named "knowledge in the Real," the acephalous knowledge, which can never be subjectivized, since

> it involves no inherent relation to truth, no subjective position of enunciation—not because it dissimulates the subjective position of enunciation, but because it is in itself nonsubjectivized, or ontologically prior to the very dimension of truth (of course, the term ontological becomes thereby problematic, since ontology is by definition a discourse on truth). Truth and knowledge are thus related as desire and drive: interpretation aims at the truth of the subject's desire (the truth of desire is the desire for truth,

as one is tempted to put it in a pseudo-Heideggerian way), while construction provides knowledge about drive.[14]

In this vein we could also posit a counterargument to a pertinent contemporary criticism of Žižek's work, Bruno Bosteels's article "Badiou without Žižek." Bosteels presents some inner obstacles of Žižek's understanding of the materialist dialectics in comparison to the work of Alain Badiou, which are in his view also problematic as regards the possibility of constitution of a positive political project. This criticism aims at the question of repetition as the basis of the materialist dialectic in Žižek, which lacks the movement or the turn of the dialectic and therefore gets stuck in the inability (anxiety), as the repetition of negativity, to produce a new truth, a new enthusiastic, courageous project of fidelity to the Event. Bosteels sees the problem with Žižek's "ultra-dialectic" in the following way:

> ultimately, the problem with this logic is its complete inability to conceive of the transformative power of an event other than as the effect of a structural reiteration, even though the indefinite repetition of mark and place generates a semblance of dialectical movement that claims to be more radical than anything: "One could speak of a kind of 'ultra-dialectic,' a theory of movement such that it becomes impossible not only to grasp but more radically to determine the movement itself." At best, the passage from one term to another, when they are identical, only leads to a "serial logic," that is to say, "one and then the other as minimal difference." Any attempt to turn the play of minimal difference into the greatest insight of Badiou's philosophy at the very least would have to come to terms with this profound criticism of the Hegelian or Lacano-Millerian logic, which Žižek for obvious reasons is only too happy to privilege in Badiou's *Le Siècle*.[15]

In reference to this gap of the minimal difference as the basis for the materialist dialectic, I claim that Bosteels's argument for the logic of repetition as the serial logic fails, if we take for granted that Real as the minimal difference in recent Žižek's work is presented as the Real of the sexual difference. If the critique implies that the structuralist repetition of the Lacano-Millerian suture does not imply movement, that it is a nondialectical repetition of the One, Žižek claims that Lacan's "y'a de l'un" is exactly the bar of the minimal difference and strictly correlative to the sexual difference as Lacan's "il n'y a pas de rapport sexuel": "the two sexual partners are never alone, since their activity has to involve a fantasmatic supplement that sustains their desire, it is actually the couple of three: $1 + 1 + a$, "the 'pathological stain that sustains their desire."[16] In this sense the movement of the dialectic as repetition resides within this supplement. Bosteels is further exposing the problem of the possibility of the emergence of a new truth in Žižek: "is there or is there not a truth of the real? . . . It seems to me, however, that the question is still very much open if and how we can get here from there: can we ever expect to get to the act as radical change by starting from the act as real, or from the act as confrontation with the vanishing cause of the real, after traversing the fundamental fantasy?"[17]

Žižek's answer would here again be: the act of the introduction of the gap of the sexual difference, separating the Master signifier and *objet a* is actually the Real as new consistency. It is the gap that divides the One into the always already deferred One and the material remainder. According to Žižek it could be named the Democritian *den* (the object, which in the ontological sense refers to the "more than something, but less than nothing"):[18]

> this brings us, finally, to the most speculative aspect of the notion of su-
> ture: the purely formal difference between an element and its place func-
> tions as a pure difference which is no longer a difference between two
> positive entities; and, as we have already seen, this pure difference is
> the condition of symbolic differentiality. The paradox is thus that what
> sutures a field is not a unifying feature but the pure difference itself—
> how? . . . Badiou's (and Deleuze's) name for this (parallax) shift is "a
> minimal difference": In Lacanese, what occurs is the addition or subtrac-
> tion of the objet a from the thing, of the unfathomable X which stands
> for the inscription of the subject itself (its gaze or desire) into the object.
> This minimal difference can only be detected at the moment of shortest
> shadow when, as Nietzsche put it in *Beyond Good and Evil*, "at midday it
> happened, at midday one became two."[19]

If we conclude, Žižek's parallax gaze is actually the Real as the *jouissance* (*jouis-sense*) in late Lacan. Although, as Žižek has pointed out, it is problematic to talk about the knowledge and not truth in reference to ontology, it is exactly the point of Žižek's criticism of Badiou's theory of the Event, namely, that we have to reintroduce the transcendentality (the gaze as the Real) back into the immanence of Being, and by that also the question of knowledge. Perhaps we have to understand it as the gaze of Being as such.[20] Žižek is most recently basing his argument particularly in Lacan's theory of "y'a de l'un" as the gap of the sexual difference. As Žižek particularly underscores, the later Lacan transposes his concept of the relation between the Symbolic and the Real from the search of some kind of mutual inner kernel and in the direction of the gap of pure difference, which holds them (the Master-Signifier and the *objet a*) together, a nonreciprocal relation:

> in *Lituraterre* he [Lacan] finally drops this search for the symbolic pineal gland (which for Descartes marked the bodily point at which body and soul interact) and endorses the Hegelian solution: it is the gap itself that forever separates S and J, which holds them together, since this gap is constitutive of both of them: the symbolic arises through the gap that separates it from full jouissance, and this jouissance itself is a specter produced by the gaps and holes in the symbolic. To designate this interdependence, Lacan introduces the term littorale, standing for the letter in its "coast-like" dimension and thereby "figuring that one domain [which] in its entirety makes for the other a frontier, because of their being foreign to each other, to the extent of not falling into a reciprocal relation. Is the edge of the hole in knowledge not what it traces?" So when Lacan says that "between knowledge and jouissance, there is a littoral"; we should hear in this the evocation of jouis-sense (enjoy-meant), of a letter reduced to a sinthome, a signifying formula of enjoyment. Therein resides late Lacan's final "Hegelian" in Sight: the convergence of the two incompatible dimensions (the Real and the Symbolic) is sustained by their very divergence, for difference is constitutive of what it differentiates. Or, to put it in more formal terms: it is the very intersection between the two fields which constitutes them.[21]

In conclusion I shall try to outline Žižek's subjective position within his writing that depends upon this shift of the gaze back into the question of ontology, which wards off some of the contemporary criticisms of his work. If we take as an example one of the more or less recent criticisms of Žižek's work and the method he is using, that of Ian Parker in *Slavoj Žižek: A Critical Introduction*, more precisely the chapter where Parker tackles the problem of assymetry, the mechanism, the object, and the application in Žižek's work. According to the abovementioned text, it becomes clear, how the author misses the crucial point.

In the section just quoted, Žižek explains that the Symbolic arises simultaneously with the Real. It constitutes itself through this gap ex nihilo, as a simultaneous move from the Real. However, there is simultaneously the Real, which is the spectre produced by the very gap that separated it from the Symbolic. It is precisely the eruption of the difference between the Symbolic and the Real ex nihilo, as this difference. Parker misses the following point. The assymetrical rendering of Hegel and Lacan and Marx in Žižek's work is not the product of the Real, which glows through the Symbolic. On the contrary, it is the product of the bar (gap) separating and engendering the Symbolic and Real at once. His interpretation of Žižek's assymetrical anamorphical application of Lacan in the matrix of Hegel, Lacano-Hegelian interpretation of Marx, and presumably random skipping from one topic to another as the consequence of a certain Žižek's *simptome* as "particular, 'pathological,' signifying formation, a binding enjoyment, an inner stain resisting communication and interpretation, a stain which cannot be included in the circuit of discourse, of social bond network, but it is at the same time a positive condition of it,"[22] is still an interpretation that is based on the understanding of the relation between the Symbolic and the Real in classical Kantian transcendentalist frame.

If we remind ourselves again of the second Hegelian twist of the transcendentalism of the late Lacan in Žižek, this spectral gap within Being (the gaze) is therefore no longer the symptom of the subject but the *sinthome*, which goes beyond the transcendental subject. We are here no longer dealing with the Lacanian simptome but with sinthome:

> but when we take into account the dimension of the sinthome, it is no longer sufficient to denounce the "artificial" character of the ideological experience, to demonstrate the way the object experienced by ideology as "natural" and "given" is effectively a discursive construction, a result of a network of symbolic over-determination; it is no longer enough to locate the ideological text in its context, to render visible its necessarily

overlooked margins. What we must do (what Gillian or Fassbinder do), on the contrary, is to isolate the sinthome from the context by virtue of which it exerts its power of fascination in order to expose the sinthome's utter stupidity. In other words, we must carry out the operation of changing the precious gift into a gift of shit (as Lacan put it in his *Seminar XI*), of experiencing the fascinating, mesmerizing voice as a disgusting, meaningless fragment of the real. This kind of "estrangement" is perhaps even more radical than is Brechtian Verfremdung: the former produces a distance not by locating the phenomenon in its historical totality, but by making us experience the utter nullity of its immediate reality, of its stupid, material presence that escapes "historical mediation." Here we do not add the dialectical mediation, the context bestowing meaning on the phenomenon, instead we subtract it.[23]

Therefore my claim is that Žižek's writing is not about him transversing his own fantasm on one side (being the analyst of himself) or about assuming the place of the Big Other (*sujet suppose savoir*), assuming the place of an analyst in front of us, his hysterical readers,[24] but that his writing position is actually the registration of the self-analysis of Being as such, of its sinthome. His writing position is situated precisely within this gap (the gaze) of the sexual difference, or what Žižek tries to transmit through his writing, is the awry look (the gaze) of Being itself, the Real as the enjoyment of Being itself. We can thus say that Žižek's writing is not about pointing at our blind spot in the picture, that is, the blind spot that we can only see if we look at it from the different angle, as the effect of our transcendental limitation, but the blind spot that is actually there in the picture as its own immanent transcendental limitation. So the charge that Žižek in his philosophical work applies Lacan to Hegel and Lacano-Hegel to Marx in an assymetrical, anamorphous way is in a way correct, but for the wrong reasons. As I have already pointed out, the assymetricity is the result of the gap, bar of the sexual difference, which is inscribed within the coordinates of Being itself. Žižek's work lies merely in the act of registering it.

As I have already shown, this preceding void, the void of the death drive, is doubly split. The gap of sexual difference is double, which means that it is simultaneously the cause of the assymetry and noncoincidence of the Real within the symbolic fiction (the Real as the vanishing cause) and the spectral supplementation as the attempt to cover it. So, if we turn from this point of view yet again to the charge that Žižek's style of writing is hasty, always trying to retroactively anticipate and in advance nullify the enemy's or even his own ideas, we have to refer yet again to Lacan's idea of the sinthome. Therefore in terms of the question of time, it is no longer the question of anteriority and anticipation of the simptom, but of the pure cut within time, the sheer simultaneity, as the gap that divides the time in Nietzsche's high noon.

The analyst's discourse, which Žižek presumably assumes in his work, is thus the position of the gaze of Being, which is simultaneously doing away with the Real as the vanishing cause, the Real of the symbolic fiction, and simultaneously with all the spectral apparitions (even his own) that are trying to fill in this void. He is actually assuming the position of the gap that redoubles the void, the gap that engenders the homology between the lack and the void as the filling, which tries to cover up this lack, thus the place of the gap of the sexual difference. From the point of view of temporality, we could conclude that Žižek's working resides not on the loop of the retroactivity of the death drive but in the high noon of the sexual difference.[25]

Notes

1   Slavoj Žižek, *Looking Awry: An Introduction to Jacques Lacan through Popular Culture* (Cambridge, MA: MIT Press, 1991), 125.

2   See Merriam Webster *Thesaurus and Dictionary*, www.merriam-webster.com/, my italics. This type of problem most recently arose with the Chinese moon rover *Jade Rabbit*. BBC News, January 27, 2014. See www.bbc.co.uk/news/world-asia-china -25908527.

3   Slavoj Žižek, "From Purification to Subtraction," in *Think Again: Alain Badiou and the Future of Philosophy*, ed. Peter Hallward (London: Bloomsbury, 2004), 168.

4   See Slavoj Žižek, *Organs without Bodies: On Deleuze and Consequences* (New York: Routledge, 2004), 101.

5   Žižek, *Organs without Bodies*, 91–92.

6   See Slavoj Žižek, *Ticklish Subject: The Absent Centre of the Political Ontology* (London: Verso, 2000).

7   Adrian Johnston, *Žižek's Ontology: A Transcendental Materialist Theory of Subjectivity* (Evanston: Northwestern University Press, 2008), 286.

8   Žižek, *Organs without Bodies*, 91.

9   Slavoj Žižek, *Less Than Nothing: Hegel and the Shadow of Dialectical Materialism*, 598. My emphasis.

10 Žižek, *Less Than Nothing: Hegel and the Shadow of Dialectical Materialism*, 598.

11   Johnston, *Žižek's Ontology*, 23. Quotation from Paul Verhaeghe, *Beyond Gender: From Subject to Drive* (New York: Other Press, 2001), 147.

12   Žižek, *Less Than Nothing*, 805.

13   Žižek, *Less Than Nothing*, 101.

14   Slavoj Žižek, "Desire: Drive = Truth: Knowledge," in *(U)mbra: On the Drive*, ed. Joan Copjec, 1997. www.lacan.com/zizek-desire.htm.

15   Bruno Bosteels, "Badiou without Žižek," *Polygraph* 17 (2005).

16   Slavoj Žižek, *Organs without Bodies*, 99.

17   Bosteels, "Badiou without Žižek."

18   Žižek, *Less Than Nothing*, 495.

19   Žižek, *Less Than Nothing*, 616–17.

20   Another prominent Slovenian philosopher, Rado Riha, has recently devoted a book to the similar problematic, but in my view perhaps even from the angle of subjectivation of such Lacanian "knowing in the Real" (as the third type of the Lacanian Real Žižek is referring to; see Žižek, *Organs without Bodies*, 103) as part of the accomplishment of Kant's system of critiques. It is tackling the so-called second transcendental turn in Kant, where Rado Riha focuses on the "new," the third subject of Kant's *Third Critique*, which is actually the transcendental subject, which has, after the completed system of the transcendental critique has appeared, namely the subjective constitution of reality or subjectified reality, as such appeared within the empirical world, which is in contrast to the idea of the knowledge in the real as nonsubjectifiable. Riha is staking his argument on the ontology of the ideas of Reason, which are nonexistent for the objective world. See Rado Riha, *Kant in drugi transcendentalni obrat v filozofiji* [Kant and the second transcendental Turn in philosophy] (Ljubljana: Založba ZRC, 2012).

21   Žižek, *Less Than Nothing*, 819.

22   Ian Parker, *Slavoj Žižek: A Critical Introduction* (London: Pluto Press, 2004), in Slovenian translation: *Slavoj Žižek, Kritični uvod* (Ljubljana: Ropot, 2009), 152.

23   Slavoj Žižek, *Looking Awry: An Introduction to Jacques Lacan through Popular Culture* (Cambridge, MA: MIT Press, 1992), 129.

24   See Parker, *Slavoj Žižek*. For the illustration I cite Bruno Bosteels's recapitulation of Lacan's words: "The act happens precisely when something of the real passes into a form of knowledge capable of transmission and as a result of which something drops out of the existing arrangements of knowledge, including their guarantee in the subject who is supposed to know." See Bosteels, "Badiou without Žižek."

25   In this sense we can say that the retroactivity and temporal loop in Žižek's use of the Real as the death drive against the philosophical truth of Alain Badiou, in terms of psychoanalysis, would mean that the discourse of the analyst and the negativity of the death drive always already outsmart the hysterical discourse of the philosoper's attempt to posit the consistency of a new truth, and often even his own truth (in the case of presenting his autocriticism as prior to his original work). See Bosteels, "Badiou without Žižek." Recall Bosteels's witty presentation of the philosophical dispute between Žižek and Badiou on the question of the truth and knowledge (desire and drive) as the joke about the fight between two hospitalized madmen in the asylum, scorning

to each other: "You're a fool!" and "No, you are!" and concluding with one of them saying, "Tomorrow I will wake up at 5 o'clock and write on your door, that you are a fool!" and the other one (in our case Žižek) replying, "And I will wake up at 4 o'clock and wipe it off!" as the invincible logic of the retroactivity of the death drive. I, however, say that if Žižek, as I have tried to show, assumes the position within the gap of the pure difference, then he will wake up at high noon and wipe both inscriptions off the door at once. This is perhaps a less funny and more horrifying image.

Oxana Timofeeva

In the chapter titled "The Animal That I Am" of his *Less Than Nothing*, Žižek mentions two cats. The first one belongs to Derrida. This cat opens up what could be a Derridean perspective on animals.[1] However, it would be problematic even to say "a Derridean perspective on animals," since, after Derrida, saying "animals," or "animal," while referring to a certain generalized nonhuman animality, is almost illegitimate, or rather "asinine," as Derrida himself puts it. It is asinine to talk about the animal as compared to the man, either in terms of some homogeneous continuity between man and other animals or in terms of a discontinuity, a rupture, or an abyss between them. This binary itself is asinine; a fundamental difference between the two effectively erases actual differences between the many of the animals themselves. And, again, how can one talk about animals themselves; how can their irreducible multiplicity be thought, if not from the point of view of the alleged integral subjective unity of man? The latter is the case, according to Derrida, of many philosophers, who are looking at animals or at the animal in general from the point of view of the so-called humanity proper, which is nothing other than asininity, *bêtise*. Descartes, Heidegger, Levinas, and Lacan are first in this list—albeit very differently, they are all deeply infected with asininity of anthropocentrism.

Derrida aims to break this faulty tradition, first of all, by inverting a viewpoint. Thus, instead of a Derridean perspective on animality, one would rather talk about an animal perspective on Derrida, which Derrida himself attempts to grasp. Another impossible enterprise, but isn't an impossible enterprise what philosophy is all about? Anyway, his book starts from an animal that is looking at man. No, not an animal, but *the* animal: it is a cat. Not a cat in general, not a metaphoric, not a symbolic cat, not a figure of the cat, not one of those cats from various parables and poems: it's a real cat who now stares at Derrida. He never stops repeating, that the cat is *real*. What a suspicious word.

The real cat Derrida is talking about is the one who lives in his house; it's just as simple as that: his real small cat, a female one. Derrida just woke up and makes his way to the bathroom, naked. The cat follows him there; apparently, she is asking for some food, she was already anticipating this moment of Derrida's awakening. She is running ahead, or behind—this is not quite clear, who follows whom (you know these little cats, sometimes they just get under one's feet), but this moment of following is very important for Derrida: here, he is followed by the gaze. The gaze belongs to the cat; she looks at Derrida, who is naked. Derrida reacts to this gaze with an incredible outburst of shame. He is ashamed of his nakedness, in front of this small and silent female cat.

Shame is reflective. Derrida feels shame not simply because he is seen, but because he is seen being seen naked. Shame supposes that one sees oneself, or rather one is seen being seen. That's original sin, that's what all the history of (Western, Christian) humanity starts from—to be ashamed, to be seen being seen naked. Derrida opens his book on the animal (not on the animal in general, as philosophers would put it, but on the one that he is) with this scene of the original sin of being seen being seen naked, exposed before the gaze of the real animal. The cat is also naked, by the way. But she does not know it, as they say. She does not have knowledge of her nakedness, she is not ashamed being seen.

The naked cat who is staring at Derrida does not occupy the same structural position as, say, a human fellow creature in Paradise, with whom the first man shares his shame of being seen naked. But this absence of reciprocity does not really make things simpler (as if he was not really seen, and therefore did not have reasons to be ashamed). As Žižek has commented, "the cat's gaze stands for the gaze of the Other—an inhuman gaze, but for this reason all the more the Other's gaze in all its abyssal impenetrability. Seeing oneself being seen by an animal is an abyssal encounter with the Other's gaze, since—precisely because we should not simply project onto the animal our inner experience— something is returning the gaze which is radically Other. The entire history of philosophy is based upon a disavowal of such an encounter."[2]

At this point, Žižek is thoughtfully following Derrida's analysis and even introduces another image of a cat. This time, the gaze of the Other intervenes as particularly striking and deranging: "I remember seeing a photo of a cat after it had been subjected to some lab experiment in a centrifuge, its bones half broken, its skin half hairless, its eyes looking helplessly into the camera—this is the gaze of the Other disavowed not only by philosophers, but by humans 'as such.'"[3] This image reinforces Derrida's radical ethical stance, apparently shared by Žižek.

Take Levinas, whose Other is strictly limited by its species: Levinas's Other is the one with a human face, the face of the Other is the beginning of human-to-human compassion and relation; beasts do not count. For Derrida, Levinas is of those who do not see themselves seen by an animal, those who do not feel shame in front of animals. Or take Descartes, who considered animals to be machines without reasoning, without a thinking soul (the absence of which he could see in their dissection, when animals were still alive and their muscles and veins continued to function for some time as stupid automatons). The right question, repeats Žižek after Derrida (who, in his turn, repeats it after Bentham), would be not "Can animals reason and think? Can they talk?" but "Can they suffer?"

As far as the animal suffering is concerned, Žižek recalls, again, after Derrida, a motive of the "great sorrow of nature," picked up by Heidegger and Benjamin after the German Romantics and Schelling. Derrida criticizes this motive for being, after all, another logocentric trick, since mute nature here supposed to be relieved in humanity and language, which becomes its telos. According to Derrida, animals suffer not so much because of a certain preexistent sorrow of nature as such (as the Romantics thought, and therefore hoped that this suffering could be redeemed through language) but precisely because of the fact of being violently caught by language, by being named.

Žižek, in his turn, proposes to dialectically invert this teleology. The question must be not "What is nature for language? How can we grasp this silent and suffering unhuman realm?" but "What is language and human for this silent nature?" or, as Žižek puts it, traditionally, in Hegelese, "instead of asking what Substance is for the Subject, how the

Subject can grasp Substance, one should ask the obverse question: What is (the rise of the) Subject for (pre-subjective) Substance?" If we address this question to the two aforementioned primal scenes with cats, it will not be "Can they see?" but "What do they see?" This is precisely what Žižek does:

> so, to return to the sad and perplexed gaze of the laboratory cat, what it expresses is perhaps the cat's horror at having encountered The Animal, namely ourselves, humans: what the cat sees is us in all our monstrosity, and what we see in its tortured gaze is our own monstrosity. In this sense, the big Other (the symbolic order) is already here for the poor cat: like the prisoner in Kafka's penal colony, the cat suffered the material consequences of being caught in the symbolic gridlock. It effectively suffered the consequences of being named, included in the symbolic network.[4]

It might seem that Žižek here pushes forward and radicalizes Derridean argument, almost in solidarity with Derrida's criticism of previous philosophers, and brings this criticism up to a new level, where, in order to deal with this "inhuman core of the human,"[5] we still need psychoanalysis to intervene, because deconstruction is not enough. It's not enough to rehabilitate animality, so unfairly disavowed in philosophical tradition, so far as this animal not only sees, but it sees *us* humans in our monstrosity, and this necessarily brings us back to the problem of the constitution of the human subject and its symbolic order, which only psychoanalysis now seriously takes into account. However, this is only a part of the story, and at this point, I have to refer to Žižek's own criticism of deconstruction, which he introduces in this very small chapter.

In fact, Žižek starts from this criticism of what he defines as "the common sense of deconstruction."[6] Thus, talking about animals, Derrida addresses his philosophical predecessors with questions undermining their ideas that animals differ from man according to certain generalized criteria—absence of language, of thought, of an exclusive access to being, of knowledge, of awareness of death, of unconscious, of face (as it is said that only human beings have faces), or whatever they consider to be specifically human features. Animals thus merge into some homogeneous unit, whose very existence serves to shadow an arbitrariness and tyranny of anthropocentric categories. All these categories of differentiation should be therefore deconstructed: "as Derrida emphasizes again and again, the point of this questioning is not to cancel the gap that separates man from (other) animals and attribute also to (other) animals properly 'spiritual' properties—the path taken by some eco-mystics who claim that not only animals, but even trees and plants communicate in a language of their own to which we humans are deaf. The point is rather that all these differences should be rethought and conceived in a different way, multiplied, 'thickened'—and the first step on this path is to denounce the all-encompassing category of 'the animal.'"[7]

In his criticism of this "common sense" Žižek makes at least two clear points. First of all, he brings up a Hegelian argument according to which a notorious human-animal distinction can nevertheless be important and useful. As he says: "to put it in Hegelese, it is not only that, say, the totalization effected under the heading 'the animal' involves the violent obliteration of a complex multiplicity; it is also that the violent reduction of such a multiplicity to a minimal difference is the moment of truth. That is to say, the multiplicity of animal forms is to be conceived as a series of attempts to resolve some basic antagonism or tension which defines animality as such, a tension which can only be formulated from a minimal distance, once humans are involved."[8] Thus, according to Žižek, the human must still be distanced from the rest of the animal kingdom, but this time not so much in order to violate animals via language as in order to acquire their animality via its own antagonism. Not in order to see, but in order to be seen.

To develop this argument, Žižek even refers to Marx's metaphor for the general equivalent from the first edition of the first volume of *Capital*: "it is as if, alongside and external to lions, tigers, rabbits, and all other actual animals, which form when grouped together the various kinds, species, subspecies, families, etc. of the animal kingdom, there existed in addition *the animal*, the individual incarnation of the entire animal kingdom."[9] For Žižek, this metaphor of capital as the animal as such, which, indeed, does not exist, can also serve, in a way, as an illustration of Derridean criticism of the animal as an empty generalized idea. But, at the same time, the nonexistent animal, running alongside the pack, is a kind of negative for the human as a spectral being. It draws a minimal difference, necessary to create "an oppositional determination."[10] And again: "perhaps this is how animals view humans, and this is the reason for their perplexity."[11]

Thus, both Žižek's reading of Hegel and his Hegelian reading of Marx, paradoxically, provide a kind of animal perspective on the human. How is this possible? Here, I would allow myself to step further and to recall Hegel's famous definition of truth from paragraph 20 of *Phenomenology of Spirit*:

> The truth is the whole. However, the whole is only the essence completing itself through its own development. This much must be said of the absolute: It is essentially a *result*, and only at the *end* is it what it is in truth. Its nature consists precisely in this: To be actual, to be subject, that is, to be the becoming-of itself. As contradictory as it might seem, namely, that the absolute is to be comprehended essentially as a result, even a little reflection will put this mere semblance of contradiction in its rightful place. The beginning, the principle, or the absolute as it is at first, that is, as it is immediately articulated, is merely the universal. But just as my saying "*all* animals" can hardly count as an expression of zoology, it is likewise obvious that the words, "absolute," "divine," "eternal," and so on, do not express what is contained in them;—and it is only such words which in fact express intuition as the immediate. Whatever is more than such a word, even the mere transition to a proposition, is a *becoming-other* which must be redeemed, that is, it is a mediation. However, it is this mediation which is rejected with such horror as if somebody, in making more of mediation than in claiming both that it itself is nothing absolute and that it in no way exists in the absolute, would be abandoning absolute cognition altogether.[12]

One should not neglect "all animals" from this paragraph as a routine example, among possible others, of a certain whole that does not coincide with itself if taken as something immediate. In the present case, animals, who are, of course, never all, are a main concern; it is not random that they are mentioned together with the absolute, divine, and eternal. They are of the same nature; these words express an immediate intuition, or a mere universal. But there is always more than all animals; moreover, *whatever* is always more than that, that is to say, all animals (as well as the absolute itself) are still less than whatever.

Such is the dialectics of truth, in which the Other (the whatever) demands its redemption via mediation, or becoming. The Other needs to be redeemed, the Other than all animals, the not-all of animals, without whose negative intrusion there is no truth, no language, no animals, no nothing. Isn't then "All animals," which Derrida deconstructs, is an immediate intuition? In the Hegelian process of truth, it will be differentiated and mediated, animality as such will redefine itself again and again—particularly through the mediation of a species that thinks of itself as a part of this multiplicity, but at the same time as excluded from it, a particular not-all of animals. Instead of denying this exception, albeit for the sake of multiplying differences in order to give room to the Other, Žižek tries to push it forward and to radicalize ontological and political potentials of human-animal distinction.

Let me move on to the second point of Žižek's criticism of "a common sense of deconstruction." Žižek introduces it in a very subtle way, by turning Derrida's argument against himself. Of course, Derrida is right—by attributing to animals some negative characteristics (speechless, worldless, deprived of reason, of unconscious, of awareness of death, and so on) or giving them some false positive determinations (like automatism of instinctual behavior), philosophers not only totalize, but, in such a blind totalizing, obliterate them. The same goes for the attitude of the moderns toward the so-called primitive, tribal people:

> Do we not encounter the same phenomenon in traditional Eurocentric anthropology? Viewed through the lenses of modern Western "rational" thought taken as the standard of maturity, its Others cannot but appear as "primitives" trapped in magic thinking, "really believing" that their tribe originates from their totemic animal, that a pregnant woman has been inseminated by a spirit and not by a man, etc. Rational thought thus engenders the figure of "irrational" mythical thought—what we get here is (again) a process of violent simplification (reduction, obliteration) which occurs with the rise of the New: in order to assert something radically New, the entire past, with all its inconsistencies, has to be reduced to some basic defining feature.[13]

After drawing this parallel, Žižek immediately applies the same logic to Derrida himself and argues that Derrida, basically, treats his philosophical predecessors the same way they treat animals or moderns treat "primitives." In his deconstructive mode, Derrida, according to Žižek, generalizes previous philosophical tradition under the headings "phallogocentrism" or "metaphysics of presence."[14] What could seem like a joke suddenly transforms Derrida from a radical critical thinker into a kind of anthropologist, who discovers a tribe of Descartes, Heidegger, Levinas, Lacan, and many other naïve believers in *the* animal in general as opposed to human. He generalizes "the generalizers." Coming back to what I've said with a reference to Hegel's definition of truth, Derrida deconstructs philosophers' immediate intuition of all animals, but immediately replaces it with an immediate intuition of all philosophers.

This logic, however, can be expanded. Isn't it that Žižek himself naïvely believes that Derrida naïvely believed that philosophers of the past naïvely believed in a human-animal binary? The line goes from primitive animals to primitive people, and further to primitive classical philosophers, or primitive philosophers of deconstruction. Perhaps it is not a line, but rather a vicious circle. I do not even pretend to step outside it, and I am not sure if it really has an outside. Instead, I would suggest following Žižek's initial proposal to try to look back at our naïve forefathers, and to be seen by them—by cats, by tribal people, by Descartes, Heidegger, Levinas, Lacan, Derrida, Žižek, and all those messy animals that they are. To be seen by them and to be ashamed.

Meanwhile, there is one more point of potential criticism, or rather a point of minimal difference between Derrida's and Žižek's animals, that I will try to outline, as my own kind of "Žižekian" variation on Derrida. For this purpose, I will go back to cats. In this particular chapter from *Less Than Nothing*, both for Derrida and Žižek himself, the cat "stays for the Other." But it stays differently. The concept of the Other, which is actually of principal significance, I have already mentioned here and there. Elsewhere, in his various works, Žižek gives it a proper Lacanian development. In order to estimate the complexity of this concept, one should at first differentiate, following Lacan, between the Real, the Imaginary, and the Symbolic Other. For which of these Others does the cat stay, after all?

As I have already emphasized, for Derrida, the cat is *real*. By real he means, of course, not a Lacanian real, which is in no way meant to coincide with reality as something supposedly independent from the symbolic dimension of language. I naïvely believe that Derrida starts from his naïve belief in a really existing cat. However, a subjective experience, in which his cat involves him, opens for the reality of the cat some new horizon.

Let us go back to this scene. Derrida is ashamed not merely because he is seen naked. Shame comes from the doubling of the gaze, from the fact of being seen being seen naked. An immediate assumption that the cat does not see it the same way as another fellow human being would do, a suspended status of her gaze, requires something else, some confirmation of the fact that what she sees is *really* seen. Another gaze, one more instance of vision. Which could, of course, be counted as Derrida's own seeing of himself being seen, or a mere reflection ("what if this cat sees me naked?"). But, according to such an account, in fact, the cat as the Other would be rather an unnecessary supplement for this entire narcissistic construction. No, the cat should *really* see, the cat as the Other should have its own Other who guarantees the fact that the cat sees. As if there is someone who observes them both and who puts Derrida to shame.

Symbolic order, or the big Other—for example, a cultural law, prohibiting people from hanging around naked in front of others—is not strong enough to make one feel shame in front of the animal Other, which if not completely excluded from this order, then at least does not follow it and does not respect the same prohibiting law. Why feel shame? Isn't it that behind the big Other (Symbolic) there should be yet another Other? Thus, we have the (imaginary) cat Other, on whom we project our own gaze, the Symbolic Other, which is the Law, and the Other of the Other, or the Real Other, with its invisible metagaze for which the little cat stays, as a lamb stays for God (a sacrificial animal, after all).

Lacan's lesson, which Žižek never stops to repeat, is that the big Other does not exist, as well as the Other of the Other, which could provide a guarantee of its existence.[15] Its inexistence, however, actively affects our social being, captured in the chain of signifiers. In the absence of the Other of the Other the inverse of the Law turns into an arbitrary violation, which makes bloody ruptures in the body of the natural real (a Žižekian lab cat, a Kafka's prisoner). The gaze of the animal does not provide us with meaning (unless we are stuck between imaginary projections onto the animal Other of our own meanings and fantasies); an encounter with this gaze bears therefore a strange threat of breaking the chain of signifiers and returning to us an impossible truth of the real, which is itself a rupture, a cut. This is not a rupture between something and something different, or something that was at the beginning and what comes after, but rather a pure difference itself: at the beginning, there was no nothing. This active nothingness was already described by Hegel in his famous passage as the night of the world: "Man is this Night, this empty nothing that, in its simplicity, contains everything: an unending wealth of illusions and images which he remains unaware of—or which no longer exist. It is this Night, Nature's interior, that exists here—pure self—in phantasmagorical imagery, where it is night everywhere . . . where, here, shoots a bloody head and, there, suddenly, another white shape—only to disappear all the same. We see this Night whenever we look into another's eye—into a night that becomes utterly terrifying—wherein, truly, we find the Night of the World suspended."[16] What we see in the gaze of the animal is the dark of the night, which we are, and no God. It is this dark that philosophy is trying to redeem in its gray-on-gray paintings. In this dark, all cats are gray.

Notes

1 Jacques Derrida, *The Animal That Therefore I Am*, trans. David Wills (New York: Fordham University Press, 2008).
2 Slavoj Žižek, *Less Than Nothing: Hegel and The Shadow of Dialectical Materialism* (London: Verso, 2012), 411.
3 Žižek, *Less Than Nothing*, 411.
4 Žižek, *Less Than Nothing*, 413.
5 Žižek, *Less Than Nothing*, 394.
6 Žižek, *Less Than Nothing*, 408.
7 Žižek, *Less Than Nothing*, 408–9.
8 Žižek, *Less Than Nothing*, 408–9.
9 Karl Marx, *Value: Studies*, trans. Albert Dragstedt (London: New Park, 1976). Quotation from marxist.org. Accessed July 28, 2014. www.marxists.org/archive/marx/works/1867-c1/commodity.htm. Quoted by Žižek, *Less Than Nothing*, 410.
10 Žižek, *Less Than Nothing*, 410.
11 Žižek, *Less Than Nothing*, 410.
12 G. W. F. Hegel, *Phenomenology of Spirit* (Oxford: Oxford University Press, 1977), 11.
13 Žižek, *Less Than Nothing*, 410.
14 Žižek, *Less Than Nothing*, 409.
15 See, for example Slavoj Žižek, "The Big Other Doesn't Exist," *Journal of European Psychoanalysis*, Spring–Fall 1997. Accessed July 28, 2014. www.lacan.com/zizekother.htm.
16 G. W. F. Hegel, *The Jena System, 1804–05: Logic and Metaphysics* (Montreal: McGill-Queens University Press, 1986).

PART II **psychoanalysis**

7

"Father, Don't You
See I'm Burning?"
Žižek, Psychoanalysis,
and the Apocalypse

Catherine Malabou

In his article "Descartes and the Post-Traumatic Subject," Slavoj Žižek develops a very insightful critique of the current neurobiological and neuropsychoanalytic redefinition of the unconscious, as well as of the new approach to the notion of "psychic event" that follows from it.[1] Already, in *The Parallax View*, he had insisted on the importance of the current neuroscientific contribution to the understanding of the psyche and of its wounds.[2] He remains nevertheless doubtful that these new elaborations can substitute for the Freudian and Lacanian definitions of traumas.

While developing their own critique of psychoanalysis, namely of Freud and Lacan, neurobiologists would not have been aware of the fact that Freud and Lacan, precisely, had already said what the neurobiologists thought they had not said. The neurobiologists would thus have been ventriloquized by Freud and Lacan at the very moment when they thought they were talking from another point of view than that of psychoanalysis.

According to Žižek, contemporary approaches to trauma would then remain unaware—out of disavowal or of desire—of Lacan's most fundamental statement: trauma has *always already* occurred, that is, *before* any empirical or material shock or wound. A specific trauma may happen only because the originary trauma has always already happened. Such is its apocalyptic structure. As we know, *apocalyptô*, in Greek, literally means revealing and unveiling. It also refers to destruction and catastrophe. Therefore, apocalypse is a truthful annihilation, a mean-ingful collapsing of all things. The apocalyptic structure of revelation is the transcendental structure of destruction. It is because the uncon-scious is structured by the arche-trauma that something like an external or contingent event may occur and be experienced as such. The external accident is always a revelation of what it internally destroys. Such is the apocalyptic economy of the Real. The neuroscientific and neuropsycho-analytic approach to trauma would not destitute in the least the law of the always already. It would only be a repetition, in other words, of what has already occurred and been said.

To state that trauma has already occurred means that it cannot occur by mere chance, that every empirical accident or shock impairs an al-ready or previously wounded subject. There is an obvious rejection of chance in Freud and Lacan. This is what I want to advocate here, as an echo to my book *The New Wounded*, which is also challenged in Žižek's article.[3] I intend to secure the fact that there is a "beyond the always already principle," that a trauma may occur without referring to any "al-ready," a purely contingent accident, as neurobiologists admit. This is something that Lacan would never have said, something that escapes the always already's authority, and gives a chance to chance.

In my view, the Lacanian distinction between the Real and the Sym-bolic follows from a reelaboration of the Freudian conception of the psychic event as a meeting point between two meanings of the event: the event conceived of as an internal immanent determination (*Erleb-nis*) and an encounter that takes place from outside (*Ereignis*). In order for an accident to become properly a psychic event, it has to trigger the subject's psychic history and determinism. The "*Ereignis*" has to unite with the "*Erlebnis*." The most obvious example of such a definition of the psychic event is the example, often taken by Freud, of the war wound. When a soldier, on the front, gets traumatized by a wound, or fear of the wound, it appears that the current real conflict he is involved in is a repe-tition of an internal conflict. Shock is always a reminder of a previous shock. Freud would then have considered PTSD to be the expression of the always already character of the conflict or trauma.

Neurobiologists on the contrary admit that severe trauma (1) is funda-mentally an "Ereignis," that is, something that happens by mere chance from the outside, and (2) thus dismantles the *Ereignis/Erlebnis* distinction to the extent that it severs the subject from her reserves of memory and from the presence of the past. After severe brain damage, which always produces a series of disconnections and holes within the neural network, a new subject emerges with no reference to the past or to her previous identity. A neural disconnection does not trigger any previous conflict. Instead, the posttraumatized subject disconnects the structure of the always already. The posttraumatized subject is the never more of the always already. In that sense, neurobiology breaks the apocalyptic loop.

It is then possible to state that a neural disconnection cannot belong to either of the three terms that form the Lacanian triad of the Imaginary, the Symbolic, and the Real, to the extent that this triad is rooted in the transcendental principle of the always already. I propose to introduce a fourth dimension, a dimension that might be called the "material." From a neurobiological point of view, the trauma would be taken to be a material, empirical, biological, and meaningless interruption of the transcendental itself. This is why posttraumatic subjects are *living examples of the death drive* and of the dimension *beyond the pleasure principle* that Freud and Lacan both fail to locate or to expose. Beyond the always already principle lies the genuine beyond the pleasure principle.

Žižek affords a certain validity to these ideas but rejects them out of hand for three main reasons:

1. These statements are seemingly ignorant of the Lacanian distinction between pleasure (plaisir) and enjoyment (jouissance). Enjoyment in itself is precisely beyond pleasure. It is this painful surplus of pleasure that resists being contained within the framework of the pleasure principle. Enjoyment is the always already confronting us with death, and without which we would be trapped in pleasure only. In other words, neurological trauma cannot be but a form of enjoyment. Lacan has always already said that disconnection, separation from the past, lost of memory, and indifference are modalities or occurrences of "jouissance": "What is beyond the pleasure principle is enjoyment itself, it is drive as such," writes Žižek.[4] The unconscious is always already ready for its own destruction.

2. The second objection concerns destruction itself in its relation to what Lacan calls the Thing (la Chose). The Thing is the threat of

death. Without this threat, which mainly appears to the subject as the threat of castration, any empirical objective danger or hazard would remain meaningless to the psyche. Here comes the always already again: "castration is not only a threat-horizon, a not yet/always to come, but, simultaneously, something that always already happens: the subject is not only under a threat of separation, it is the effect of separation (from substance)."[5]

3. This last sentence expresses the main objection: according to Žižek, the subject is, since Descartes, a posttraumatic subject, a subject structured in such a way that it has to constantly erase the traces of its past in order to be a subject. Thus, and once again, the experience of being cut off from oneself is a very old one. Neurobiology doesn't teach us anything new on that point, it rather confirms the very essence of the subject: "the empty frame of deathdrive is the formal-transcendental conditions" of subjectivity: "what remains after the violent traumatic intrusion onto a human subject that erases all his substantial content is the pure form of subjectivity, the form that already must have been there."[6] Further: "if one wants to get an idea of cogito at its purest, its 'degree zero,' one has to take into a look at autistic monsters (the new wounded), a gaze that is very painful and disturbing."[7] Here again, erasure and destruction cannot be but revealing, that is apocalyptic, movements. What erases the subject accomplishes the essence of subjectivity.

To answer these objections one may insist that the motif of chance, conceptualized and elaborated in a certain way, deconstructs the "always already," which appears to be a barrier to what it is supposed to be, that is, a barrier to destruction. If destruction has always already happened, if there is something like a transcendental destruction, then destruction is indestructible. This is what, in Freud and in Lacan, remains extremely problematic: destruction remains for them a structure, the repetition of the originary trauma, an arrangement which, in itself, resists all annihilation. What if the "always already" might explode? What if the "always already" were self-destructive and able to disappear as the so-called fundamental law of the psyche?

In order to address these issues more specifically, let's concentrate on the status of chance in a dream that Freud analyzes in chapter 7 of *The*

Interpretation of Dreams, the dream of the "burning child,"[8] a dream that Lacan comments on in his turn in his seminar 11, *The Four Fundamental Concepts of Psychoanalysis,* in chapter 5, "*Tuché* and *Automaton,*" and chapter 6, "The Split between the Eye and the Gaze."[9]

Freud writes:

> A father had been watching beside his child's sick bed for days and nights on end. After the child had died, he went into the next room to lie down, but left the door open so he could see from his bedroom into the room in which the child's body was laid out, with tall candles standing round it. An old man had been engaged to keep watch over it, and sat beside the body murmuring prayers. After a few hours sleep, the father had a dream that his child was standing beside his bed, caught him by the arm and whispered to him reproachfully: "Father, don't you see I'm burning?" He woke up, noticed a bright glare of light from the next room, hurried into it and found that the old watchman had dropped out to sleep and that the wrappings and one of the arms of the beloved child's dead body had been burned by a candle that had fallen on them.[10]

The issue immediately addressed by Freud is to know whether we can consider such a dream a wish-fulfillment. Isn't it on the contrary an objection, a counterexample to his theory of dreams?

Let's consider Lacan's answer to this issue. First of all, after having reminded us of this dream, Lacan posits that psychoanalysis is "an encounter, an essential encounter—an appointment to which we are always called with a real that eludes us."[11] This essential missed encounter, or misencounter, with the real is the encounter with the trauma. According to Lacan, this dream stages such an encounter. The Freudian question comes back at that point: if this dream stages the encounter with the trauma, how can we consider it a wish-fulfillment, as a fulfillment of a desire?

We need to understand more precisely what the very notion of "encounter with the real" means. This formula is contradictory to the extent that "encounter" refers to something contingent, accidental, something that may or may not happen, and "real," on the contrary, designates for Lacan the necessary and determined mechanism of repetition, the always already of the trauma. How then can we "encounter"—contingently— the necessity of trauma? Here, the notion of chance is emerging. How can we encounter—by chance—the necessity of the trauma that has always already been here?

On this point, Lacan refers to Aristotle, who distinguishes in his *Physics* two regimes of events or of causality. First, *"tuché,"* which means fortune, contingency; then *"automaton,"* the blind necessity of the repetition mechanism, the compulsion to repeat as such. We then have chance on the one hand, determinism on the other. According to Aristotle, everything that comes to pass is due to one of these two modes of temporality. *Tuché* will decide if you will meet by chance a friend in the agora today. *Automaton* governs the cycle of sunset and sunrise, or the seasons' cycle, and so on. Lacan comments on these two modes: *"tuché*, he says, is good or bad fortune."[12] *"Automaton* is the Greek version of the compulsion to repeat."[13] Even if this encounter between two regimes of events and two modes of causality is said to be a missed encounter, it is nonetheless an encounter. Again, how is this possible?

Here begins the analysis of the dream. In this dream, what does belong to *automaton* and what to *tuché*? As Lacan puts it: "where is the reality in this accident?" And where is the accident in this reality?[14] Obviously, what belongs to *tuché* is the falling of the candle and the burning of the child's arm. This is the reality, Lacan says, but not the Real. The Real is the *unreal* "resurrection" of the child and the words "Father, don't you see I am burning"? And here, Lacan starts to analyze *tuché* as a secondary kind of causality or of reality. The child's burnt arm is not the real accident in this dream, it is not the Real. The Real comes with the speech, the son's address to his father. *Tuché* has no autonomy, it is in fact only a means for the Real or the *automaton* to emerge. There would only be one mode of happening, that of *automaton*, with a disguised version of it, a mask, *tuché*.

Chance, or fortune, is only an appearance, an "as if." What happens "as if" by chance is in fact always the automatism of repetition, the primary trauma: "What is repeated, in fact, is always something that occurs *as if by chance*."[15]

Lacan asks himself what is genuinely burning in the dream: is it the child's arm or the sentence uttered by the child: "Father, don't you see that I'm burning"? "Does not this sentence, said in relation to fever, asks Lacan,

suggest to you what, in one of my recent lectures, I called the cause of
fever? . . . What encounter can there be with that forever inert being—even
now being devoured by the flames—if not the encounter that occurs precisely at the moment when, by accident, as if by chance, the flames come
to meet him? Where is the reality in this accident, if not that it repeats
something more fatal *by means* of reality, a reality in which the person
who was supposed to be watching over the body still remains asleep, even
when the father reemerges after having woken up?"[16]

It is clear that contingent reality is always a means for the Real to come
to light; it is then always secondary. When Lacan asks what the reality is
in this accident, he means that there is something other, in the accident,
than the accident: "Is there no more reality in this message than in the
noise by which the father also identifies the strange reality of what is happening in the room next door?"[17]

The contingent external encounter of reality (the candle collapses and
inflames the cloth covering the dead child, the smell of the smoke disturbs the father) triggers the true Real, the unbearable fantasy-apparition
of the child reproaching his father. Again, what burns are the words, not
the arm. "Father, don't you see I'm burning? This sentence is itself a fire-
brand—or itself it brings fire where it falls."[18] Further: the veiled meaning
is the true reality, that of the "primal scene."

In other words, there is a split between reality and the Real.

Now is the moment for approaching the problem of wish-fulfillment.
Lacan writes: "it is not that, in the dream, the father persuades himself
that the son is still alive. But the terrible version of the dead son taking
the father by the arm designates a beyond that makes itself heard in the
dream. Desire manifests itself in the dream by the loss expressed in an
image at the cruel point of the object. It is only in the dream that this
truly unique encounter can occur. Only a rite, an endlessly repeated act,
can commemorate this . . . encounter."[19]

This dream would then be a kind of fulfillment to the extent that
it would render the encounter with "jouissance," enjoyment, possible.
The fulfillment is not always linked with pleasure, says Lacan, but it
can be linked with jouissance. We remember that "jouissance" is defined by Žižek as the beyond of the pleasure principle, the excess or surplus of pleasure which transforms itself into a kind of suffering which

is the very expression of the death drive. Because we can only encounter "jouissance" in dreams, then this particular dream is, in its way, a wish-fulfillment. The way in which Lacan distinguishes two kinds of realities in this dream, a true one and a secondary one, is highly arguable. Cannot we think that the accident of the candle falling on the child's arm is traumatizing per se, that it does not necessarily trigger the repetition mechanism of a more ancient trauma? This accident would then be as real as the words it provokes.

If there is something "beyond the pleasure principle," can we still understand it as being "a beyond chance," "beyond the accident" or "beyond contingency"? Such an understanding is precisely no longer possible from the perspective of contemporary neurobiology. When the victims of traumas are "burning," we certainly don't have a right to ask: where is the reality in these accidents? We certainly don't have a right to suspect contingency of hiding a more profound or different kind of event, for being the veiled face of the compulsion to repeat: to split reality from the Real, contingency from necessity, the transcendental from the empirical, good or bad fortune (*tuché*) from necessity (*automaton*). Reading this Lacanian interpretation, one cannot help but visualize the psychoanalyst as a fireman looking at the catastrophe and saying: "there must be something more urgent than the fire I am actually seeing, I am due to take care of a more originary, hidden but nevertheless more urgent, emergency."

The accident never hides anything, never reveals anything but itself. We need to think of a destructive plasticity, that is, a capacity to explode, that cannot, by any means, be assimilated by the psyche, even in dreams.

The answer we can give to the second objection, concerning the castration as something that has always already occurred, is that the threat of castration is what helps Lacan to always see, even if he says the contrary, the Symbolic at work within the Real.

Castration is for Freud the phenomenal form of the threat of death. Because it means separation, it gives death a figurative content. About separation, Lacan declares: "We must recognize in this sentence [Father don't you see I'm burning?] what perpetuates for the father those words forever separated from the dead child that are said to him."[20] Here, separation, the child's death, the separation from the child, is the trauma, the

automaton. But since this separation can be expressed by another separation, that of words—words separating from the body—then trauma encounters the Symbolic and never escapes it. The Real is separated from
itself thanks to words, thanks to the Symbolic. The child's words make
the trauma meaningful.

The presence of the Symbolic in the Real is irremissible, which domes-
ticates linguistically the traumatic wilderness. Whatever Lacan may say,
there is no such thing as a "pure" Real.

What brain damage allows us to see is that the violence of traumatizing lesions consists in the way they cut the subject, as we already noticed,
off from its reserves of memory, of symbolic and linguistic resources.
Traumatized victims' speech does not have any revelatory meaning.
Their illness does not constitute a kind of truth with regard to their past.
There is no possibility for them of being present, even in dreams, to their
own fragmentations or wounds. In contrast to castration, there is no representation, no phenomenon, no example of separation that would allow
the subject to anticipate, to wait for, to fantasize what can be a break in
cerebral connections. One cannot even dream about it. There is no scene
for this Thing. No words. We have to admit that something like a total
absence of meaning is the meaning of our time.

There is a global uniformity of neuropsychological reactions to traumas, be they political, natural, or pathological traumas. Žižek accepts
the necessity to consider this new uniformized face of violence:

> first, there is the brutal external physical violence: terror attacks like 9/11,
> street violence, rapes, etc., second, natural catastrophes, earthquakes,
> tsunamis, etc.; then, there is the 'irrational' (meaningless) destruction of
> the material base of our inner reality (brain tumors, Alzheimer's disease,
> organic cerebral lesions, PTSD, etc.), which can utterly change, destroy
> even, the victim's personality. We would not be able to distinguish be-
> tween natural, political and socio-symbolic violence. We are dealing today
> with a heterogeneous mixture of nature and politics, in which politics
> cancels itself as such and takes the appearance of nature, and nature dis-
> appears in order to assume the mask of politics.[21]

Žižek doesn't seem to admit that a new form of violence is emerging
today, one implying a new articulation of the concept of the Real, we

might also say the concept of what is burning. An articulation that would give chance a chance, a chance that would never be an "as if," an "as if by chance."

Let's turn to the third and last objection. We remember that for Žižek, posttraumatic subjectivity is nothing other than the contemporary version of traditional Cartesian subjectivity. The subject as Descartes defines it capable of erasing all substantial content in order always to be spontaneously present to itself and the world. Such a concept of the subject traverses the whole history of metaphysics.

This might be true, but it is difficult to believe that traumatic erasure can occur without forming each time a different subject, unaware of the previous one. Repetition is plastic, it gives form to what it destroys, a new person emerges each time, which is not the transcendental subject, but the amnesic one, the deserted one, the brain-damaged one. A subject which does not say "I think therefore I am," but "I no longer think, nevertheless I am." The plasticity of contingency has the power to bestow its own form on the subjects that it shocks. A subject that is *really* burning.

What is a shock? A trauma? Is it the result of a blow, of something that cannot, by any means, be anticipated, something sudden, that comes from outside and knocks us down, whoever we are? Or is it on the contrary an always already predestined encounter? Something that would force us to erase the "whoever you are" from the previous sentence to the extent that an encounter presupposes a destination, a predestination, something that happens to you, to you proper, and to nobody else? According to this second approach, a shock or a trauma would necessarily result, as Freud states, from a meeting between the blow itself and a preexisting psychic destiny.

Is this Freudian conception still accurate to characterize current global psychic violence, or don't we have to consider that blows, shocks, strike any of us without making any difference, erasing our personal histories, destroying the very notions of psychic destiny, childhood, past?

For Freud and for Lacan, it seems clear that all external traumas are "sublated," internalized. Even the most violent intrusions of the external real owe their traumatic effect to the resonance they find in primary psychic conflicts. When it comes to war neuroses, Freud, in his introduction to "Psycho-analysis and the War Neuroses," declares that the genuine cause of a trauma is never the accidental one. The accident only awakens an old "conflict in the ego." The genuine enemy is always an "internal enemy."[22]

According to Freud, there is only one possible kind of "neurosis etiology": the sexual one. Some passages from "Sexuality," and "My Views on the Part Played by Sexuality," both published in *The Aetiology of the Neuroses*,[23] are very clear.

In the former, Freud states: "the true aetiology of the psychoneuroses does not lie in precipitating causes."[24] In the latter, Freud sums up his whole theory of infantile trauma and recapitulates the modifications he has brought to it through time. He says that he was forced to give up the importance of the part played by the "accidental influences" in the causation of traumas.[25] Traumas are not caused by effective events or accidents but by phantasms depending on individual psychic constitutions: "Accidental influences derived from experience having receded into the background, the factors of constitution and heredity necessarily gained the upper hand once more."[26]

For Freud, brain injuries and brain lesions, since they are regarded as merely external, cannot have a real causal power. The brain has no responsibility in the course of our psychic life and the constitution of our subjectivity. The brain is not responsible, which also means that it cannot bring a proper *response* to the issue of the relationship between hazard and the psyche. It is exposed to accidents but remains alien to their symbolic and psychic meaning. Sexuality for Freud does not refer to "sexual life" in the first place but fundamentally designates a specific kind of causality, which alone is able to explain the constitution of one's personal identity, one's history, and one's destiny. Even if the frontier between the inside and the outside is being constantly redrawn in Freud, there remains a wide gap between external and internal traumatic events in psychoanalytic theory. The determinant events of our psychic life cannot have an organic or a physiological cause. Sexuality is never accidental.

In *Beyond the Pleasure Principle*, Freud goes so far as to state that the emergence of a neurosis and the occurrence of an organic lesion are antithetic and incompatible: "in the case of the ordinary traumatic neuroses two characteristics emerge prominently: first, that the chief weight in their causation seems to rest upon the factor of surprise, of fright; and secondly, that a wound or injury inflicted simultaneously works as a rule *against* the development of a neurosis."[27]

Freud here recognizes the importance of surprise and terror. He seems to acknowledge the power of chance and the impossibility of anticipation. However, this power either causes a physical wound or a psychic wound. In the first case, there is a narcissistic bodily investment that takes care of the wound, as if organic injuries were able to cure themselves without any psychic therapy. As if a physical wound and a psychic wound had nothing in common unless the former would let itself be translated into the language of the latter, thus becoming a "symptom." Which means that for Freud, people suffering from brain diseases do not obey psychoanalytic jurisdiction.

Psychic life (contrarily to organic life) is indestructible:

> The primitive mind is, in the fullest meaning of the word, imperishable. What are called mental diseases inevitably produce an impression in the layman that intellectual and mental life have been destroyed. In reality, the destruction only applies to later acquisitions and developments. The essence of mental disease lies in a return to earlier states of affective life and functioning. An excellent example of the plasticity of mental life is afforded by the state of sleep, which is our goal every night. Since we have learnt to interpret even absurd and confused dreams, we know that whenever we go to sleep we throw out our hard-won morality like a garment, and put it on again next morning.[28]

Even if Lacan displaces many Freudian arguments, he also shares many Freudian statements on the indestructibility of psychic life, which is another name for the "always already."

Neurobiology puts this so-called psychic immortality into question. Sociopolitical reality shows multiple versions of external intrusions, traumas, which are just meaningless brutal interruptions that destroy the symbolic texture of the subject's identity and render all kind of internalization/interiorization impossible. Nothing, in cerebral life, is indestructible, and if brain and the psyche are one and the same, then nothing, in psychic life, is indestructible either.

Žižek evokes the possibility that neurobiologists would only project their own desire, without mentioning it, in their account of neurobiological victims and meaningless trauma: "does [the neurobiologist] not forget to include [himself or herself], [his or her] own desire, in the observed phenomenon (of autistic subjects)?"[29] But we might of course reverse the objection: does not Žižek omit to include his own desire for the "always already"? Even if he is one of the most accurate and generous readers of current neurobiology, as it is manifest in so many passages of his books, we might interpret here the meaning of such a desire as Žižek's traumatic fear of being forever separated from Lacan.

Notes

1   See Slavoj Žižek, "Descartes and the Post-Traumatic Subject," in Catherine Mala- bou's *Les nouveaux blessés* (Paris: Bayard, 2007), translated as *The New Wounded: From Neurosis to Brain Damage*, trans. Steven Miller (New York: Fordham University Press, 2012), in *Qui Parle*, 17, 2 (2009), 123–47, revised version in *Filozofski vestnik* (Ljubljana) 24, 2 (2008), 9–29.

2   Slavoj Žižek, *The Parallax View* (Cambridge, MA: MIT Press, 2009).

3   Catherine Malabou, *The New Wounded: From Neurosis to Brain Damage*, op. cit.

4   Žižek, "Descartes and the Post-Traumatic Subject," 136.

5   Žižek, "Descartes and the Post-Traumatic Subject," 141.

6   Žižek, "Descartes and the Post-Traumatic Subject," 144.

7   Žižek, "Descartes and the Post-Traumatic Subject," 146.

8   Sigmund Freud, *The Interpretation of Dreams*, vol. 5 of *The Standard Edition of the Complete Psychological Works of Sigmund Freud* (London: Hogarth Press, 1957).

9   Jacques Lacan, *The Four Fundamental Concepts of Psychoanalysis*, trans. Alan Sheridan (New York: Norton, 1978).

10 Freud, *The Interpretation of Dreams*, 5: 547–48.

11 Lacan, *The Four Fundamental Concepts of Psychoanalysis*, 53.

12 Lacan, *The Four Fundamental Concepts of Psychoanalysis*, 69.

13 Lacan, *The Four Fundamental Concepts of Psychoanalysis*, 67.

14 Lacan, *The Four Fundamental Concepts of Psychoanalysis*, 58.

15 Lacan, *The Four Fundamental Concepts of Psychoanalysis*, 54.

16 Lacan, *The Four Fundamental Concepts of Psychoanalysis*, 58.

17 Lacan, *The Four Fundamental Concepts of Psychoanalysis*, 58.

18 Lacan, *The Four Fundamental Concepts of Psychoanalysis*, 69.

19 Lacan, *The Four Fundamental Concepts of Psychoanalysis*, 59.

20 Lacan, *The Four Fundamental Concepts of Psychoanalysis*, 58.

21 Žižek, *Descartes and the Post-traumatic Subject*, 125.

22 Sigmund Freud, "Psycho-Analysis and the War Neuroses," in *The Standard Edition*, 17: 210.

23 Sigmund Freud, "Sexuality," in *The Aetiology of the Neuroses*, in *The Standard Edition*, vol. 3.

24   Sigmund Freud, "My Views on the Part Played by Sexuality," in *The Standard Edition*, 7: 250.

25   Freud, "My Views on the Part Played by Sexuality," 7: 275.

26   Freud, "Sexuality," 3: 250.

27   Sigmund Freud, *Beyond the Pleasure Principle*, in *The Standard Edition*, 18: 12.

28   Sigmund Freud, *Thoughts for the Times on War and Death*, in *The Standard Edition*, 14: 285–86.

29   Žižek, *Descartes and the Post-Traumatic Subject*, 137.

8

Enjoy Your Truth:

Lacan as Vanishing

Mediator between

Bruno Bosteels   **Badiou and Žižek**

I rise up in revolt, so to speak, against philosophy. What is certain is that it is something finished, even if I expect to see some reject grow out of it. Such outgrowths are common enough with things that are finished.
—Jacques Lacan, "Monsieur A," March 18, 1980

Triangulations

In what follows I propose once more to study the relations between Alain Badiou and Slavoj Žižek starting from the notion of "antiphilosophy" that Jacques Lacan proudly assumed as his own in the 1970s as the name for his position toward philosophy and that Badiou systematically took up in the mid-1990s in a series of seminars on Nietzsche, Wittgenstein, Lacan, and Saint Paul.[1] The occasion for such a return to the scene of the crime—Nietzsche after all calls the philosopher "the criminal of criminals"—is provided by the fact that in the last few years Badiou has published several books from that series, including the complete transcript of the original seminar on Lacanian antiphilosophy as well as two shorter studies, coauthored with Barbara Cassin, on Lacan's late text "L'étourdit."[2] Meanwhile, over the course of the same period, Žižek repeatedly has been at pains to argue that Lacan is actually no less of a philosophical hero despite the fact that in 1975, in "Perhaps at Vincennes . . ." (published in the first issue of his journal *Ornicar?*), Lacan proposed antiphilosophy as a subdiscipline, together with linguistics, logic, and topology, in which all analysts in his school would have to be trained.[3] As recently as in *Less Than Nothing: Hegel and the Shadow of Dialectical Materialism*, the Slovenian thinker thus minimizes the importance of the explicit references to antiphilosophy in the late Lacan. For Žižek, in fact, antiphilosophy has more to do with the standard deconstructionist and multiculturalist rejection of universal truths, whereas Lacan is seen as a worthy heir to the long sequence of German idealist philosophy after Kant and Hegel.[4] Yet from Badiou's point of view, even if he has not made this point explicitly, it is not only Lacan but also undoubtedly Žižek himself who could and perhaps should be read as antiphilosophers.[5] My aim is not to settle this debate once and for all, let alone to adjudicate good and bad points in what could only be a dry schoolmasterly fashion, but to sort out the fundamental stakes behind the polemic and reconstruct the general problematic in which these thinkers operate.

It is of course undeniable that the giant figure of Lacan serves as the principal mediator in the ongoing polemics between Badiou and Žižek.[6] Yet mediation in this context does not mean the dialectical overcoming of a gap or distance, the forging of a unified articulation, but quite the opposite: I would argue that Lacan functions as an obstacle that forever keeps apart the likes of Badiou and Žižek—albeit by a minimal distance. In this sense, he is the name for something like a point of the real that cuts through the imaginary identifications and the no-less-imaginary mutual rejections (the likes and dislikes) between his latter-day admirers. Lacan is a stubborn obstacle, rather than a mediating third term in any straightforward dialectical sense, first of all, because Badiou and Žižek obviously have their own specific interpretation of the work of the French psychoanalyst; second, because these interpretations cannot be distributed evenly into pros and cons as if they were referring merely to different takes on the same corpus of fundamental concepts whose stable meaning we would be able to grasp beforehand; and finally, because even if we were able to reconstruct them in detail, such divergent interpretations of what Lacan meant by antiphilosophy are still a long way from helping us figure out the concepts of philosophy, psychoanalysis, and antiphilosophy as they are mobilized over time in the works of Badiou and Žižek. There is always a risk that by choosing the path of Lacanian psychoanalysis in order to triangulate the relation between Badiou and Žižek, we end up trapped in a merely exegetical exercise that fails to capture the true stakes of the polemics between the two. But the same could be said about choosing Badiou to triangulate between Lacan and Žižek; or about Žižek to triangulate between Lacan and Badiou. Despite the obvious proximities and frequent declarations of influence, loyalty, and complicity, I have yet to see an exegesis that would satisfy diehard followers of all three figures at once: Badiou, Lacan, and Žižek. At least one and often two of these cohorts is likely to be unconvinced by a reading that they can always claim is unfaithful to their favorite source of exegetical authority and unduly biased toward the others. ("Badiou completely fails to understand what Lacan means by the death drive," "Žižek misses the most basic ideas behind Badiou's metamathematical ontology," "Žižek's Lacan changes so much over time as to become monstrously unrecognizable," and so on and so forth.)

In the hands of Badiou even the notion of antiphilosophy takes on a meaning of its own that is far from being restricted to whatever signification Lacan attributed to this same notion. Thus, Badiou in his seminar is able to interrogate Lacan from the point of view of a much broader antiphilosophical tradition, now including Pascal, Rousseau, Kierkegaard, Nietzsche, and Wittgenstein, in which the French psychoanalyst can then be said to fall short of, complicate, or even contradict the general matrix of a notion that he nonetheless was the first to assume openly after its original coinage by the so-called *antiphilosophes*, that is, the mostly religious and now long-forgotten opponents who in the eighteenth century resisted the atheism and new materialism of French *philosophes* such as Diderot or Voltaire.[7] Even in the most faithful reconstruction of Lacan's understanding of antiphilosophy, therefore, we would be hard pressed to recognize the profile of the antiphilosopher drawn in Badiou's systematization. Rather, we are likely to end up with what Jean-François Lyotard calls a differend, in which the concerned parties or their followers are unable to settle their accounts because they do not share the same language or dwell in the same universe of discourse. If we tried to bring them together, we would have to betray one party's convictions by translating them into the idiom of the other; or else we would have to accept defeat in our effort at mediation between the different discourses, by acknowledging that their incommensurability is in fact insuperable. For translation at the level of thought or theory is never a neutral passage from one theoretical idiom to another, insofar as each idiom comes with its own conceptual presuppositions, ideological commitments, and subjective dispositions. These presuppositions, commitments, and dispositions can only rarely, if ever, be flattened out into a neutrally transmissible message. Rather, they point toward the presence of something that is not of the order of scholastic or exegetical precision but hearkens back to an existential decision.

This, too, may well be a crucial lesson to be learned from the confrontation between philosophy and antiphilosophy as mediated in this case by psychoanalysis. Indeed, the reference to the subject behind the act of thinking—so crucial for the analytical practice, as summarized for instance in the role of the subject of enunciation as opposed to the subject of the enunciated—tends to push up against the walls of philosophy's conceptual bulwark in favor of experiential intensity at the level of desire, affect, drive, or will to power. To apply this antiphilosophical principle of the privileging of subjectivity over systematicity, of affect over concept, to our investigation would entail that we inquire into the inscription of theory in the practice of the speaking and thinking subject. In other words, the point is not just to come to an exact understanding of Badiou's reading of Lacan in contrast to Žižek's reading of Lacan but rather to understand why these two contemporary thinkers return again and again, as if in a compulsory repetition, to the work of Lacan as a symptomatic site, and from there to redefine the stakes of what, in the Althusserian school to which both Badiou and Žižek paid their dues in their formative years (separated, to be sure, by a good twenty years), was once called "theoretical activity" or "theoretical practice," without as yet prejudging its philosophical or antiphilosophical qualities. Indeed, if there is one principle that Badiou and Žižek share without hesitation, over and beyond their disagreements, it is an undivided faith in the urgent and invigorating role of thought in a context of ongoing crisis, global war, and general ideological disorientation. In the end, we should never lose sight of this shared conviction, even when dealing with the specific differences regarding the place each of them assigns to philosophy, psychoanalysis, politics, mathematics, love, art, sexuality, and so on: When in doubt—Badiou and Žižek seem to want to tell us time and again—do not give in to the spontaneous coercion to act at all cost but dare to think! Nonetheless, the stickier question is the one that points to whatever precedes this imperative at the level of subjective motivation, desire, or drive: Where exactly does this imperative stem from?

Motives

To be sure, in his answer to the question "What is Enlightenment?" Immanuel Kant already proposed the imperative: *Sapere aude*, that is, "Dare to think" or "Dare to know."[8] Behind this imperative to show autonomy and courage in thought, however, we can detect a great many contradictory motives and impulses. Badiou and Žižek certainly do not come to accept this obligation to think in the same way, or from the same place. In fact, if we take into account their subjective trajectories, these two thinkers almost seem to be at cross-purposes and to trace something like a chiasm of desiring lines. What is more, to understand this disjunction at the level of personal dispositions or impulses will prove to be a crucial step toward grasping the respective takes of each thinker on the place of philosophy and antiphilosophy. As I suggested before, it could very well be the only step needed—the one basic insight to which we will have to return at the end of our investigation. After all, Kant's injunction alone is still insufficient, and in the background of this entire debate we must always try to hear echoes of Lacan's rightly famous "Kant with Sade."[9] This programmatic title can and must be read in two intimately related ways. It is not just that Sade reveals the dark and perverse underside of Kant's Enlightenment; rather, the crucial point not to be missed is that there is also a Kantian maxim of universalization—a moral law—to be found within the logic of Sadean perversion. Mutatis mutandis, is this not how we should try to read "Badiou with Žižek," especially if we take into account Žižek's own follow-up question: "Is Sade—in the Lacanian reading—not the antiphilosopher to Kant, so that Lacan's 'avec' means to read a philosopher through his antiphilosopher?"[10]

What I propose to call the chiasmic structure of desire that underpins Badiou's and Žižek's disposition toward the philosophical or antiphilosophical nature of thought is best understood as an effect of two very different trajectories. When Badiou in the 1990s decided to take up the gauntlet in a series of four seminars devoted to as many great antiphilosophers, he had in fact just consolidated his name as a quintessential philosopher, proud author of a *Manifesto for Philosophy* to accompany the presentation of his grand system of thought in *Being and Event*. Here, then, was someone who claimed to stand up for Plato over and against the prevailing anti-Platonism of all those contemporaries of his who had been calling for the end of philosophy, from Martin Heidegger to Richard Rorty. If, at this precise time, Badiou also begins to be interested in reconstructing the generic matrix of antiphilosophy, this is still only or primarily to put to the test his own protocol for the systematic regrounding of philosophy. The point is always courageously to traverse antiphilosophy, but for the sake of a reenergized consolidation of philosophy. Badiou's single overarching question in his seminar therefore consists in asking: "How does the antiphilosophical Lacan identify philosophy?"[11] On the other hand when Žižek in the same years began to acquire international fame with the publication of his English books *The Sublime Object of Ideology* and *For They Know Not What They Do: Enjoyment as Political Factor*, he was coming out of a long training and analysis with Jacques-Alain Miller in France, the result of which had just been published in two volumes, *Le plus sublime des hystériques* and *Ils ne savent pas ce qu'ils font*, in a book series especially reserved for theoretical work in the Lacanian psychoanalytical field.[12] And yet, even when very soon thereafter the unstoppable success story of Žižek's work in English took off, this story would largely remain confined to the field of cultural studies, foreign to the psychoanalytical and philosophical background of the Slovenian school of Lacanians of which he was becoming such an important part. This tragic misrecognition explains, in my eyes, why Žižek, over and above his well-deserved fame in cultural studies, would feel the need not only to underscore his own credentials as a philosopher — someone who is ultimately far more interested in Hegel than in Hitchcock — but also to refute the antiphilosophical elements in Lacan — now reread, in a way that Badiou already anticipated in his *Theory of the Subject*, as our contemporary Hegel. Thus, whereas Badiou after the completion of *Being and Event* speaks from within the bastion of a classically or neoclassically styled philosophy, waving the banner of Platonism with sufficient self-confidence to accept the challenge of an antiphilosopher such as Lacan, Žižek is still at pains to downplay the late Lacan's antiphilosophical provocations for the sake of gaining respectability as a philosopher. Anecdotally, we could illustrate this by noting how, the longer and seemingly more systematic Žižek's books become, the less can he leave unchallenged the customary antiphilosophical portrayal of Lacan that we find in Badiou.

Again without wanting to give out good or bad grades in any dogmatic sense, I have no doubt that we could pinpoint certain institutional factors that overdetermine this crossed encounter between Badiou and Žižek on the subject of Lacan. But more than in what could quickly threaten to become a predictable Bourdieu-inspired sociology of the field of intellectual production, with the contest of faculties laying the ground for the structure of the modern university, it is the desires that are funneled into and more often than not come to die in the institutions that interest me. Consider, for example, how from beginning to end Badiou's life as a philosopher has been inscribed within one of the official strongholds of French philosophy. In fact, when seen in this light, his career can be said to have come full circle. Not only did he start out as a young chain-smoking student who first hit the limelight as the up-and-coming talent interviewing the likes of Jean Hyppolite, Paul Ricœur, Michel Foucault, and Georges Canguilhem for French public television in a program called *The Philosopher in the Street*.[13] But, at the end of his career, he also was able to return to the Philosophy Department of his alma mater, the École Normale Supérieure in rue d'Ulm, where he would go on to occupy the chair of his former mentor Louis Althusser and where to this day, following his retirement, he regularly continues to offer his seminar on Wednesdays.

Žižek's case, as far as I know, could not have been more different in this sense. Neither in Ljubljana (at the Institute of Sociology) nor in Birkbeck (at the Institute for the Humanities) can he be seen as affiliated with the disciplinary structures or institutional apparatuses of philosophy strictly speaking. Furthermore, compared to the grin of irony and self-assurance with which Badiou already dared to interrogate the great French thinkers of the 1960s—all the luminaries and mentors of what later would come to be called disparagingly *la pensée '68*, or "thought of May 1968," Žižek's proverbial nervousness could also be read as a confirmation of the uncertain status of his discourse. More than a sign of simple performance anxiety, we could almost say that this is anxiety itself being performed, including in the analytical sense of anxiety as the affect that never lies. Žižek thus acts out the hysteric's discourse in contrast to the master's discourse of a stoically unfazed Badiou. Or at least this is how it seemed until recently. Ever since he began publishing increasingly voluminous attempts at a more systematic outline of his thought, from *The Ticklish Subject* to *The Parallax View* to *Less Than Nothing*, while still displaying equal amounts of nervousness on stage, Žižek has in fact toned down the antiphilosophical attacks and openly sought to add a mature philosophical and political rejoinder to his long-standing personal friendship for Badiou.

Lacan's case, once again, contains aspects of both these trajectories without allowing us to settle comfortably on any synthesis. So then, let us ask: What about Lacan's desire—the desire of the analyst—in this context? Why does he feel the need to present himself as an antiphilosopher? And, on top of his subjective motivations, wishes, and needs, are there any objective reasons that come to frame and overdetermine them? Perhaps we might answer these questions starting from what I take to be the most important institutional factor in this regard, namely, the potentially poisoned invitation on the part of Althusser to bring Lacan to the École Normale Supérieure in rue d'Ulm. Indeed, could we not say that Lacan's animosity against philosophy—his enraged insurrection against the philosopher in the 1970s—is a belated reaction, or abreaction, to Althusser's invitation?[14] What was, after all, the effect of this invitation? Or rather, what did this invitation confirm in terms of a potential risk that was already eating psychoanalysis from within like a polyp, ever since the late Freud's incursion into the domains of cultural, religious, or so-called civilizational matters? Nothing less than the risk of becoming a philosophical worldview, or weltanschauung—something that Freud himself explicitly sought to resist, for example, in the name of science, in the last one of his *New Introductory Lectures on Psychoanalysis*. Thus, when Lacan accepted Althusser's invitation, he was in a sense entering the lion's den, and it should not come as a surprise to see him inveigh so viciously against his audience, especially once the students all too obediently returned to his seminar after the failed revolt of May '68 that had caused him prematurely to break off his lectures planned for 1967–1968 on *The Psychoanalytical Act*.

However, Lacan's veritable addressee—the real target of his invectives—is actually not the philosopher. On this issue Badiou makes an important distinction, which asks us to separate the object from the addressee of Lacan's antiphilosophical attacks. For Lacan, even though he thus may seem to be biting the hand that feeds him, the philosopher is always already a lost case. In fact, though otherwise paradoxical, such relative indifference to actual philosophers is true for all antiphilosophers, according to Badiou. Just as Pascal or Rousseau, for example, address not the philosopher but the libertine or the sensible person who alone has any hope of salvation, so too does Lacan address not the philosophers but the analysts in his seminar room. They are the ones whom Badiou, in an open homage to Gilles Deleuze's notion of the "conceptual characters" of philosophy, calls the "counter-characters" of the antiphilosopher. They alone—the present and future analysts in the Lacanian school(s)—are the ones who are at risk and need to be saved from the temptation of turning psychoanalysis into yet another philosophical doctrine or worldview, that is, into a false quest for speculative reassurance, systematic completeness, and consolatory meaning.

This is yet another way in which all the parties involved in this ongoing debate continue to find themselves at cross-purposes. Whereas Lacan is consistent with the long line of antiphilosophers who, according to Badiou, seek to mock and discredit the professional philosophers, but without really ever addressing them, since the philosopher in the eyes of Nietzsche, Wittgenstein, or Lacan is really beyond salvage, Žižek by contrast directly used to provoke Badiou in the past with frequent criticisms and polemical rejoinders, nearly all of them unreciprocated—at least on paper. This also means that as soon as we move beyond the academic reconstruction of each thinker's position, we may end up contradicting the very impulse behind their work, for example by considering Žižek an antiphilosopher against his own will, or by telling Badiou that Lacan is actually more of a philosopher along the likes of Kant and Hegel than the analyst himself claims to be.

Mathematics

Badiou organizes his interpretation of antiphilosophy in the late Lacan around four basic statements. The first three of these actually articulate crucial insights that no philosopher can afford to ignore, insofar as they address what Badiou calls the "conditions" of philosophy, that is, the "generic procedures" that alone are capable of producing truths that philosophy is then supposed to seize and shelter in a space of shared possibility, or compossibility. To be exact, the three truth procedures that are at stake in this interpretation are science (or mathematics), politics, and love. What Lacan argues about these conditions is that philosophy by definition fails to grasp even the slightest thing about them. To do so he adopts a guiding image that may well be borrowed from Freud, who was fond of quoting the following line of Heinrich Heine about the philosopher: "with his nightcaps and the tatters of his dressing-gown he patches up the gaps in the structure of the universe."[15] Thus, too, images of blockheaded philosophers, clogged pipes, and patched-up gaps run through each of the three statements from Lacan studied by Badiou. But the real difficulty comes into view when we realize that Badiou's response, in turn, is not the same for each of the criticisms contained in Lacan's statements, nor can we simply extend the latter without further ado so as to attribute the positions and commitments implied therein to Žižek.

In the first statement Lacan charges philosophy with being blind to the value of mathematics while he himself defends mathematical formalization and more generally opposes the truth of science to the speculative-hermeneutic quest for meaning or sense that he associates with philosophy: "To be the most propitious language for scientific discourse, mathematics is the science without conscience which our good Rabelais promised, the one to which a philosopher cannot but remain blocked."[16] In this sense, incidentally, we can already see how Lacan is separated from the broader matrix of contemporary antiphilosophy, insofar as most of his predecessors, in particular Nietzsche and Wittgenstein, reduce mathematics to a merely formal question of grammar or logic, to which they then oppose the force of life, value, or sense—not the propositional sense of statements *about* the world but the suprapropositional sense *of* the world as such; also not this or that table of values, but the value of value, that is, life, which itself cannot be evaluated. Lacan, by contrast, holds up a notion of scientific truth, especially in his early works from the 1950s and 1960s, as witnessed in what is no doubt one of the most crucial writings or *écrits* for all of Badiou's generation: "Science and Truth" was not for nothing published for the first time as the opening salvo in *Cahiers pour l'analyse*, the influential journal of Althusserian-Lacanian students of the rue d'Ulm.[17]

Initially Badiou responds to this statement by inverting the charge and accusing Lacan himself for being a bit blockheaded about the true nature of the relationship between philosophy and mathematics. For Badiou, it is not the philosophers but rather the working mathematicians who remain blind to the grandeur of their axioms, theorems, and proofs, which it falls to philosophy to unlock in terms of their ontological implications. Beyond this initial inversion, however, Badiou admits that Lacan's argument contains a genuine lesson. On the one hand it is indeed the case that philosophy harbors a tendency to veer off in the direction of a religious or hermeneutic search for meaning or sense, against which the purely axiomatic operations of mathematics serve as a powerful corrective. On the other hand philosophy can be shown—even at the most sublime heights of its speculative ambition as in Plato or Hegel—to have recognized this power of mathematics, capable of demonstrating infinity in the immanence of its discourse, as a weapon in the battle against hermeneutics.

Thus, in one sense, Lacan splits philosophy from itself in relation to mathematics. However, this can be said to be the case only if we ignore the many passages in which we see a wholesale rejection of philosophy as being blind to mathematics in general. In another sense, therefore, we can say that this wholesale rejection relies on an undivided image of the entire tradition of philosophy in a way that brings Lacan much closer to Heidegger's destruction of the history of Western metaphysics—except that the author of *Being and Time* includes science and technology in this history, whereas science and mathematics in the eyes of Lacan promise a salvific break from all philosophical elucubrations of meaning, which ultimately are no different from religion. Lacan himself, in fact, introduces a split within science between mathematics and what he calls the matheme. If mathematics consists in rigorous formalization, based on the axiomatic consistency of its own discourse, then the matheme, as a formula of writing that is connected to the real, aims at the impasse of such mathematical formalization. Here we touch on a need that can be found among all antiphilosophers, according to Badiou: the need to provide some form of access to a domain or realm—the value of life for Nietzsche, or the sense of the world for Wittgenstein—that would be radically different from the empty quests for meaning of the professional philosophers. In the case of Lacan, this implies the possibility of accessing and transmitting a point of the real as a hole in our imaginary or symbolic representations of reality—including a hole in whatever discourse produces at the level of mathematical formalization. And the matheme, in the Lacanian sense, promises to enable precisely the universal demonstration and transmission of such a point of the real. "We are thus justified in saying that the matheme is what inscribes the real as impasse," concludes Badiou. "That which must be kept silent, for Lacan, is indeed this real which cannot be said but only written or inscribed. Such is properly speaking the matheme."[18]

If now we approach Žižek in light of this dispute about mathematics between Lacan and Badiou, what immediately strikes the eye is the complete absence of any treatment of mathematical formalization in the works of the Slovenian. If anything, Lacan and Badiou might agree that it is Žižek who remains stubbornly blocked, or *bouché*, to the insights of mathematics. On closer inspection, however, I wonder if we cannot locate a resource in Žižek's writing that performs a function similar to that of the Lacanian matheme, as distinct from mathematics, that is, the function of transmitting an impasse or—to use Žižek's preferred term for the impasse of formalization—a deadlock. Indeed, can we not say that popular culture in general and jokes in particular serve the purpose of conveying a point of the real that both reveals and interrupts the obscene functioning of our ideological fantasies about reality? Far from being reducible to matters of mere taste, whether good or more often than not bad, obscene jokes and the inevitable references to blockbuster movies and gadgets of all kinds thus have a strictly formal function in Žižek's analytical apparatus. They are to the Slovenian what nonorientable surfaces and other mathematical objects are to Lacan.

Politics

The triangulation is no less complicated in the case of the second statement that Badiou culls from his reconstruction of antiphilosophy in the late Lacan. Here, flirting once more with the Heideggerian vocabulary of the history of metaphysics, Lacan accuses philosophy of blocking or clogging up the hole of politics. "To my 'friend' Heidegger, evoked with the highest respect that I have for him, may he hold still for a moment," writes Lacan in the German edition of his *Écrits*, "I express this purely gratuitous wish because I know only too well that he won't be able to do so—hold still, I say, before the idea that metaphysics has never been anything else and will not be able to prolong itself except to busy itself with plugging the hole of politics. That is its mainspring."[19] In responding to this charge Badiou adopts a strategy that is almost the reverse of his answer to the first accusation. Instead of either turning the objection back against psychoanalysis or else accepting the lesson that philosophy is split on the subject of mathematics, Badiou in a sense will argue that it is Lacan who is divided on the subject of politics, while fundamentally agreeing with the Lacanian characterization thereof.

Badiou agrees with Lacan that politics has nothing whatsoever to do with the fiction of a just society, nor with the equally fictitious representation of the good revolution. Instead, politics is of the order of an interruption to which is conjoined a hasty and always haphazard act of intervention. Contrary to Lacan's disparaging comments, however, Badiou argues that philosophy has always been obliged to recognize this multiple, precarious, and contingent aspect of politics: "Even at the culmination of its foundational will—and God knows that this is the case of Plato's *Republic*—philosophy identifies in politics something which cannot be sutured but remains subject to a kind of contingent gap that even foundational thought cannot reduce."[20] By contrast, if we inquire into the possibility of an antiphilosophical position with regard to politics, a position that would not plug up its gaps with the rags of a social fiction, there is little or nothing to be learned from Lacan, according to Badiou. This is because the view of the collective—whether as a group, school, party, or any other institution—as necessarily being under the effect of an imaginary unity cannot allow for an organized thought-practice that would deserve to be named a politics. There is only a semblance of politics because politics is never anything but a matter of semblance as the necessary "glue" or *colle* that in Lacan's pun holds together the "school effect," as both *effet d'école* and *effet de colle*, always to be avoided in harsh acts of self-dissolution imposed by the severe and solitary founder.

Only dissolutions, but no lasting foundations—such would be the political nonlesson to be gleaned from Lacan. Except for just another semblance, the most we obtain is a pure world of vanishing absences, like a whirl of atoms swerving in the void, which even in Lacan's case does little more than combine the old utopia of direct democracy with a tyrannical perseverance in left-wing anarchism. "There has been no Lacanian political creation, no institution or installation of Lacanian politics. Which in the end would not be an objection if it were not for the fact that Lacan, for his part, did object to philosophy for plugging the hole of politics," claims Badiou in his seminar, before going one step further in his conclusion: "I would even say—though this is not Lacan's expression—that his profound thought holds that there is no politics at all, there is only political philosophy."[21]

For Badiou, in sum, Lacan fails to be the Lenin to Freud's Marx that he claims to be: "There are astonishing local analyses. But Lacan did not write *What Is To Be Done?* I say this because on numerous occasions he compares himself to Lenin. He says he is the Lenin for whom Freud would be Marx."[22] At best the mystery and at worst the necessary ignorance surrounding the practice of the cure suggest that this claim has been disappointingly unfounded. On this account, Žižek may lately have come to a point of near-complete agreement with Badiou insofar as he too criticizes the limited political potential of Lacan, for example, in *Less Than Nothing*: "Lacan unveiled the illusions on which capitalist reality as well as its false transgressions are based, but his final result is that we are condemned to domination."[23] In fact, in the case of politics, it is Žižek who sides with Badiou against Lacan, as witnessed in the ongoing international collaboration around the communist Idea. Nevertheless, the question remains as to whether this political fidelity does not imply a necessary betrayal of the fundamental lesson of psychoanalysis, particularly with regard to the role of enjoyment and the death drive.

Enjoyment

The key questions in the various triangulations at work thus seem to come down to the following: Can there be a politics of enjoyment? Beyond the recognition of enjoyment as the kernel of idiocy on which the administration of public life erects social fictions and fantasies of all kinds, can the recognition of the death drive also serve as the leverage for a minimal political act—or one that would not amount, once again, to an act of dissolution as a way of laying bare the symptomatic void at the heart of the social? Put differently, if what Žižek appreciates above all in Badiou is a politics of truth, can we enjoy this truth or does the psychoanalytical account of enjoyment run counter to this notion of truth, so cherished—even loved—in the philosophical tradition? What else does Lacan teach to the analysts of his school, if not that they should not enjoy the truth too much—lest they stoop to the level of the dogmatic slumber of the philosophers with their nightcaps and tattered sleeping gowns? After all, what is this love of truth that defines philosophy?

This is where Badiou invokes the third statement, drawn from Lacan's Seminar XVI, *The Other Side of Psychoanalysis*, which took place at the École Normale Supérieure in the year immediately following the revolt of May 1968: "The love of truth is the love of this weakness whose veil we have lifted, it's the love of what truth hides, which is called castration."[24] This is a slippery statement if ever there was one, for the simple reason that the connotation of the category of truth changes in the course of the sentence itself, as indicated by the fact that elsewhere in the same seminar the "truth" of analysis frequently seems to require quotation marks. What Lacan suggests is that philosophy deludes itself in its love for truth; that the "truth" for psychoanalysis is always the fact of a barred possibility, or an impossibility, the analytical name for which is castration; and that the philosopher's love of truth is premised on the constitutive disavowal of this "truth" laid bare—or unconcealed, in yet another flirtation with Heidegger—in the clinical practice of psychoanalysis: the face-to-face confrontation with a certain real, that is, the fact that there is no such thing as a sexual relationship.

And yet, this last objection runs the risk of ruining the hoped-for political alliance between the likes of Badiou and Žižek. Nothing indeed has been more common for Žižek than to attack Badiou precisely on the grounds that he completely fails to understand the first thing about love, desire, enjoyment, and the death drive. Such an attack can take the typically antiphilosophical form of a disparagement, as when Žižek accuses Badiou of falling to the level of sheer nonthought: "When Badiou adamantly opposes the 'morbid obsession with death,' when he opposes the Truth-Event to the death drive, and so on, he is at his weakest, succumbing to the *temptation of the non-thought*."[25] Or else, especially in Žižek's more recent works, the accusation can mask itself behind more respectable philosophical labels, such that Badiou turns out to have been blind to the role of pure negativity, or radical finitude, as a prior condition—the tabula rasa of all fantasies that alone clears the ground for a genuine ethical or political act. Thus, except for the sobered-up tone, in

Less Than Nothing we are still within the same problematic as the one in *The Ticklish Subject*. "Negativity (whose Freudian name is the 'death drive') is the primordial ontological fact: for a human being, there is no 'animal life' prior to it, for a human being is constitutively 'out-of-joint.' Every 'normality' is a secondary *normalization* of the primordial dislocation that is the 'death drive,' and it is only through the terrorizing experience of the utter vacuity of every positive order of 'normality' that a space is opened up for an Event."[26] Finally, what emerges as the fundamental stake in the ongoing disputes between Badiou and Žižek on the subject of Lacan is the problematic of the different relationships between truth, knowledge, and the real of enjoyment.

Truth or Knowledge

Indeed, if in a first, more classical period, as I mentioned earlier, Lacan defended science and truth over and against the religious quest for meaning that threatened even psychoanalysis with its temptation, then in his late writings, seminars, and allocutions he tends to subordinate truth to the functioning of the real in knowledge. For Badiou, this shift can be summed up in a fourth and final statement, pulled from Lacan's 1970 "Closing Allocution to the Conference of the Freudian School of Paris": "Truth may not convince, knowledge passes in the act."[27] Only philosophers pine away for the truth, which may not be convincing. But what the experience of the psychoanalytical act teaches Lacan — if not the analysts in his School — is that at best a small piece of the real may pass into knowledge. The dominant notion for the late Lacan, beginning in the 1970s, is no longer truth or science but the act of knowledge in the real: the passage or passing of a piece of the real into knowledge. In French, there is even an additional benefit to the expression that Lacan typically uses in this context, since *passe en savoir* is also a homonym for *pas sans savoir*, meaning "not without knowing" or "not without knowledge."

We could thus conclude by returning to Kant's maxim: *Sapere aude*. If we translate the Latin expression as "Dare to think," we can uphold a certain love of philosophical truth that, in spite of everything, has been a constant from Kant to Heidegger to Badiou, including "thinking" as a privileged name for postmetaphysical philosophy, but we still risk being blind to the dissolving power of enjoyment as death drive or pure self-relating negativity. On the other hand if we translate Kant's maxim as "Dare to know," then we are perhaps better equipped to lift the veil of the obscene fantasy of enjoyment about which psychoanalysis provides us with passing bits of knowledge, but only at the cost of forsaking any lasting political experiment that would not be the sheer repetition of our own private symptoms. In the end, at the crossover point between all the chiasmic lines that are the result of the triangulations attempted here between Badiou and Žižek with Lacan as their vanishing mediator, we thus find an impossible imperative: Enjoy your truth![28]

Notes

1   Previously I have dealt with Badiou's reconstruction of antiphilosophy in general and with his treatment of Ludwig Wittgenstein and Friedrich Nietzsche in particular, in Bruno Bosteels, "Radical Antiphilosophy," *Filozofski Vestnik* 2 (2008), 155–87; translator's introduction to Alain Badiou, *Wittgenstein's Antiphilosophy*, ed. and trans. Bruno Bosteels (London: Verso, 2011), 1–66; and "Nietzsche, Badiou, and Grand Politics: An Antiphilosophical Reading," in *Nietzsche and Political Thought*, ed. Keith Ansell-Pearson (London: Bloomsbury, 2013), 219–39.

2   See Alain Badiou, *Lacan: L'antiphilosophie*, vol. 3 (Paris: Fayard, 2013); and Alain Badiou and Barbara Cassin, *Il n'y a pas de rapport sexuel: Deux leçons sur "L'étourdit" de Lacan* (Paris: Fayard, 2010).

3   Jacques Lacan, "Peut-être à Vincennes . . . ," *Ornicar?* 1 (January 1975), 3–5, reprinted in *Autres écrits*, ed. Jacques-Alain Miller (Paris: Seuil, 2001), 313–15; see also my epigraph, drawn from Jacques Lacan, "Monsieur A," *Ornicar?* 21–22 (Summer 1980), 17.

4   Slavoj Žižek, "Badiou and Antiphilosophy," in *Less Than Nothing: Hegel and the Shadow of Dialectical Materialism* (London: Verso, 2012), 841–58. Compare already Slavoj Žižek, *Tarrying with the Negative: Kant, Hegel, and the Critique of Ideology* (Durham, NC: Duke University Press, 1993), 3–4.

5   For a rare portrait of Žižek as a typical antiphilosopher, see Alain Badiou, *Logics of Worlds: Being and Event*, vol. 2, trans. Alberto Toscano (London: Continuum, 2009), 565.

6   Or is G. W. F. Hegel perhaps the more important reference? On the one hand this is what Žižek himself affirms: "My ongoing debate with Badiou could be read as a series of variations on the motif of how to redeem Hegel," in *Less Than Nothing*, 805. On the other hand even Badiou might not disagree with this claim, insofar as Lacan for him is in fact our contemporary Hegel: "Lacan, I said earlier, is our Hegel, that is, he presents the (idealist) dialectic of our time," so that our task is to divide him: "like Hegel for Marx, Lacan for us is essential and divisible." See Alain Badiou, *Theory of the Subject*, trans. with an introduction by Bruno Bosteels (London: Continuum, 2009), 132–33.

7   For an intellectual history of the original eighteenth-century antiphilosophes, see

Didier Masseau, *Les Ennemis des philosophes: L'antiphilosophie au temps des Lumières* (Paris: Albin Michel, 2000).

8   Immanuel Kant, "An Answer to the Question: 'What Is Enlightenment?,'" in *Political Writings*, ed. Hans Reiss (Cambridge: Cambridge University Press, 1991), 54. The official translation reads: "have courage to use your *own* understanding." I will leave aside for the moment the specific difference of translating "sapere" as "to understand," "to think" or "to know," until the moment in my conclusion, when we will be better equipped to address this issue in light of Badiou and Lacan's discussion of truth and knowledge, or *savoir* in French, as derived from the Latin *sapere*.

9   Jacques Lacan, "Kant with Sade," in *Écrits*, trans. Bruce Fink (New York: Norton, 2006), 645–68.

10   Žižek, *Less Than Nothing*, 18n17. For an earlier attempt to read the dispute in this way, see Bruno Bosteels, "Badiou without Žižek," in *The Philosophy of Alain Badiou*, ed. Matthew Wilkens, special issue of *Polygraph* 17 (2005), 221–44.

11   Badiou, *Lacan*, 141.

12   Slavoj Žižek, *Le plus sublime des hystériques: Hegel passe* (Paris: Point Hors Ligne, 1988), and *Ils ne savent pas ce qu'ils font: Le sinthome idéologique* (Paris: Point Hors Ligne, 1990).

13   See *Badiou and the Philosophers: Interrogating 1960s French Philosophy*, trans. Tzuchien Tho and Giuseppe Bianco (London: Bloomsbury, 2013).

14   To this early invitation François Regnault adds an additional factor, namely, the later institutional rivalry between the Department of Philosophy and the Department of Psychoanalysis at the University of Paris-VIII of Vincennes, which would further explain the animosity of Lacan in the 1970s against philosophy—with antiphilosophy now appearing as a direct reply to Gilles Deleuze and Félix Guattari's antipsychiatry and the huge following they garnered in the wake of their anti-Oedipus. See François Regnault, "L'antiphilosophie selon Lacan," *Conférences d'esthétique lacanienne* (Paris: Agalma, 1997), 57–80.

15   Sigmund Freud, "The Question of a *Weltanschauung*," in *New Introductory Lectures on Psychoanalysis*, trans. James Strachey (New York: Norton, 1965), 141.

16   Jacques Lacan, "L'étourdit," *Scilicet* 4 (1973), 9, reprinted in *Autres écrits*, 453, and quoted in Badiou, *Lacan*, 39.

17   Jacques Lacan, "La science et la vérité," *Cahiers pour l'analyse* 1 (January 1964), 6–28, in English, "Science and Truth," in *Écrits*, 726–45. For the intellectual context of the Althusserian-Lacanian project behind the *Cahiers pour l'analyse*, see the two volumes *Concept and Form*, ed. Peter Hallward and Knox Peden (London: Verso, 2013).

18   Badiou, *Lacan*, 44–45.

19   Jacques Lacan, "Introduction à l'édition allemande d'un premier volume des *Écrits*," *Scilicet* 5 (1975), 11–17, reprinted in *Autres écrits*, 5: 54–55. The text is dated October 7, 1973.

20   Badiou, *Lacan*, 150.

21   Badiou, *Lacan*, 154 and 214.

22   Badiou, *Lacan*, 218.

23 Žižek, *Less Than Nothing*, 18–19. Admittedly, Žižek is paraphrasing Badiou and Lardreau, but later statements in his own name appear to confirm the criticism of Lacan's limitations.

24 Jacques Lacan, *The Seminar of Jacques Lacan, Book XVII: The Other Side of Psychoanalysis*, ed. Jacques-Alain Miller, trans. Russell Grigg (New York: Norton, 2007), 52, quoted in Badiou, *Lacan*, 159.

25 Slavoj Žižek, *The Ticklish Subject: The Absent Centre of Political Ontology* (London: Verso, 1999), 145.

26 Žižek, *Less Than Nothing*, 835.

27 Lacan, "Allocution sur l'enseignement," *Scilicet* 2–3 (1970), 391–99, reprinted in *Autres écrits*, 305, and quoted in Badiou, *Lacan*, 18.

28 Compare with Žižek's statement that from a first maxim dear to the classic structuralist Lacan—"Dare the truth"—we move closer in the second or late Lacan to something like a forced choice—"Truth or dare": "at the level of *jouissance*, truth is simply *inoperative*, something which ultimately doesn't matter." See Slavoj Žižek, "Foreword to the Second Edition: Enjoyment within the Limits of Reason Alone," in *For They Know Not What They Do* (London: Verso, 2002), lxvii.

9

Henrik Jøker Bjerre and

Brian Benjamin Hansen

The Discourse of the

Wild Analyst

The aim of this chapter is to identify the particular version of psycho-analysis that prevails in Slavoj Žižek's work. By this is not meant his interpretation of Sigmund Freud or Jacques Lacan, or the employment of them in the "short circuit" of classical, especially German philoso-phy from Kant to Hegel. Rather, our wager is that Žižek's analytical approach to contemporary society can, and should, be seen in the light of his specific operationalization of the terminology and analytical re-sources of the tradition from Freud and Lacan. Žižek's analytical take on society and culture remarkably fits what Freud called "wild analysis," but rather than denying or excusing this, we want to make the case for a positive understanding of wild analysis—and we end up formalizing this understanding in what we term the discourse of the wild analyst; as a short circuit, in itself, if you will, of Lacan's famous four discourses.

The End of Analysis

Beginning from the end, Žižek's approach to psychoanalysis could be framed through a comparison to Freud's and Lacan's conceptions of the end of analysis. Roughly said, one could say that to Freud analysis was completed when the techniques of the analyst had made possible suffi-cient progress in the patient's self-awareness and well-being, whereas to Lacan it consisted much more in a new relation of the analysand toward his or her situation—a change in perspective, in position, and in rela-

tions to other people. In Žižek, in turn, the very idea of an end of analysis is applied to the social field as such—to the "fall of the big Other"
in political revolutions, for example, when the social bond disintegrates
and new openings suddenly become possible. This shifting emphasis reflects different approaches to psychoanalysis, in its practice as well as in
its relation to the world outside the clinic.

In his text "Analysis Terminable and Interminable," Freud treated the
question of the end of analysis in a rather pragmatic fashion. Analysis
simply ends, as he wrote, "when analyst and patient cease to meet for
the analytic session,"[1] although this definition should be complemented
by the observations that the patient should no longer experience suffering, and that the analyst should regard the work as successful. Patients
may of course suffer setbacks or experience new traumas after analysis
has been ended, and strictly speaking one could say that no one ever becomes entirely sane (whether in analysis or not), but Freud maintained
that the end of analysis was a matter of practice and not a theoretical
question of the complete transparency of the unconscious. Theoretically,
however, analysis could in fact be seen as interminable ("infinite," as the
German original has it). There are always residues of repressed material
and resistance, and if analysis should ever really be over without any
reservation, it would imply a rather implausible conscious awareness of
all hitherto unknown motivations—a complete "draining of the Zuider
Zee," as it was called in another text.[2] With a technique, you may reach
a certain level of effect, a certain point of clarification, but you may also
have to accept that you will never reach the point of complete conversion
between the theoretical conception of what ending analysis would mean
and practical reality, where what we can hope for is to be able to live
more or less normally ("work and love"), without analysis.

In Lacan, there is also a practical dimension to the end of analysis,
but it is not merely a question of deciding that the patient seems more
or less okay—the end of analysis involves a kind of solution, even in a
theoretical sense, in a way which it does not in Freud. There is of course
no purely sane conception of the human being in Lacan either—indeed,
the common philosophical novelty of Freudo-Lacanian psychoanalysis
could be said precisely to be that there is no such thing as the "normal"
or "unpathological" way of living. But in Lacan, the emphasis is nonetheless different. The end of analysis is in fact possible, because it does

not concern an approximation to a theoretical idea of complete sanity, displaced into an infinite horizon, but a different way of relating to this impossibility. The end of analysis is not a pragmatic acceptance of the always only partial redemption of the infinite possible approaches and clarifications, but a change of attitude, a possibility of relating to the whole field of one's emotional investments and traumas in a different way—a traversing of the fundamental fantasy.[3] As a Danish analysand told his analyst toward the end of his analysis: "I feel that everything has changed, and yet I am still the same as when I came here the first time."[4] What changes at the end of analysis, one could almost say, is not really the analysand, but rather his or her position with respect to the Other; the question is how the analysand relates to that which he or she is in the face of the others who define and form the background for the subject's social being. What *can* change through analysis could almost be understood as acquiring the ability to speak in another way, maybe more freely, maybe in a way that acknowledges and assumes the impossibility of escaping language/discourse, the medium of the Other, once and for all—creating a new relation to the world and oneself. Recapitulating, Lacan saw his interventions and approaches as potential for such changes in the analysand's relation to the Other.

In Žižek, this point is radicalized. The end of analysis in his work first of all indicates the moments when the big Other falls, and now, the Other is not the imaginary guarantor of the stability of an individual phantasm, but the social bond as such—the secret accord between for instance the citizens of a state—which maintains that the Other functions, even if no one in particular truly believes in it. The end of analysis, in Žižek's version, is the dissolution of this social bond, as when the people no longer step back in the face of state authority, or when an institution or an order suddenly appears to have been undermined, maybe even without its subjects being aware of it. If the subject in analysis, in Lacan's perspective, has to realize that the Other does not exist, in Žižek the question is much more that the Other itself has to realize this. As the story about the man, who thought he was a grain, goes: he was hospitalized and received intensive therapy to cure his anxiety of being eaten by a chicken, but when released, he immediately returned. "Why are you coming back," his doctor asked, "you know very well now that you are not a grain." "Yes, of course," replied the man, "but does the chicken know it?!" The end of analysis is only achieved when the chicken knows it as well, and there-fore Žižek's interventions in public and philosophical debates could very often be seen as attempts at identifying points and acts that might pro-voke such a realization—hence his support of Syriza in Greece as the possible intervention into European economic policies, for instance.

Although such a short summary as this does of course not do justice to the obvious similarities that also exist between the three, one could say that the impossibility of overcoming that which requires analysis is (theoretically) placed at an "infinite" horizon in Freud, whereas it is more like a turning point in Lacan: the analysand "turns around" this impossibility and suddenly finds him- or herself in a different relation to the Other. In Žižek, the impossible itself *happens*; it cannot take place, the Other cannot be overcome, since it is the very (unconscious) belief in the Other's omnipotence that prevails even in the face of its flaws, mis-takes, and so on—but nonetheless it happens. And the aim of political interventions should precisely be to identify or, more precisely, enact this happening of the impossible.

Where Does Analysis Take Place?

The three different ontologies of the end of analysis have consequences for analysis itself; that is, the very process of analyzing as played out in the relation between analyst and analysand. We find it fruitful to present this as three different practico-theoretical constructs of what analysis is about, where Freud stands for technique, Lacan for discourse (as in the discourse of the analyst), and Žižek for intervention.

Freud, in his practice as well as in several texts on the subject mat-ter, defended technique as the means to distinguish a true psychoanalyst from laypersons, quacks, and "wild analysts." Wild analysts are seen as those who burst out with their diagnosis much too quickly (without let-ting the patient arrive at his or her own conclusions through free asso-ciation and careful interpretative assistance) and thereby risk creating great animosity in the patient, which might seriously impede or even make impossible further treatment. Technique is thus the "medical tact" of psychoanalysis, Freud argues in his text on wild analysis,[5] and the sci-entific doctrine and technical skills that pertain to psychoanalysis can and must even be institutionalized in order to be able to defend the reputation of psychoanalysis. In the same text, he thus also argues for and legitimizes the founding of the International Psycho-Analytical Association (IPA), which took place earlier in the year 1910.

It is well known that the very association that Freud founded in 1910 was the same that Lacan (in his own words) was "excommunicated" from in 1963, especially due to his experiments with, maybe even going beyond, technique. As Freud always maintained that analysis could not be shortened, and thus valorized patience and a respectful contract or working alliance with the patient,[6] Lacan engaged in the so-called short sessions; sessions ending at an unspecified time, with the effect of shocking or surprising the patient and attacking his or her ego. The question of technique thus in fact centers on the question of the ego: as Freud upheld that a strong ego was necessary for recovery and maintained that psychoanalysis was a work of culture, Lacan, in practice as well as theory, spent all his years attacking the ego and thus reopening Freud's initial discovery: the subject, the subject of the unconscious. This changes the approach to the very practice of analysis: as Pierre-Gilles Guéguen has remarked in an article on Lacan's short session, what Lacan does is to "put the frame into the picture, a topological operation that makes of the Lacanian session now and forever something more than an IPA session cut short."[7] What Guéguen here means by topological operation is that psychoanalysis is not only about offering the analytical session as something to be put on top of the rest of the analysand's life (as a medium for intellectual reflection Woody Allen–style) but also about disturbing (scandalizing, punctuating) the life of the analysand through the session, folding the frame of the session into the very life of the patient. What Lacan does with his short session, in other words, is form a new vision of the connection between life and sessions. Whereas analysis for Freud happens only in the clinic, analysis for Lacan happens at the border between the clinic and the life of the patient, or at the border of the clinical practice and culture at large. This is of course also why Lacan worked hard to create a theoretical liaison between psychoanalysis and structuralism: The signifier is not something whose function is limited to the clinic (where the dreams and symptoms of the patient can be talked through using the technique of free association), the signifier works in reality: social reality and culture. Analysis is in relation with the whole of the patient's signifying system, as Guéguen remarks,[8] which means that it enters into relation with the whole of the system of culture, as well as the discourses (as they are presented in Lacan's seminar *The Other Side of Psychoanalysis* as the discourse of the master, the hysteric, the analyst and the university),[9] upholding, questioning, or in other ways partaking in various domains of culture or the social.

From this basis we can envision what has been and is Žižek's project: To bring analysis the last step from the clinic and into the very signifying systems that underpin subjectivity, thus not reinventing psychoanalysis as a self-contained discipline and technique, but reinventing it through philosophical approaches that contribute to the analysis of subjectivity, social antagonism, and cultural formations. If Freud's analyses of culture were "scientific" in the sense of being modestly explorative, proceeding with caution into the domain of culture from a few basic insights from psychoanalysis, Lacan changed the game with his engaged remarks on different types of discourses, played out in different social arenas (the arena of production, the arena of the university, etc.) and their potentials. In the case of Žižek, however, the analysis of culture does not mean to apply the theory of the psyche to cultural formations; nor does it only mean to point out that there is a discourse of the analyst that is distinct from the discourse of the master, the hysteric, and the university. Rather, it means to invest this discourse of the analyst in culture itself. This is what Žižek aims at when he mocks "snobbish French Lacanians" who are against translating *jouissance* as "enjoyment" and who like to tell the story of how "Lacan, on his first visit to the United States, watched in Baltimore a TV commercial with the motto "Enjoy Coke!" and, dismayed at its vulgarity, emphatically claimed that his *jouir* is NOT this 'enjoy.'"[10] Why not, Žižek writes, claim that this is exactly *jouir* in its superego imbecility? What Lacan has "produced" with his models of the discourses, or in prolongation of his readings of Freud or Greek tragedies, is thus not bound to psychoanalytical experience, or to a certain psychoanalytical-academic vision, but *is out there*, in culture itself, where we can find the exact same vulgarity and obscenity developed à propos jouissance. In Žižek, it is even as if culture is always also in the process of analyzing itself, meaning that breakthroughs and revolutions can happen as if an analysis was going on, if not completed, *without* the aid or authority of a clinically trained psychoanalyst. Once again, this could be the case with Syriza, and Žižek has also recently pointed to the Arab Spring and

Occupy Wall Street as examples of such breakthroughs: what the occupiers at Wall Street accomplished was the insight that there is no ground beneath the feet of the brokers and bankers at Wall Street, thus in praxis reminding them of and enacting the scenario of the inexistence of the big Other (telling them "Hey, look down!"), and in this way possibly paving the way for new social models. Žižek's focus on the concept of the "act" throughout the years points in the same direction: The act is seldom referred to in clinical terms but in Žižek's own blend of theoretical considerations and very practical references to Lenin, Keyser Söze, or other figures from either literature, popular imagination, or political contexts.

It has become commonplace to define Žižek's project as "Hegel with Lacan," as if he is saying and writing a lot about Lacan (and about culture, from toilets to politics) but *really* wants to say something about German idealism in the light of Lacan.[11] What we claim is that it might be equally, if not more, pertinent to claim the opposite as well: Žižek's writings could also meaningfully be seen as "Lacan with Hegel." The Lacanian subject is brought into the streets with the help from Hegel, because Hegel enables an understanding of subjectivity as a matter of much more than what appears in a clinical setting. (Substance itself is subject, as it is famously put in the preface to the *Phenomenology of Spirit*.)[12] It is via the Hegelian perspective of a "Weltgeist," already engaged in its own analysis, that Žižek is able to bring psychoanalysis the last step from the clinic to the streets. The interventions of the wild analysis are, in other words, supposed to bring forward the subjectivity already secretly at work "out there." Such interventions ideally mark the point where "a form of life has grown old," as it is called in the preface to the *Philosophy of Right*,[13] and thus indicate the transition to a new mode of being or a new form of consciousness.

Wild Analysis

So what does it mean to invest the discourse of the analyst in culture itself, as we said? This is exactly where we think it makes sense to speak of a "discourse of the wild analyst." We conceptualize it as a discourse, because it relates to the subject as part of a broader signifying system. And we insist on wild analysis, because, contrary to Freud and Lacan, we think that there are ways of conceptualizing the relation between analyst and analysand that open up a much broader scope for psychoanalysis in terms of interventions in culture, society, politics, and so on.

Let us risk a formalization of this discourse, which has become Žižek's in his interventions in especially political debates. In good, wild analysis faith, we take on Lacan's four discourses from his seventeenth seminar and rearrange them a little bit:[14]

$$a \rightarrow S_2$$
$$S_1 \quad \$$$

Like in the discourse of the analyst, *a* is speaking in the discourse of the wild analyst. What is at stake is the processing of the desire and enjoyment that remains to be articulated. However, unlike the discourse of the analyst, desire is not articulated in an address to the subject but to the culture at large—knowledge, S_2—where the wild analyst intervenes with a message about desire that culture (not the individual subject) did not know that it already secretly knew. In addition, unlike the discourse of the analyst, it is not knowledge that resides as the truth beneath the discourse of the wild analyst but the master signifier. Think of Žižek in a university panel debate: he does not usually present his knowledge in traditional, academic style, with all the relevant reservations and caveats, but much more seeks an engagement with his audience to make them reflect on certain questions of the cultural field. He thus in a way takes on the role of the analyst, but not to hear what people have to say—on the contrary: to provoke them to start thinking. The master signifier, which is the truth of the discourse of the wild analyst, therefore suddenly springs forward and is sometimes openly acknowledged (in contrast to the university discourse, which more or less completely represses the power structures in e.g. academia), as when Žižek displays his Stalin poster, speaks in favor of Hugo Chavez, says "Fuck you" to a moderator, and so on. Or think of the entire gesture of his oeuvre; hanging on to the language and project of emancipatory politics in times when this is ridiculed, even criminalized—and doing this through Philosophy, one of the classical master discourses according to Lacan.

In Lacan's discourses the upper level of all the discourses, for example, from *a* to *s* in the analyst's discourse, are characterized by impossibility. It is impossible for the analyst to "totalize" the object-cause of the analysand's desire without destroying analysis altogether (this would amount to something like hypnosis). However, in the discourse of the wild analyst it is not the imaginary relation between analyst and analysand that is at stake. At stake is the real (*a*) as that which resists symbolization (S2), as one of Lacan's famous articulations of the real goes. The real is what remains impossible in the discourse of the wild analyst—no wonder, then, that "the real" has been the focus point of the weightiest of Žižek's theoretical investigations throughout the years, as well as the focus point for numerous analyses of society, politics, and phenomena from popular culture. Žižek is indeed "interrogating the real," as the title of a collection of his texts goes. He is not analyzing concrete patients, he is analyzing ideology, Hollywood film, commodities, technological gadgets, the war in Iraq, and so on as traces or effects of the structuring, but impossible real at the core of social reality. The Abu Ghraib scandal can be dismissed as a flaw, triggered by some bored soldiers who momentarily went crazy, but it can also be seen as an expression of the "unknown known" of the entire logics of the war in Iraq, "the disavowed beliefs, suppositions, and obscene practices we pretend not to know about, although they form the flipside of public morality."[15] To hit the real, Žižek cannot aim at it directly but must traverse the American culture from the TV show Jackass that performs excessive, popularized rites of initiation, over Donald Rumsfeld's epistemology and the New York art scene, to the plethora of inconsistent arguments on why to wage war, the disavowed need for Western control of oil reserves, and so on. He must conduct some kind of analytical alchemy. To extrapolate a surprising interpretation of what is not immediately understandable, because it forms the very nonthematized framework for our entire mode of understanding, he must connect seemingly incoherent elements from popular culture, philosophy, and political economy. In formal terms, he must dis- and reconnect the S2s available in order to make them point to the *a* they are circling around. He must not "read" the S2s as in ordinary literary analysis, but somehow make a wager that there is an *a* (some libidinal investment) somewhere in them, and using himself, his own bewilderment at the more or less crazy social reality we live in, he must "construct" this *a*. (Notice the way Žižek often presents a case he wants to analyze, for example, saying "isn't it crazy that . . . [e.g. in the U.S. you can buy a chocolate laxative],"; or notice the overwhelming number of rhetorical questions in his texts, e.g., "aren't we here confronting Lacan's *objet a* in pure form . . ."; "isn't this a perfect example of *jouissance* . . ."; etc.)

The parallel to ordinary psychoanalytic practice is of course clear. To hit the real, the analyst focuses on exactly that which doesn't "fit," the slips, the repetitions, the excessive emotional engagement, and so on. However, the radical difference between clinical psychoanalysis and Žižekian analysis of contemporary society is also very obvious. In the clinic, there is only one voice, which is occasionally interrupted or redirected. In analysis of contemporary culture, there is a sea of language that operates on a number of levels. The analyst in the clinic normally intervenes as little as possible and only by addressing things said, in order to make one and the same speaker articulate related chunks of his or her unacknowledged libidinal investments. In analysis of society, you do not get a subject on a couch with a fundamental willingness to be interrupted and redirected. Thus, as we have argued, what is left for the analyst is to intervene, and every analysis (as e.g., the above one on Abu Ghraib) turns into an intervention. The intervention consists in interpreting the symptom on behalf of the subject (culture, society); although the analysis is careful and learned, it is performed on a subject that cannot reply in the ordinary sense of the term. We are simply presented with Žižek's own interventionist interpretation of our cultural trends, political behavior, and so on.

One could argue that Žižek, in his writing and lecturing, seems to be more of an analysand than an analyst, with all his excessive jokes, tics, and endless explanations. We would argue, however, that this seemingly neurotic anxiety should be seen in the light of the anxiety of the analyst, even though not in the usual meaning of this term. The anxiety of the analyst usually concerns the right moment to intervene in the speech of the analysand, facing the danger that the timing can be wrong and the analysand will relapse. However, intervening as a wild analyst in culture is not anxiety-provoking in this way: culture simply grinds on, no matter how much you provoke it. Žižek's wager is another. It does not concern the intervention as such but rather concerns the very construction of transference "behind" the intervention. In clinical psychoanalysis the analysand contacts the analyst, and the work of and with transference can already begin from session one. In wild analysis there are at the outset no analysands knocking at the analyst's door, and transference has to be created ex nihilo. This establishes a very fine balance between functioning as *a* in terms of a point of identification (as some kind of fetish in the shape of the great Philosopher, Revolutionary, etc.) and on the other hand in terms of a point for the renewal of thought. The anxiety-provoking question for Žižek is: Does the wild analysis work? Not in terms of the recovery of the subjects addressed, or their philosophical *Aufklärung* of some sort, but in terms of it producing thought beyond identification, fetishism, and so on. Here, Žižek wavers back and forth between complete denial (or maybe a very conscious strategy of casualness) of the effects of his interventions (as when he allows editors to cut up his texts, even rewrite them, before publishing them in his name) and a high degree of sensitivity to "failed" interventions, which he returns to over and over again, as for example one unfortunate debate with Bernard-Henri Lévy, where they found themselves in some kind of fake agreement.

Something like an "ethics of the wild analyst" is played out at this level. Žižek positively assumes the role of the analyst, and of the subject supposed to (know/speak), but only to ultimately deny that role. First of all, readers generally search in vain for an emancipatory-political manual in his writings. There may be a staging of the truth of our predicament, in the sense of an unveiling of certain unacknowledged beliefs and libidinal investments, but there is hardly ever anything remotely resembling a manifesto. This can be seen as a deficit in Žižek's work, but it certainly also has a systematic significance, which deserves to be acknowledged. Although Žižek has changed his political stance since *The Sublime Object of Ideology* in 1989, in the direction of a heightened interest in political action that doesn't necessarily remain within the frames of the "democratic," he has consistently abstained from trying to assume the role of a Master of any actual political movement.

In summa, wild analysis is at the same time dogmatic and modest, or—going back to the original Lacanian discourses—one could say that it is part master's discourse and part analyst's discourse. It is part master's discourse because it directs itself to a sea of language and voices, to cultural formations, and so on: it has to break in, interrupt, without knowing whether the timing is right. Wild analysis is, however, a master discourse of the new, so to speak, dogmatically insisting that the impossible can happen. And this, to be sure, does not mean to be "infinitely demanding" or the like. Rather, it goes with a certain kind of modesty on behalf of the analyst: all that the discourse of wild analysis aims for is for thought to be produced; to insert the specter of the subject into philosophy and politics once again, as Žižek puts it in *The Ticklish Subject*. The new, the breakthrough, is the very reason for doing wild analysis, but this new is not controllable, as it can happen anywhere, anytime. Wild analysis is not a raid toward the new in the sense of ever more provocative statements and transgressive exercises, but is simply a beginning from the basis of the question: What if the end of analysis, though impossible, happens, and a thinking subject appears?

Notes

1   Sigmund Freud, "Analysis Terminable and Interminable," in *International Journal of Psychoanalysis* 18 (1937), 375.

2   Sigmund Freud, "The Dissection of the Psychical Personality," in *The Standard Edition of the Complete Psychological Works of Sigmund Freud*, vol. 22 (New York: Vintage, 1999), 79.

3   Jacques Lacan, *The Seminar of Jacques Lacan: The Four Fundamental Concepts of Psychoanalysis, Book XI*, ed. Jacques-Alain Miller, trans. Alan Sheridan (New York: Norton, 1998), 273.

4   K. H. Enemark, "Den psykoanalytiske akt, 1. del" [The psychoanalytical act, part 1], in *Drift — Tidsskrift for psykoanalyse* (Copenhagen: University of Copenhagen, 2003), 69, our translation.

5   Sigmund Freud, "'Wild' Psycho-Analysis," in *The Standard Edition of the Complete Psychological Works of Sigmund Freud*, vol. 10, *Five Lectures on Psycho-Analysis, Leonardo da Vinci and Other Works* (New York: Vintage, 1999), 225.

6   Freud writes: "psychoanalytic intervention, therefore, absolutely requires a fairly long period of contact with the patient. Attempts to 'rush' him at first consultation, by brusquely telling him the secrets which have been discovered by the physician, are technically objectionable." "'Wild' Psycho-Analysis," 225.

7   Pierre-Gilles Guéguen, "The Short Session — and the Question Concerning Technique with Lacan," in *The Symptom 10*, Spring 2009. http://www.lacan.com/thesymptom/?p=216.

8   Guéguen, "The Short Session."

9   Jacques Lacan, *The Seminar of Jacques Lacan, Book XVII: The Other Side of Psychoanalysis*, ed. Jacques-Alain Miller, trans. Russell Grigg (New York: Norton, 2007).

10 Slavoj Žižek, *Enjoy Your Symptom!: Jacques Lacan in Hollywood and Out* (New York: Routledge, 2001), vii.

11 This claim can of course be backed up by Žižek's self-descriptions, from *The Sublime Object of Ideology*, which claims to "accomplish a kind of 'return to Hegel' — to reactu-

alize Hegelian dialectics by giving it a new reading on the basis of Lacanian psycho-analysis" (Slavoj Žižek, *The Sublime Object of Ideology* [London: Verso, 1989], 7), to *Less Than Nothing*, where we are told to bear in mind that "Lacan's theory is here interpreted as a repetition of Hegel" (Slavoj Žižek, *Less Than Nothing: Hegel and the Shadow of Dialectical Materialism* [London: Verso, 2012], 5). There is a constant insistence in Žižek that everything is really about Hegel, or that at least *from now on*, everything is really about Hegel.

12   G. W. F. Hegel, *Phänenomenologie des Geistes*, in 6 vols. (Hamburg: Felix Meiner Verlag, 1999), 2: 22.

13   G. W. F. Hegel, *Grundlinien der Philosophie des Rechts*, in 6 vols. (Hamburg: Felix Meiner Verlag, 1999), 5: 17.

14   As Levi R. Bryant has recently pointed out, there are six possible universes of Lacanian discourses, and Lacan can be said to have explored the universe of the master's discourse (the order of S_1, S_2, a, s turned around its own axis), as well as opened up the universe of the capitalist's discourse (s, S_2, a, S_1—Bryant is attempting to explore the remaining three discourses in this universe). As to the four remaining universes, Bryant writes: "the additional four universes of discourse have not been named as it has not yet been established whether or not they, in fact, exist in our social world. They are virtual without being actual"; Levi R. Bryant, "Žižek's New Universe of Discourse: Politics and the Discourse of the Capitalist," *International Journal of Žižek Studies* 2, no. 4 (2008). http://zizekstudies.org/index.php/ijzs/article/view/163/257. What we claim is thus that (at least) the discourse of the wild analyst is actual, and that Žižek should be acknowledged as the one who actualized it, or pointed to its existence in the social world.

15   Slavoj Žižek, "Between Two Deaths: The Culture of Torture," *London Review of Books* Vol.26, Nr.11, 3.6.2004.

10

"Vers un

Signifiant Nouveau":

Gabriel Tupinambá   **Our Task after Lacan**

It is not a question of disputing authority,
but of extracting it from fiction.
—Jacques Lacan, *Autres Écrits* (2001)

The Reflective Positing of Lacan

Žižek concludes the introduction of his first book in English, *The Sublime Object of Ideology*, with the following summary of his own strategy: "it is my belief that these three aims are deeply connected: the only way to 'save Hegel' is through Lacan, and this Lacanian reading of Hegel and the Hegelian heritage opens up a new approach to ideology, allowing us to grasp contemporary ideological phenomena (cynicism, 'totalitarianism,' the fragile status of democracy) without falling prey to any kind of 'post-modernist' traps (such as the illusion that we live in a 'post-ideological' condition)."[1] This schematization could be understood as a good overview of Žižek's philosophical project: it proposes a first link, between the Lacanian logic of the signifier and the Hegelian dialectics, and another one between Hegel, now revitalized by the Freudian theory of the death drive, and the Marxist theory of ideology.[2] However, this is also a useful diagram because it reveals the limit of Žižek's own project and the beginning of a properly *Žižekian thinking*. What is missing in this schema is, of course, a third vector, binding the "new approach to ideol-

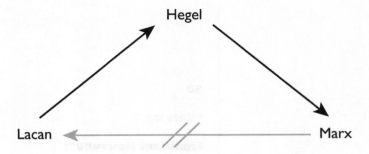

ogy" back to psychoanalysis—an investigation that, albeit increasingly present in Žižek's work, remains substantially undeveloped (fig. 10.1).[3]

In order to grasp not the singular trajectory of Žižek's thought but the general space of thinking it has founded, we must turn to a second description of his project, which appears in the introductory pages of *For They Know Not What They Do*, published two years later:

> As with *The Sublime Object of Ideology*, the theoretical space of the present book is moulded by three centers of gravity: Hegelian dialectics, Lacanian psychoanalytic theory, and contemporary criticism of ideology. These three circles form a Borromean knot: each of them connects the other two; the place that they all encircle, the "symptom" in their midst, is of course the author's (and, as the author hopes, also the reader's) enjoyment of what one depreciatingly calls "popular culture" . . . The three theoretical circles are not, however, of the same weight: it is their middle term, the theory of Jacques Lacan, which is—as Marx would say—"the general illumination which bathes all the other colors and modifies their particularity."[4]

This new presentation is in fact much richer and useful to us. First of all, it turns the implicit limit of the previous formulation—the lack of any mention to how a new theory of ideology could help us deal with the impasses of psychoanalysis—into a specific and nonessential trait of Žižek's project, and allows us instead to grasp the productive restrictions and invariances that constitute the "theoretical space" of *any* Žižekian thinking (fig. 10.2).

These restrictions, which axiomatically construct a certain logical space, are of two kinds: conceptual and topological. The conceptual invariance names the three components to be articulated: the psycho-

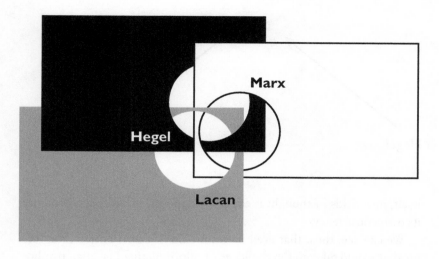

analysis of Lacan, the philosophy of Hegel, and Marx's political thinking. These three proper names delimit the specific conceptions of psychoanalysis, philosophy, and politics at stake in Žižekian thinking.

The topological invariance on the other hand concerns the "shaping"
of this general conceptual space by its "Borromean" property.[5] It imposes
two conditions on any possible trajectory connecting psychoanalysis,
philosophy, and politics. The first condition is that it prohibits one-to-
one conversions between fields of thought—it is a decision concerning
noncomplementarity: there can be no relation between Freud and Marx
without a detour through Hegel, nor a study of Hegel's relation to Marx
without a consideration of Freud, and so on. This first condition, of a re-
strictive kind, prevents conceptual strategies such as Freudo-Marxism or
"existential psychology" from appearing, since it prohibits any attempt
to use one field of thought to directly solve the impasses of another.

The second condition, equally profound, is an affirmative one, that
of an *immanent transition* between any two given fields of thought. If the
consistency of Hegelian philosophy relies on its articulation with both
Marx and Lacan, then a rigorous philosophical investigation *will eventually lead us, without ever crossing any limiting border, into politics and
psychoanalysis.* Accordingly, political thinking, *on account of the inconsistency of politics itself,* might require us to bring into play psychoanalytic
or philosophical ideas, just as psychoanalysis might have to go outside

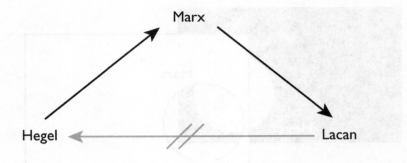

itself, into fields of thought it explicitly opposes, in order to encounter its own consistency.

We can see, thus, that even if, within Žižek's own project, the vector that would take up the challenge of reformulating Lacanian psychoanalysis through an engagement with Hegel and Marx remains mostly unexplored, such a study is nevertheless part of the horizon of Žižekian thinking.

Still, it is crucial to note that in his recent work Žižek has often treated Hegel and Lacan more separately,[6] as if unbinding them now that the work of reading Hegel through the Freudian logic of the drive has been thoroughly developed.[7] From this separation, another coupling of vectors became operative—the first proposing a Hegelian reading of Marx's theory of capital,[8] and the second sketching a critique of psychoanalytic institutions based on psychoanalysis's current alliances with neoliberal ideology (fig. 10.3).[9]

But what could the purpose of such an investigation be? From our previous remarks, we can at least already discern what it is *not*: according to the first condition described above, it cannot be an attempt to suture the current psychoanalytic impasses with political or philosophical explanations, nor, in accordance with the second condition, could it be a mere external critique of "really existing psychoanalysis" from the standpoint of other fields of thought. Instead—and following here a path that Žižek himself has tentatively elaborated—this study must operate a "reflective positing of Lacan": *an inclusion of psychoanalysis into the very field of problems it has allowed us to discern in the world.* In other words, we must produce an immanent study of psychoanalysis so as to discern how, within the clinic, the institutional impasses and the problems of

metapsychology, questions that are essentially political and philosophical, appear outside their own fields in a concrete form.[10]

In order to provide us with the basic elements for a Žižekian contribution to the psychoanalytic practice, as well as a first proof of the useful-
ness of further developing this line of inquiry, I will concern myself in this
text with constructing an alternative periodization of Lacan's teaching.

Institution, Clinic, and Concept:
Their Knotting before and after 1964

Lacan's writings must be understood, in a manner similar to political
writings, as localized interventions. Rather than providing us with schematic systematizations of his teaching—whose constant reelaborations
were in fact tracked through his yearly seminars—his *scripta* served
above all as combative answers to specific problems posed by the conjuncture of the psychoanalytic milieux of the time. This is why, in the
postface to the French edition of his eleventh seminar, Lacan warns us
that his writings were made "not to be read"—"pas-à-lire":[11] they are
meant to intervene, dislodge, or divide, rather than describe, summarize, or condense.

Two consequences follow from this realization. First of all, in order
to think with Lacan—and not merely to read him—we must consider his
writings together with the "context of struggle" in which they were produced.[12] This implies, for instance, an attention to the challenges faced
by psychoanalysis at the time of each of Lacan's interventions and a capacity to distinguish, with this reference in mind, between conditional
and unconditional preferences, between the alliances and conceptual
connections that had to be made, sometimes forcefully, for tactical reasons, and those that can be said to be intrinsic to psychoanalysis as such,
and that might perhaps only reveal themselves retroactively.

Moreover, the concern with the different battles fought by Lacan—
battles sometimes waged against his own previous positions—must be
supplemented by a refined attention to an important shift that took place
around 1963 in his relation with the French psychoanalytic situation. Before his rupture with the Société Française de Psychanalyse (SFP), Lacan's
constant engagement with the decrepit state of psychoanalysis in France,
both in its clinical inefficacy and its conceptual deviations, took mostly

the critical form of accusations, ironic retorts, and a relentless concern with the return to the basic insights of Freud's discovery. However, once Lacan lost his place within the International Psychoanalytic Association (IPA),[13] and his teaching was suddenly in danger, he was faced with a new and fundamentally different task: that of creating an alternative institution, the École Freudienne de Paris (EFP), organized according to his own ideas, and capable of positively inscribing in the world a position that, until then, had only been articulated as a critical one.

The relevance of this second consequence cannot be underestimated—in fact, it constitutes perhaps the only periodization of Lacan's work that truly distinguishes two separate moments in his teaching. There are, of course, some convincing and useful ways to divide Lacan's seminars into discernible conceptual sequences, but the distinctions between two Lacanian "classicisms,"[14] or between the "six paradigms of enjoyment,"[15] rarely account for the heterogeneous problems that resisted the previous conceptual sequence and demanded the subsequent reformulations. Only the break that distinguishes a before and an after the founding of Lacan's own School, in 1964, could possibly refer to institutional, conceptual, and clinical changes simultaneously.

The institutional break is somewhat evident: Lacan was suddenly faced with the difficult task of combining his relentless critique of the psychoanalytic establishment with a formative project that did not succumb to any of these same deviations. The conceptual break, if we consider solely the rupture I have already observed, concerning Lacan's "founding act," was equally profound: an aspect that is quite clear throughout Lacan's seminars that took place after the famous "interrupted seminar" of 1962 was his concern with the problem of *rigor* in psychoanalysis—namely, the problem of how to distinguish between conceptual markers developed in order to rectify the metapsychological and clinical import of psychoanalysis and their use as identificatory traits by his disciples and followers. Concerning the clinic, the break is even clearer: Lacan became quite infamous in the French psychoanalytic scene precisely because of some of his clinical inventions, such as the variable-length session, and these matters were brought up as reasons for his expulsion from the SFP. It follows, then, that these technical procedures would finally find their place in his own School, which so openly invited psychoanalysts to reinvent the Freudian practice in accordance with their own time. But the

Lacanian teaching before 1964:
Extrinsic linkage through the
critique of the forgetting of the
Freudian experience

Lacanian teaching after 1964:
Intrinsic linkage through the
formulation of the forgetting of an
immanent procedure to Lacan's
teaching itself

crystallization of Lacan's theory of logical time into a general principle of the analytic practice was not the most evident of the changes that followed from the break of 1964: the most important clinical development was surely the invention of the *passe*[16] — an invention that was not only clinical but also in fact confirms that the founding of Lacan's School concerned simultaneously the three registers I have just outlined, given that the passe was supposed to be, at the same time, the marker of the end of analysis (clinic), a communal and formative procedure (institution), and a source of theoretical developments and problems for psychoanalysis (concept).

My proposition is thus the following: the actual break in Lacan's teaching is the one that distinguishes between a first moment when the relation between the clinic, the concept, and the institution was held together—even if critically or negatively—by the psychoanalytic situation already established in Europe since the creation of the IPA, and the latter one when it fell upon a singular site, Lacan's teaching, to *immanently* knot these three dimensions of psychoanalysis together (fig. 10.4).[17] Moreover, this rupture does not merely divide Lacan's work into two equally consistent sequences, it rather divides two distinct notions of fidelity—one in contradiction with the psychoanalytic situation of the time and another *in contradiction with itself*:

it is known, in effect, that the originality of Lacan's reading of Freud resides in the affirmation of his Freudian orthodoxy and in his refusal of all post-Freudian "detours." According to this perspective, his entry into dissidence was not possible if not as a renewal of the Freudian rupture, and only as such. Well, by creating a school of his own, Lacan found himself constrained, if not to confess himself a Lacanian, at least to validate the political existence of a "Lacanism." Through this self-recognition, his movement entered into a contradiction with the very doctrine which sustained it and which defines itself as Freudian.[18]

However, this important break cannot be understood as an instantaneous cut—it cannot be read, as it is sometimes intuited, even by Lacan himself, as a cut marked exclusively by the "interrupted seminar" of 1962, on the Names of the Father.[19] When the first signs of an irresolvable difference between his teaching and the general orientation of the SFP began to appear, Lacan did everything in his power to remain within the French branch of the Freudian society, and these disputes took many years before culminating in the actual break. Accordingly, during these difficult years we find Lacan already working through the first necessary elements for a theory of the immanent linkage of the Freudian clinic, metapsychology and community. The most telling of these is, perhaps, a short but critical mention of Freud's text *Group Psychology and the Analysis of the Ego*, found in the class of May 31, 1961:

> It could be said of what I am trying to do here, with all reservations that this implies, that it constitutes an effort of analysis in the proper sense of the term, concerning the analytic community as a mass organized by the analytic ego-ideal, such as it has effectively developed itself under the form of a certain number of mirages, in the forefront of which is that of the "strong ego," so many erroneously implicated there where one believes to recognize it. To invert the pair of terms which constitute the title of Freud's article to which I have referred before, one of the aspects of my seminar could be called *Ich-Psychologie und Massenanalyse*.
>
> Moreover, the *Ich-Psychologie*, which was promoted to the forefront of analytic theory, constitutes the jam, constitutes the dam, constitutes the inertia, for more than a decade, which prevents the re-start of any analytic efficacy. And it is insofar as things have gotten to this point that it is

convenient to interpellate as such the analytic community, allowing some
light to be shed on this matter, on what comes to alter the purity of the
position of the analyst regarding the one to whom he responds, his analysand, insofar as the analyst himself inscribes himself and determines himself through the effects which result from the analytic mass, namely, the
mass of analysts, in the current state of its constitution and discourse.[20]

This crucial passage, which mediates Lacan's remarks about transference and identification, the themes of his current and following seminars,
respectively, must be at least schematically reconstructed. What is the
movement implied by the inversion of terms in the title of Freud's famous
text? Lacan's reasoning could be sketched as follows:

1. the analytic mass has organized itself—despite everything—in the
   very way that Freud described the formation of groups through the
   "introjection" of a trait into a shared ego-ideal;[21]
2. given that the group of analysts is the set of those who position themselves in a certain way within the clinical space—in a distant resonance with the scientific community—the trait that binds the analytic
   mass could not be located inside the psychoanalytic societies in the
   figure of a leader, but must rather appear as an ideal for the clinic;[22]
3. this trait, whose function was mainly to organize the analytic society,
   had nevertheless a place within the clinic itself: it served as the index
   in the relation between analyst and analysand that verified one's belonging to the group of analysts. Accordingly, the sense of *permanence*
   and the clear division between *inside and outside*, both proper to relations of membership, returned in the clinic as the ground for a particular metapsychological deviation—namely, the "strong ego"—and
   the series of technical restrictions associated with the direction of
   treatment that assumes such a "muscular" egoic force of defense and
   control as its guideline.

The structure of Lacan's argument binds together, therefore, institutional, clinical, and conceptual dimensions around a problem that is irreducible to any one of the three domains: *How to identify and group
together the set of those whose only shared property is to dissolve group identifications?*

But why would such a construction require Lacan to invert Freud's terms? In order to understand this shift—which so clearly reflects the change in Lacan's position before and after the foundation of his School—we need only take notice of the rather unorthodox presupposition implied in his argument: that the overlap that binds the clinic to the analytic community should not be the one between the practitioner in the clinic and the member of the Freudian society—a positive link— but should be between what simultaneously escapes the circuit of identifications in transference and the ego-ideal in the institution. However, *there is no such negative cause in Freud's theory of groups*—that is to say, there is no real of sociality as such. This is why Lacan stresses that he is engaging there in "an effort of analysis in the proper sense of the term" even though he is dealing first and foremost with an institutional problem: the proper diagnosis of the impasse that would ultimately lead him to found the EFP required a commitment with a new hypothesis, one that cannot be found as such in Freud's doctrine, even if only in order to remain faithful to Freud himself.

The question becomes, then: did Lacan ever resolve the new impasse that delimited this second period in his teaching? The answer is clearly negative: not only was the problem of how to tie together conceptual, clinical, and institutional matters in psychoanalysis never properly resolved, but it was never thematized as such by Lacan. Undoubtedly, the theory of the end of analysis as the passage from analysand to analyst, already in its very first formulation, provides us with all the necessary materials to construct the problem in a rigorous fashion, and we can easily recognize how the mechanism of the passe would itself possibly name the most consistent answer to this impasse, but it remains a fact that Lacan's School dissolved in 1980 and that the passe, as early as 1978, was considered by him "a complete failure."[23]

Desire, Act, and Discourse: Three Names for an Impasse

I have proposed the following schema as a model for the break that truly distinguishes two separate moments in Lacan's psychoanalytic trajectory (fig. 10.5). I have also shown how this new impasse, according to Lacan's own "analysis of the analytic mass," ties together, in an immanent way, the form of organization of the analytic community, the direction of treatment in the clinic, and the conceptual apparatus of psychoanaly-

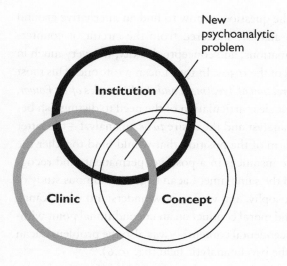

New
psychoanalytic
problem

Institution

Clinic

Concept

Lacanian teaching after 1964:
Intrinsic linkage through the
formulation of an immanent procedure
to Lacan's teaching itself

sis. The problem itself, however, is neither entirely institutional (it also concerns problems of how to handle transference and of the conceptual grasp of subjectivity) nor purely clinical (the different clinical positions in this matter informing the constitution of the analytic community as well as the place of transmission of knowledge in its consistency) or conceptual (given that different "ontological commitments" regarding the place of negativity and desire restrict in different ways the scope of the analytic practice and social link). Moreover, the excessive character of this impasse ultimately redoubles the problem: after all, does a question that cannot be assigned to any one of the domains of psychoanalysis remain strictly psychoanalytical? No matter how we respond to this enigma, it is nevertheless clear that we are dealing with a problem of *impurity*, both in the sense that this impasse taints each register with concerns belonging to the other two and in the sense that it includes in psychoanalysis itself a question that seems slightly outside of its own scope.

This problem is most clearly discernible in a comparison of Lacan's two conceptualizations of the "desire of the analyst"—first in the seminar on ethics and, after the break with the SFP, in his eleventh seminar. As

I have already shown, the question of how to find an alternative ground for the position of the analyst, sheltered from the circuit of counter-transference, group formations, and conceptual laxity, was very much in Lacan's mind by the end of the 1950s. In 1958 Lacan wrote one of his most important texts, *The Direction of Treatment and the Principles of Its Power*, in which we find the first clear articulation of the need to distinguish between the desire of the analyst and the desire *to be* an analyst—the latter being the conceptual form of the position that would bind together the different psychoanalytic instances in a positive, permanent, and recognizable point.[24] Around the same time, Lacan began his famous study of the Kantian moral philosophy, and we can now understand why: Kant's problem—how to ground moral conduct on an unconditional point without any need for a transcendental content?—was also the problem Lacan was faced with within the psychoanalytic field (fig. 10.6).[25]

Between 1958 and 1960, Lacan took it upon himself to develop an elaborated critique of Kant's position, looking for an intrapsychoanalytic instance that would serve as a ground for the ethical rectitude needed of an analyst, who would have to be capable of doubting not only the pitfalls of counter-transference but also his or her recognition as an analyst by his or her peers and the convenience of his or her own conceptual elaborations—in short, a position that would have to orient itself by maintaining a degree of distance from its own pathological attachments.[26] At this point, Lacan elaborated a conception of the desire of the analyst as a *pure desire*, as if the way to solve the impasse of immanently knotting the institutional, clinical, and conceptual dimensions of psychoanalysis could be achieved through a reference to a special kind of moral rectitude, oriented by the empty form of desire in a way akin to the role of the empty fact of Reason in Kant's second critique. However, by 1963, after the rupture with the SFP had taken place, Lacan concluded his famous seminar *The Four Fundamental Concepts of Psychoanalysis* with the following affirmation: "the analyst's desire is not a pure desire. It is a desire to obtain absolute difference, a desire which intervenes when, confronted with the primary signifier, the subject is, for the first time, in a position to subject himself to it. There only may the signification of a limitless love emerge, because it is outside the limits of the law, where alone it may live."[27]

The theme of ethics would completely disappear from Lacan's teaching

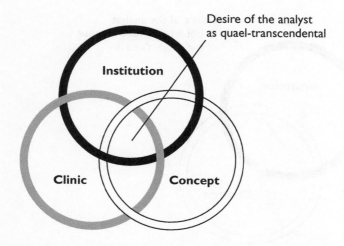

Desire of the analyst between 1958 and 1960

from then on, and the reference to the quasi-transcendental dimension of desire would be substituted for his lasting investigation of the Freudian theory of the drives. However, this shift should not be understood as a development prompted by clinical or conceptual matters alone: in fact, the claim that the desire of the analyst is not pure—in the sense of grounded in an empty form removed from pathological interests—has the fundamental consequence of *blurring the limits between analyst and analysand* in the analytic procedure. In the quotation above it already becomes somewhat clear that the kernel of the analyst's desire—and the pivot of its distinction from the "desire to be an analyst"—*is paradoxically on the side of the analysand*. In short, by bringing the theory of the drive, of the objectal dimension of the subject, to the center of psychoanalytic consideration, Lacan also shifted his theory of the desire of the analyst toward the practical capacity of anyone to sustain her- or himself at the point of an "absolute difference" *in relation to the analysand's speech*, rather than in relation to her or his own pathological interests (fig. 10.7).

This transformation is nothing short of unprecedented. To be succinct, it allows us to conceive the institutional space of psychoanalysis in a completely new way: just as the clinic would have to be reformulated, after 1963, in accordance with the principle that the "unconscious is outside,"[28] so would the analytic community have to come to terms with the

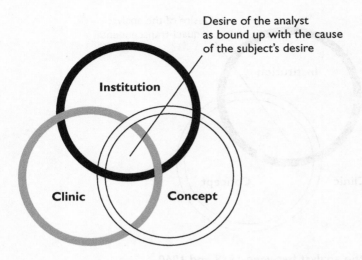

Desire of the analyst after 1964

idea that *it is a community composed only of its own exterior,* that is, a community whose esoteric center coincides with its most exoteric material, the speech of those who seek analysis on account of their suffering. But how to conceptualize this inconsistent relation between the clinical practice and the psychoanalytic School without offering its own theoretical apprehension as its point of fixation?

Lacan's new account of the desire of the analyst introduced a certain indiscernibility or vacillation at the heart of the analytic procedure, bringing closer together at the institutional level the two instances that are in "absolute difference" within the clinical scene. This indiscernibility, I believe, is the motor behind a crucial conceptual thread that cuts across Lacan's teaching in the 1960s: the investigation that takes him, in quick succession, from the notion of the *analyst's desire* to that of the *analytical act* and then of the *analyst's discourse* (fig. 10.8).

These three concepts all have one point in common: they are all different attempts to grasp the point that holds together the psychoanalytic procedure in all its dimensions simultaneously. However, the main point of distinction between them, even at a superficial level, is the extension upon which each conceptualization ties together analysts and analysands at this impossible intersection of the clinic and the analytic community.

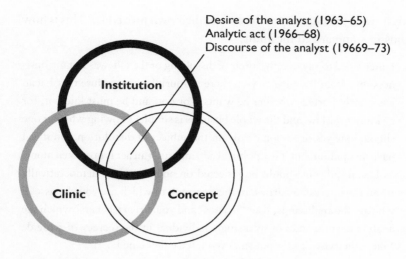

Desire of the analyst (1963–65)
Analytic act (1966–68)
Discourse of the analyst (19669–73)

Institution

Clinic

Concept

The knotting, from 1963 to 1973

This brief overview allows us, at least, to superficially trace Lacan's insistent attempts to locate, each time at a slightly different register, through different formal procedures, the impurity that decenters the position of the analyst, making it conditional on an instance, the subject's division, that paradoxically only exists as such within analysis. He would soon stop referring to the analyst's discourse as well, and what is known by exegetes as "Lacan's last teaching" would supposedly begin from that point on.[29] It is quite interesting to consider that the Borromean knot became central in Lacan's investigations precisely at the moment that the impasse I have been tracking lost any explicit reference in his teaching. It was also during this new conceptual moment that the École Freudienne de Paris slowly disintegrated.

Still, at the very moment of failure of Lacan's original institutional project, we find a very special event that should serve us as an indelible reminder of the necessity of returning to the challenge that haunted Lacan at least since 1964. We are indebted here to none other than Louis Althusser. Althusser had already played a crucial role in 1963, when he offered Lacan a new place to teach, his own students for its audience, and a renewed reading of Marx that clearly influenced Lacan's subsequent elaborations. But on March 15, 1980, at the last meeting of the EFP, Althusser showed up—uninvited—in order to confront the psycho-

analysts with the impurity at the core of their own procedure. This is how
Althusser summarized the affair:

> I intervened to say that the affair of dissolving of the EFP was not my busi-
> ness, but from listening to you, there is a juridical procedure that Lacan
> has clearly started, whether he wants it or not, and he must know it, for
> he knows the law, and the whole business is simple: knowing whether one
> should vote yes or no tomorrow on the subject of dissolution. On that I
> have no opinion, but it is a political act, and such an act is not taken alone,
> as Lacan did, but should be reflected on and discussed democratically
> by all the interested parties, in the first rank of which are your "masses,"
> who are the analysands, your "masses" and your "real teachers" which the
> analysands are, and not by a single individual in the secrecy of 5 rue de
> Lille; otherwise, it's despotism, even if it's enlightened. . . .
>   Whatever the case, I told them, in point of fact, you are doing politics
> and nothing else; you are in the process of doing politics and nothing else.
> . . . In any event, when one does politics, as Lacan and you are doing, it
> is never without consequences. If you think you are not doing any, wait
> a little; it will come crashing down on your heads or rather, and alas, it
> won't come crashing down on your heads, since you are well protected
> and know how to lie low. In fact, it will come crashing down on the unfor-
> tunates who come to stretch out on your couch and on all their intimates
> and the intimates of their intimates and on to infinity.[30]

Althusser's intervention touches at the two sides of the impurity I have
previously observed. First, it points to the role of analysands in the constitution of the analytical procedure, that is, the dependence of analysts
on their "real teachers." Second, it distinguishes the redoubled or excessive dimension of the knotting of this procedure by naming it *a political
act* (fig. 10.9).

Psychoanalysis, Politics, and Philosophy: The Axiom of Žižekian Thinking

What is, then, the enigmatic relation between politics and psychoanalysis? As I have now demonstrated, at the heart of psychoanalysis itself we
find a certain political surplus, distinct in its import from the political ap-

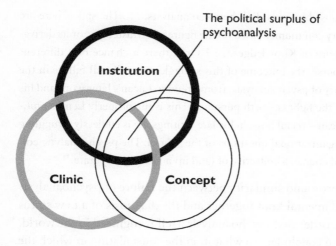

The political surplus of psychoanalysis

Institution

Clinic   Concept

Althusser's Intervention in 1980

plications of psychoanalytic theory, as well as from Freudo-Marxist ambitions: the immanently psychoanalytic problem of how to bind together the complex issues surrounding the idea of the desire of the analyst and the role of the analysands in the composition of the "analytical mass." Accordingly, I am now in a position to supplement my initial hypothesis concerning the essential break in Lacan's teaching with a further proposal, namely, that the problem that guided his work in the 1960s—and that was named by Althusser, in 1980, as the problem of the "political act" immanent to the psychoanalytic procedure—is the open problem that defines what it means to be faithful to Lacan today.

It is only in light of this impasse that we can fully appreciate Žižek's wager that there is a certain failure at the kernel of Lacan's project that should be once more taken up:

> when Lacan introduces the term "desire of the analyst," it is in order to
> undermine the notion that the climax of the analytic treatment is a mo-
> mentous insight into the abyss of the Real, the "traversing of the fantasy,"
> from which, the morning after, we have to return to sober social reality,
> resuming our usual social roles—psychoanalysis is *not* an insight which
> can be shared only in the precious initiatic moments. Lacan's aim is to
> establish the possibility of a collective of analysts, of discerning the con-

tours of a possible social link between analysts. . . . The stakes here are high: is every community based on the figure of a Master . . . , or its derivative, the figure of Knowledge . . . ? Or is there a chance of a different link? Of course, the outcome of this struggle was a dismal failure in the entire history of psychoanalysis, from Freud to Lacan's later work and his *École*—but the fight is worth pursuing. This is the properly Leninist moment of Lacan—recall how, in his late writings, he is endlessly struggling with the organizational questions of the School. The psychoanalytic collective is, of course, a collective of (and in) an emergency state.[31]

In light of the profound similarity between the failure of psychoanalysis to hold its fundamental knot together and the diagnosis of a new status of the symbolic order that psychoanalysis itself recognized in the world, Žižek goes on to conclude: "so what if, in the constellation in which the Unconscious itself, in its strict Freudian sense, is disappearing, the task of the analyst should no longer be to undermine the hold of the Master-Signifier, but, on the contrary, to construct/propose/install *new* Master-Signifiers? Is this not how we should (or, at least, can) read Lacan's '*vers un signifiant nouveau*'?"[32] In this way, we can see that the problem of psychoanalytic thinking today *is not different from the one that it diagnoses everywhere else*: the same vacillation of the signifier that analysts are prone to recognize in unconscious formations today is at stake in psychoanalysis as an institution, a conceptual framework, and a practice. We should not accept any diagnoses of the contemporary impasses of the clinic that cover up psychoanalysis's own difficulties—its conceptual and institutional deadlocks. This embedding of psychoanalysis in the very field where it attempts to think is not only a point of obscurity or blindness but also a condition for the development of truly effective clinical interventions.

Notes

1   Slavoj Žižek, *The Sublime Object of Ideology* (London: Verso, 1989), 7.
2   The epigraph to this chapter is from Jacques Lacan, *Autres Écrits* (Paris: Éditions du Seuil, 2001), 258.
3   The earliest exercise in revealing "a different Lacan . . . one extremely sensitive to the shifts in the hegemonic ideological trends," can be found in Slavoj Žižek, *On Belief* (London: Routledge, 2001), 29.

4 Slavoj Žižek, *For They Know Not What They Do: Enjoyment as a Political Factor* (London: Verso, 2002), 2.

5 Charles Livingston, *Knot Theory* (Washington, DC: Mathematical Association of America Textbooks, 1993), 10; see also the theoremic definition of the Brunnian link in Akio Kawauchi, *Survey on Knot Theory* (Basel: Birkhäuser, 1996), 38, and the presentation of the different possible links of a knot's components in David W. Farmer and Theodore B. Stanford, *Knots and Surfaces: A Guide to Discovering Mathematics* (Rhode Island: American Mathematical Society, 1995), 73.

6 Todd McGowan, "Hegel as a Marxist: Žižek's Revision of German Idealism" in *Žižek Now*, ed. Jamil Khader and Molly Anne Rothenberg (New York: Polity, 2013), 41–42.

7 An important study remains to be pursued concerning the connection between several traits that distinguish two orientations in Žižek's work: the first, of his early works, has Laclau as its privileged interlocutor, has democracy as a political ideal, and mostly espouses Marx's critique of religion, the second, discernible after *The Ticklish Subject* (1999), has Badiou as an interlocutor, has the communist hypothesis as a political emblem, and revitalizes Hegel's Christology. The true conceptual connection between this shift and the possibility of a more critical stance toward psychoanalysis's ideological deviations is nevertheless still unclear.

8 Slavoj Žižek, *The Parallax View* (Cambridge, MA: MIT Press, 2005), 16–67; *Living In the End Times* (London: Verso, 2010), 181–243; *Less Than Nothing: Hegel and the Shadow of Dialectical Materialism* (London: Verso, 2012), 241–64.

9 Slavoj Žižek, *On Belief* (London: Routledge, 2001), 29–33; *The Parallax View*, 252–70, 298–308; *Less Than Nothing*, 963–1010.

10 Žižek's early reading of Alfred Sohn-Rethel's (otherwise forgotten) work is a brilliant example of precisely such an immanent and noncomplementary relation between philosophy and politics: "we are now able to formulate precisely the 'scandalous' nature of Sohn-Rethel's undertaking for philosophical reflection: he has confronted the closed circle of philosophical reflection with an external place where its form is already 'staged.' Philosophical reflection is thus subjected to an uncanny experience similar to the one summarized by the old oriental formula 'thou art that': there, in the external effectivity of the exchange process, is your proper place; there is the theatre in which your truth was performed before you took cognizance of it. The confrontation with this place is unbearable because philosophy as such is defined by its blindness to this place: it cannot take it into consideration without dissolving itself, without losing its consistency"; Slavoj Žižek, *The Sublime Object of Ideology* (London: Verso, 1989), 17.

11 Jacques Lacan, *Le Seminaire: Livre XI—Les Quatre Concept Fondamentaux de la Psychoanalyse* (Paris: Éditions du Seuil, 1973).

12 Lacan, in his "Petit Discours aux Psychiatres," in 1967, affirms: "there is something quite astounding, which is that those who do quite well the work of transmission, [by doing it] without actually naming me, regularly lose the opportunity, which is quite visible in the text, of contributing with the little idea that they could have presented there! Little or even quite big. . . . Why is it that they would produce a small innova-

tion? It is because, in citing me, in the very fact of citing me, they would presentify . . . the context of struggle [contexte de bagarre] in which I produced all of this. From the sole fact of stating it within the context of struggle, this would put me in my place, and would allow them to produce then a small innovation." Jacques Lacan, "Petit Discours aux Psychiatres," in *Lettres de l'École*, vol. 2, no. 25 (Paris: Éditions du ECF, 1979), 66.

13   The SFP was a French "branch" of the IPA. A very useful diagram of the psychoana-lytic institutions from Freud's time up to the present can be found as an appendix in Elizabeth Roudinesco's biography of Lacan. See Roudinesco, *Jacques Lacan* (New York: Columbia University Press, 1994), 443.

14   J. C. Milner, *L'Oeuvre Claire* (Paris: Éditions du Seuil, 1995).

15   J. A. Miller, "Os seis paradigmas do gozo," in *Opção Lacaniana* 26 (São Paulo: Edições Eólia, 2006), 30–45.

16   See Jacques Lacan, "Proposition of 9th of October of 1967 on the Psychoanalyst of the School," in *Autres Écrits*, 243.

17   What is missing here is the step-by-step construction that would demonstrate that this knotting must be understood as a Borromean link, that is, a linkage between institution, clinic, and concept where each domain is tied up to the other two with-out thereby establishing any relation of complementarity with any one of the other domains. Leaving this demonstration in suspense, and trusting the reader's intuition, I will use a very rudimentary form of visualization, akin to Venn diagrams, in which this complex conceptual linkage is not directly visualizable.

18   See Erik Porge, *Os Nomes do Pai em Jacques Lacan* (São Paulo: Companhia de Freud, 1998), 71–72.

19   In his study *The Names of the Father in Jacques Lacan*, Erik Porge tracks the astonish-ing recurrent juxtapositions, throughout Lacan's teaching, of mentions of the inter-rupted seminar of 1962, the "excommunication" from the IPA, and the concept of the names-of-the-father. See Porge, *Os Nomes do Pai em Jacques Lacan*.

20   Jacques Lacan, *Le Seminaire: Livre VIII — Le Transfert* (Paris: Éditions du Seuil, 1991), 316.

21   Sigmund Freud, *Psicologia das Massas e Análise do Eu* (Rio de Janeiro: Companhia das Letras, 2011), 65.

22   Freud, *Psicologia das Massas e Análise do Eu*, 55.

23   Jacques Lacan, "Conclusão das Jornadas de Deauville da EFP," in Lacan, *Lettres de l'EFP* (Paris: EFP, 1978), 181.

24   Jacques Lacan, *Écrits* (New York: Norton, 2006), 512.

25   Lacan speaks, in *Kant with Sade* of a "critique of Reason [based] on the linchpin of impurity." See Lacan, *Écrits*, 654.

26   Jacques Lacan, *The Seminar of Jacques Lacan, Book VII: The Ethics of Psychoanalysis, 1959-1960*, (New York: W. W. Norton & Co, 1992), 300–301.

27   Jacques Lacan, *The Seminar of Jacques Lacan, Book XI: The Four Fundamental Concepts of Psychoanalysis, 1964* (New York: W. W. Norton & Co., 1998), 276.

28   Lacan, *The Seminar of Jacques Lacan, Book XI*, 123.

29 Milner, *L'Oeuvre Claire*.
30 Louis Althusser, *Writings on Psychoanalysis* (New York: Columbia University Press, 1999), 132.
31 Žižek, *The Parallax View*, 305–6.
32 Žižek, *The Parallax View*, 305–6.

11

Mourning or Melancholia?
Collapse of Capitalism and
Delusional Attachments

Fabio Vighi

This essay is divided into three sections, all meant to expand on Slavoj Žižek's thought in the direction of a critique of the current capitalist crisis. The first section provides a theoretical introduction to the argument by presenting the fundamental ontological problem posed by Žižek; the second argues for an approach to crisis informed by Lacan's discourse theory; the third focuses on what is at stake, in libidinal terms, when developing a critical conscience regarding today's capitalist deadlock.

A Crack in Everything, or: What to Do with a Dialectical Ontology of Lack

One way of understanding Lacan's critique of the University discourse, which is articulated with particular conviction in *Seminar XVII*, is to highlight how it differs from the critique of modern rationality that fuels the tradition of critical theory as represented by the Frankfurt School. While University discourse and critical theory might seem to stand for the same thing—namely the critique of the epistemic autonomy of modern scientific reason—their crucial divergence can be measured by answering the following question: From which standpoint is such critique launched? The standpoint is clearly not the same: as is the case with Adorno, Horkheimer, and Benjamin, the critical theorist's damning dissection of instrumental reason tends to be sustained by the reference to a utopian/messianic "vanishing point" situated outside the warped domain of Western rationality; with Lacan on the other hand the contra-diction is *inherent* in any knowledge apparatus, though its role and posi-tion vary. To be more precise, the implicitly Hegelian point of Lacan's discourse theory resides in positing its deadlock—the negative moment that threatens to derail discourse qua social link—as something gener-ated by the linguistic essence of discourse itself rather than as something that a priori escapes it. From a Lacanian perspective, in other words, Adorno's key theme of the "preponderance of the object"—the materi-alistic kernel at the heart of his negative dialectics—corresponds to a fundamental theoretical error inasmuch as it (paradoxically, for a dia-lectician like Adorno) hypostatizes, thus a priori excluding it from dia-lectical mediation, the very kernel of objectivity as by definition resistant to conceptual identification.

Lacan's critique, then, is more faithful to Hegel's dialectic than Adorno's, and the Frankfurt School's in general. With Lacan, it is the sig-nifier (language) that, by grafting itself on the body, brings about "sub-ject" and "world": there is no access to a prelinguistic or utopian dimen-sion; all we have is the alienated condition of identification brought in by the signifier. Negativity and contradiction, in Lacan, are categories that emerge with the intervention of the signifier. In this sense, Lacan begins exactly where Hegel sets off in his *Science of Logic*: pure being equals pure nothing, and thus needs to be mediated in order to acquire any sort of significance. When Adorno claims that the object is preponderant, he (inadvertently, perhaps) mythicizes the objectivity of being qua noth-ing, which leaves him with no other choice but to turn this objectivity into some kind of ungraspable "utopian light" that would allow reason to redeem itself from its degenerate compulsion to identify. Although Adorno firmly recoils from any endorsement of utopia as a sociopoliti-cal condition where subject and object seamlessly coalesce (which is why he prefers to depict it in aesthetic terms, as an evanescent appearance), he nevertheless remains blind to how his own tirades against instrumen-tal reason are supported by an investment in the reconciliation of sub-ject and object, which therefore, no matter how inscrutable and strictly forbidden, represents the true hinge of his philosophical system. This is to say that the preponderance of the object, in Adorno, should perhaps be understood as a symptom of Adorno's (and critical theory's) hidden desire *not* to confront the true stakes of his apocalyptic critique of the identificatory processes of instrumental rationality. Lacan offers us a different dialectical perspective, which could be summarized by the following line: "There is a *crack* in everything, that's how the *light* gets in." This quotation, which is not from Hegel but from Leonard Cohen's song "Anthem," confirms that the crack is ontological, that it pertains to *everything* we approach as human beings (in Lacanian terms, through language); crucially, the ontological fissure is also what allows "the world" to be lit, that is, to emerge as an object of knowledge—the objective world as dialectically connected with our subjective ability to try to make sense of it. This is the crucial Lacanian (and Hegelian) dialectical twist that is missed by critical theory and that should be defended as the proper theoretical weapon needed to confront the current crisis of capitalism.

Lacan makes this dialectical point emphatically: the very "crack" within discourse is ontological, in the sense that it is both responsible for its functioning and, potentially, the cause of its demise. Most important, it is produced by the signifier as a measure of its (the signifier's) constitutive instability. Lacan's "pure signifier"—the master-signifier that "quilts"[1] the endless sliding of the signifying chain—is nothing but a concretion of lack, the other side of nonsense, the necessary illusion that gushes out of being qua nothing. The signifier's arrival on the scene, which produces the necessary yet inevitably "groundless" illusion of meaning (the "light" that "gets in"), determines a situation that is akin to that of the trapeze artist, which is an accurate metaphor to define our ontological condition.[2] We are always, by definition, balanced yet at risk of falling, hanging onto, and defined by, a given signification suspended over the void from which it arises. Žižek's groundbreaking intellectual venture is erected on this paradoxical dialectical overlapping of sense and nonsense, symbolic signification and ontological "crack," as eminently reflected in the work of Žižek's two "masters": Hegel and Lacan. The invigorating novelty of Žižek's entrance in the depleted postmodern constellation in which we are still languishing has to do with his endorsing, and attempting to politicize, the ontological dimension of negativity qua antagonism. More ambitiously even: to relaunch the historically failed project of dialectical materialism by recasting it, against its worst and most sophisticated historical interpreters, as driven by its own antagonistic substance, intended as both dialectical and materialistic.

Given this theoretical introduction, my claim is that if there is a way to repeat Žižek—in the specific Žižekian sense of "insisting" on the hidden or disavowed presuppositions of his thought—this can only mean, today, to take further its dialectical ambition by developing not only the connection between the ideological universe of capitalism and its groundless presuppositions but also the opposite dialectical movement of linking the groundlessness opened by the crisis to the theorization of a new socio-symbolic framework sustained by utterly changed master-signifiers. And, as I will explicate here, such creative movement cannot abstract from the critical awareness of the real causes of the crisis. All this is the unthought of Žižek's thought, the dimension that subtends his critical theory awaiting to be translated into a dialectical project concerning a postcapitalist scenario. To paraphrase Leonard Cohen: if there is a crack in everything, then a new light must get in.

Capitalist Discourse and the Production of "Human Waste"

Although capitalism is "a wildly clever discourse," Lacan tells us, it is nevertheless "headed for a blowout." This "it will explode" has become, forty years down the line, "it is exploding." The implication is that, in a way, subtraction from capitalist ideology (the necessary presupposition for change) is already here with us, no matter how much we still feel embroiled in such ideology. The situation is similar to that described by José Saramago in his famous novel *The Year of the Death of Ricardo Reis*. On hearing of the death of Portuguese writer Fernando Pessoa, Ricardo Reis returns to Lisbon from Brazil. There he realizes that Pessoa, or rather his spirit, is still wandering through the streets of the city, failing to fathom why. In a conversation with the writer, he receives the following enlightening explanation: "before we are born no one can see us yet they think about us every day, after we are dead they cannot see us any longer and every day they go on forgetting us a little more, and apart from exceptional cases it takes nine months to achieve total oblivion."[3] Radicalizing this peculiar argumentation, we could say that, although it might well take a long time for us to "achieve the oblivion" of capitalism as our socio-symbolic order—since, as Žižek repeatedly tells us, it is "in us more than ourselves," beyond our awareness of it—we nevertheless should, in light of the devastating crisis currently unraveling, begin to consider it as good as dead: there is no future for capitalism.

By the same token, it is becoming painfully apparent that we need to begin to imagine new signifiers that might identify the "newborn social link," as its birth date is fast approaching. The reason why it is crucial to propose the right signifiers is obvious: as in the case of a newborn baby, the (new) social constellation will form its identity through the alienating mark of language. And since it will be alienated in the battery of signifiers that compose language, it is of paramount importance to begin to think of a "better form of alienation" than the one that is currently preparing its own funeral. In this respect, as happens at every respectable funeral, we will witness a mighty struggle among those heirs who will try to secure the deceased's inheritance. Here, a degree of caution should be exercised. While to engage in the struggle armed with new signifiers will be indispensable, the inheritance we should fight for, in the dialectical struggle for sublation, is first and foremost that of the Notion of capitalism, which in Hegelian terms coincides with its ultimate and founding (ontological) contradiction. Only if we manage to conceptualize the groundlessness on which capitalism has built its empire will we be able to install master-signifiers that are "new," that is, that refer to a radically changed configuration of the social.

To be clear, I want to reiterate that the demise of capitalism is self-inflicted, not the result of the triumph of the proletariat qua universal subject. Historical materialism has always tended to be, in contrast to what it claimed, profoundly idealistic. Instead, the Marx to keep faith with is the most Hegelian one; that is to say, the one who claimed that capitalism will perish at his own hands, as it will not be able to contain the specific contradiction it harbors. This brings us back to Lacan, for what Lacan put forward by introducing the discourse of the Capitalist at the start of the 1970s is precisely what explains the current capitalist crisis in Marxian terms. Here is the discourse of the Capitalist:

$$\frac{\$}{S_1} \rightarrow \frac{S_2}{a}$$

I suggest that two contiguous readings of what this discourse produces need to be expounded. First of all, let us propose that the decisive problem within the capitalist discourse has to do with what goes on in the lower level of Lacan's schema: the failed connection between the ever-expanding capitalist drive in constant search of valorization (the master-signifier in the place of truth: S_1) and the ever-diminishing realization of surplus-value (a); this is the elementary mechanism that describes today's crisis. However, a in Lacan's capitalist discourse also stands for the deeper cause of that mechanism. The double nature of the impossible relation between S_1 and a is effectively conveyed in the following passage by Robert Kurz:

> What is the ultimate cause of economic crises? It is often said that the value that has been produced cannot be realized due to a lack of purchasing power. But why is there so little purchasing power? Because, actually, very little value is being produced and this is why ordinary wages and profits are too small. And why is so little value being produced? Because competition on the world market, due to technological development and programs initiated for the purpose of cost reduction in the private economy, have rendered too much labor power superfluous. But it is precisely labor power, as the integral part of capital, which alone produces new value. For this same reason, this waste of labor power is not reducible to merely a problem of people affected by unemployment, since it is also a problem for the capitalist system.[4]

This means that what is produced by the upper-level connection between $ (the split subject in the place of agent) and S_1 (knowledge as the "battery of signifiers") is *both* the short circuit affecting capitalism and its object *and* the cause of such short circuit, namely the "wasted" labor power resulting from the blind dynamics of the development of the productive forces.

On the one hand, then, the *objet a* produced by capitalism is surplus-value. On this account, we should recall how, in *Seminar XVI* and *Seminar XVII*, Lacan had spoken of a homology between surplus-value and surplus-*jouissance*. He claimed that an inconsistency characterizes this homology, since surplus-value, precisely as a value and therefore a countable entity, represents a *distortion* of the entropic and aimless surplus that belongs to jouissance qua substance of the human being, as such inerasable from "labor power."[5] In other words, since surplus-value attempts to surreptitiously neutralize the jouissance inherent to any "knowledge-at-work" (Lacan's *savoir-faire*), such jouissance needs to find another outlet within the social link. Lacan, then, tells us that the capitalist dream of a fully valorized universe is nothing but, literally, utopia, and as such it will fail, since the entropic remainder (surplus qua lack) of the process of valorization is *ontological* and therefore inerasable. Differently put, Lacan suggests that a spectre haunts the capitalist dream of "full valorization" just as it haunts the consumerist dream of a life fully absorbed by enjoyment. More than that: value's blind pursuit of self-valorization, which is the "stuff" of the capitalist drive (that which Marx aptly called the "automatic subject"),[6] harbors lethal consequences not only for the excluded masses but also for capitalism itself, for it generates an excess that spins out of control and undermines the capitalist logic. This excess is not what Marx named the "reserve army of labor," which referred to a working class by no means expelled from work. Rather, it stands for the nightmare of absolute immiseration—or at least the condition of being radically out of work that, under the current capitalist conditions, leads to immiseration. It is here that we should read the little *a* of the capitalist discourse not only as surplus-value, but especially as "human waste." Only if we look at it parallactically do we see that what *a* actually stands for is (not just unemployment, but) a condition of irredeemable exclusion that threatens the very foundations of capitalism itself. Ultimately, the disturbing, potentially explosive "lost object" of the capitalist social link takes the form of the fundamentally displaced humanity brought about by the headless drive of profit-making.

Drive here conjures up a metaphor that fits nicely Lacan's description of the capitalist discourse as something that will "blow out." Imagine a car that accelerates against a wall; the more it accelerates, without moving an inch further, the more it burns its tires, and it soon starts dropping parts of its body, until eventually it completely breaks down. This image captures the capitalist situation at present: while the parts coming off are the excluded masses, complete systemic collapse is inevitable, since capitalism *coincides* with its accelerating drive. In this respect, "degrowth capitalism," as advocated by Serge Latouche, misses the fact that growth is the lifeblood of capitalism, not its perverse deviation. There is no such thing as capitalism without growth. As Marx put it in *Grundrisse* (in unmistakably Hegelian terms), the "inner tendency" of capitalist competition is also its "external necessity," which manifests itself in a typically disproportionate compulsion, a "drive beyond the proportion," or, in more explicit words, "a constant *march, march!*"[7]

In the present social constellation, human displacement is experienced as a devastating shock of not belonging, of having being abandoned, rejected, "dropped off." The shattering novelty of the current crisis is that it displaces masses of people who only until recently were fully included within the capitalist social order and its ideological regime of commodity enjoyment (or, in Marx's terms, of "commodity fetishism"). It is for these reasons that, as Žižek has underlined, the twilight of capitalism is and will be increasingly marked by intrinsically impotent revolts, such as the London riots of August 2011. More precisely, what is at stake is "revolt without revolution," namely the expression of "an authentic rage which is not able to transform itself into a positive programme of sociopolitical change," since it lacks the strength to confront what Hegel called "determinate negation": "What new order should replace the old one after the uprising?"[8] In this respect, I claim that the fundamental point from which to "begin anew" is the critique of the basic short circuit that is now bringing capitalism to its knees, for without this awareness we would lack the "theoretical tools" to rethink our relation to the ontological inconsistency of the social link as such. As anticipated, the reason why, with the current crisis, capitalism encounters its own absolute historical limit is that, by increasingly making labor power redundant as a direct consequence of its own competitive drive tied to technological advance, capitalism simultaneously digs its own grave, since in the "real economy" value valorizes itself only by exploiting labor power. As Lacan had perfectly grasped—before the advent of financialization in the late 1970s and early 1980s—what consumes capitalism is the blindness of its self-referential drive, its "mad" pursuit of profit, which remains totally unaware of its self-destructive logic triggered by the incessant valorization of value. If "repeating Žižek" in the context of today's crisis means something, it means first and foremost to theorize a connection between Žižek's negative ontology and a grasp of the current structural capitalist crisis that, spurred by the dramatic urgency of the situation, revisits and updates Marx's value theory, thereby preparing for the coming struggle concerning the configuration of the postcapitalist social link.

Broke but Still Flying First Class: Capitalism and Melancholia

In Woody Allen's film, *Blue Jasmine* (2013), we are given a gloomy yet sobering premonition of what will happen if we keep relating to today's crisis without both a critical conscience of it and the creative desire to completely rethink our social constellation, inclusive of its specific forms of ideological enjoyment. The film, told in a series of flashbacks, revolves around Jasmine (Cate Blanchett), a New York socialite married to wealthy yet corrupt financial trader Hal (Alec Baldwin). Although it is clear that she knows about the shady origin of her husband's wealth, she turns a blind eye in order to keep enjoying her glitzy Park Avenue lifestyle. When Hal winds up in prison, where he commits suicide, Jasmine flies to San Francisco and moves in with her adopted sister, who by contrast lives in a poor part of the city. Here it becomes apparent that Jasmine suffers from severe delusion, since she continues to act and talk as if she was still among the "1 percent," without consideration for the fact that she is broke and having to adapt to a modest, even impoverished social context. The real turning point of the film, however, is the flashback where we are told what had actually instigated Hal's downfall. Rather than being caught red-handed in a financial scandal, as we had assumed, Hal's arrest had been triggered by Jasmine. After discovering his many affairs, Jasmine had confronted her husband, demanding an explanation, only to be informed by him of his decision to leave her for another woman. In a moment of blind psychotic fury, Jasmine had then phoned the FBI, telling them about Hal's fraudulent dealings, which had led to his arrest. It is at this precise point in the narrative that the symbolic complexity and implicit political significance of the Blanchett character come to the fore, well beyond the film's morally naïve and stereotypical representation of class difference.

The striking revelation of Jasmine's betrayal is characterized by a distinct form of critical pessimism: in itself the event of the crisis, embodied by Hal's downfall as triggered by Jasmine's act, will not shift the capitalist fantasy by an inch. The dream of a world filled with commodity-induced enjoyment, the film tells us, will not suddenly evaporate with the breakdown of capitalism. In this respect, Jasmine is a modern Medea, betrayed and revengeful yet unable to let go of the alienating fantasy that, in Lacanian terms, had moulded her identity since her encounter with Hal. Lacan's message is simple: it is through the big Other (the symbolic/linguistic "density" of the world around us) that we acquire meaning. So when a world undergoes a crisis, no matter how shattering, it nevertheless survives its own death for as long as it remains supported by the subject's unrelenting desire to invest in its fantasmatic constitution, which always represented its substance. As with biological death, a systemic crash tends to be neutralized by fantasy investment. And as in the previously mentioned passage from Saramago's novel, the revenant of capitalism will continue to haunt us for a long time through the specific promise of enjoyment with which it hooks us. Jasmine loses the material substance of her world (money and status) but remains attached to it through fantasy, which therefore reveals itself to be more material and substantial than the concrete elements of that world.

The consequences of this continued investment in capitalist fantasy are, however, devastating, as is crudely shown by the film's last shot where an utterly delusional Jasmine talks to herself on a park bench, rehearsing conversations from her lost life. Jasmine, then, embodies to perfection the dangers of a politics of the event that neglects the importance of both the critical awareness of the crisis and the construction of a new fantasy sustained by new master-signifiers. A subtractive event alone does not suffice. The risk ahead is that we all become pathologically delusional like Jasmine, which will inevitably hamper any attempt at radically reconfiguring the big Other.

So what is the relevance of the discourse of the analyst, which begins precisely, we could say, from the notional truth of crisis, or else from an ontological inconsistency that is in such a position as to demand a response? Lacan suggests that, insofar as the analyst as "subject supposed to know" embodies a surplus of knowledge that draws its status from the fact that, at some point, it will reveal itself as lack of knowledge, it is only from this surplus that new master-signifiers can arise: "what he [the analyst] produces is nothing other than the master's discourse, since it's S_1 which comes to occupy the place of production. And . . . perhaps it's from the analyst's discourse that there can emerge another style of master signifier."[9] Here is the discourse of the Analyst:

$$\frac{a \rightarrow \$}{S_2 \quad S_1}$$

All the "ingredients" would seem to be in the right place here, suggesting an approach to what we are experiencing that perhaps constitutes our only chance to avoid complete collapse. In my reading, however, the analyst qua "subject supposed to know," in the position of command, is not so much a single individual but is, no doubt unwittingly, capitalism itself: it embodies a seemingly unbreakable knowledge that, nevertheless, today is clearly showing its "cracks," its fundamental inadequacy vis-à-vis the crisis it has caused. Today, those who still support capitalism as the most efficient socioeconomic system are (or should be), to borrow Lacan's colorful metaphor from *Seminar XVI*, "as embarrassed as a fish on a bicycle."[10] The awareness of the lack of knowledge that emerges from the cracks of the capitalist framework (S_2 as truth of *a* means precisely that the big Other itself is deeply inconsistent) should then set the barred subject ($) to work in an effort to produce what Lacan calls "another style of master-signifier." Here, however, the danger, as *Blue Jasmine* would seem to suggest, is that the subject might not attempt to produce anything at all but might rather turn back toward the object-cause of desire in order to desperately hang onto the substantial fantasy it embodies. The awareness that the object of desire is lacking, that it coincides with a threatening void, might not lead to the ideation of a new "universe of sense" but instead might trigger in the subject a regressive mechanism of pathological attachment to what has been lost. Hence the significance of "blue" in the title of Allen's film: Jasmine's delusion is a manifestation of her melancholic attachment to what is no more. Her position effectively tallies with Freud's elementary description of the melancholic symptoms that are normally overcome through mourning at the beginning of his well-known essay "Mourning and Melancholia": "reality-testing has shown that the loved object no longer exists, and it proceeds to demand that all libido shall be withdrawn from its attachments to that object. This demand arouses understandable opposition — it is a matter of general observation that people never willingly abandon a libidinal position, not even, indeed, when a substitute is already beckoning to them. This opposition can be so intense that a turning away from reality takes place and a clinging to the object through the medium of a hallucinatory wishful psychosis."[11] The simple question to ask here is the following: will we be able to successfully mourn the loss of capitalism, or are we condemned — as Blue Jasmine indicates — to a painful "clinging to the object," which can only harbor devastating psychological and sociopolitical consequences? Žižek's interpretation of melancholic attachment is, in this respect, particularly thought-provoking. For him,

> the melancholic is not primarily the subject fixated on the lost object, unable to perform the work of mourning on it; he is, rather, the subject who

possesses the object, but has lost his desire for it, because the cause which made him desire this object has withdrawn, lost its efficiency. . . . melancholy stands for the presence of the object itself deprived of our desire for it—melancholy occurs when we finally get the desired object, but are disappointed at it. In this precise sense, melancholy (disappointment at all positive, empirical objects, none of which can satisfy our desire) effectively is the beginning of philosophy.[12]

To anyone familiar with Lars von Trier's film *Melancholia* (2012), it will be immediately apparent that the above description perfectly captures the libidinal position of the film's heroine, Justine (Kirsten Dunst), who from the start is depicted as strangely detached from the context of her wedding, including her desired husband. What we have here is melancholy as a subtle subtractive drive that Žižek sees optimistically, as the sine qua non for "beginning anew." While I fully subscribe to this theoretical point, I nevertheless contend that the portrayal of delusional attachment to the lost object in *Blue Jasmine*—no matter how potentially motivated by an ambivalent narcissistic identification that turns into self-punishment[13]—provides a more useful metaphor for grasping the real difficulties involved in the transformative process leading to a postcapitalist society. Incidentally, perhaps a more fitting counterpart to Jasmine is Julie (Juliette Binoche) in Kieslowski's *Three Colours: Blue* (1994), a woman who manages to overcome (mourn) the sudden loss of her husband (and daughter) only when she discovers that, as it were, the object was always-already lost, since the husband had started a relationship with another woman who was expecting his child. But, again, in my view *Blue Jasmine* works as a much more realistic, sobering admonition about the resilience of the capitalist fantasy. Ultimately, that fantasy's capacity to survive systemic disintegration can only be undermined by a combined strategy that brings together the struggle to instill a critical conscience regarding the causes of today's crisis with the creative effort to rethink a socioeconomic system that makes better use of the ontological inconsistency that qualifies any socio-symbolic framework.

Notes

1   Lacan uses the expression *point de capiton* (literally, "upholstery button") to capture the idea of a given signifier that unifies a field of meaning. The expression *point de capi-*

ton has been translated in different ways ("quilting point," "anchoring point," "button tie," etc.).

2   Visually, this condition is effectively reproduced in the cover image of Žižek's *Less Than Nothing: Hegel and the Shadow of Dialectical Materialism* (London: Verso, 2012), where a naked woman attempts to prop herself up on a red line, against a black background.

3   José Saramago, *The Year of the Death of Ricardo Reis* translated by Giovanni Pontiero (Fort Washington, PA: Harvest Books, 1992), 64.

4   Robert Kurz, "Double Devalorization," *Neues Deutschland*, March 5, 2012. English translation available at *The libcom.org Collective*, http://libcom.org/library/double-devalorization-robert-kurz.

5   I develop this reading at the start of my *On Žižek's Dialectics: Surplus, Subtraction, Sublimation* (New York: Continuum, 2010), 39–58.

6   Karl Marx, *Capital*, vol. 1, translated by Ben Fowkes (Harmondsworth, UK: Penguin, 1990), 255.

7   Karl Marx, *Grundrisse* translated by Martin Nicolaus (Harmondsworth, UK: Penguin, 1993), 413–14.

8   Slavoj Žižek, "Shoplifters of the World Unite," *London Review of Books*, August 19, 2011, http://www.lrb.co.uk/2011/08/19/slavoj-zizek/shoplifters-of-the-world-unite.

9   Jacques Lacan, *The Seminar of Jacques Lacan, Book XVII: The Other Side of Psychoanalysis*, ed. Jacques-Alain Miller, trans. Russell Grigg (New York: Norton, 2007), 176.

10 The sentence is worth quoting in full: "even this [capitalist] power, this camouflaged power, this secret and, it must also be said anarchic power, I mean divided against itself, and this without any doubt through its being clothed with this rise of science, it is as embarrassed as a fish on a bicycle now"; Jacques Lacan, *Le Séminaire de Jacques Lacan, Livre XVI: D'un Autre à l'autre, 1968-1969*, ed. Jacques-Alain Miller (Paris: Éditions du Seuil, 2006), unpublished in English, lesson of March 19, 1969.

11 Sigmund Freud, "Mourning and Melancholia," in *The Standard Edition of the Complete Psychological Works*, translated by James Strachey, vol. 14 (1914–1916) (London: Hogarth Press, 1957), 243–58, quotation from 244.

12 Slavoj Žižek, *How to Read Lacan* (London: Granta Books, 2006), 67–68.

13 "The loss of a love-object is an excellent opportunity for the ambivalence in love-relationships to make itself effective and come into the open. If the love for the object—a love which cannot be given up though the object itself is given up—takes refuge in narcissistic identification, then the hate comes into operation on this substitutive object, abusing it, debasing it, making it suffer and deriving sadistic satisfaction from its suffering. The self-tormenting in melancholia, which is without doubt enjoyable, signifies, just like the corresponding phenomenon in obsessional neurosis, a satisfaction of trends of sadism and hate which relate to an object, and which have been turned round upon the subject's own self"; Freud, "Mourning and Melancholia," 251.

PART III | **politics**

Gavin Walker

An economic science inspired by *Capital* does not necessarily lead us [ne conduit pas né-cessairement] to its utilization as a revolutionary power, and history seems to require help from something other than a predicative dialectic. The fact is that science, if one looks at it closely, has no memory. Once constituted, it forgets the circuitous path by which it came into being [elle oublie les péripéties dont elle est née].
—Jacques Lacan, "La science et la vérité" (1966)

In recent years, the work of Slavoj Žižek has been closely associated with a general sense of the revival of Marxism and the rethinking of the experience and theory of communism. But this is not a new trend in his work as such. Marx has played a central role since the very earliest reception of Žižek, including questions of commodity fetishism, the relationship to Hegel, the status of the dialectic, the figure of the proletariat, the concept of alienation, the form of value, and so forth. Questions of political struggles, current strategic problems of the Left, and the evaluation of the history of revolutionary politics have also been key elements in Žižek's work over the last twenty or more years. But what specifically is the status of the Marxian critique of political economy in Žižek? What is it in this form of analysis that requires the Marxian project to be given a crucial status alongside two other instances: the Hegelian logic and the Lacanian intervention in the psychoanalytic field?

Žižek has often been the target of critical interrogation from Marxist theorists, frequently chiding him for what are perceived to be shorthand comments, rapid dislocation between arguments, a tendency toward summaries and overviews rather than sustained and deep critical engagement with the Marxian critique of political economy. This critical interrogation seems often mistaken in my view for a number of reasons, not least of which is the peculiar proprietary economy of resentment that seems to accompany it, always accusing Žižek of being, in essence, too popular, too widely published, too ready to make statements and declarations, as if we ought to all aspire to obscurity, irrelevance, hermeticism, arcane debates of an incomprehensible nature, specialized vocabulary and readerships, and so forth. In particular, this type of criticism tends to downplay the genuine contributions of Žižek to contemporary Marxist thought and critical social theory by saturating them with his more journalistic interventions, reducing his theoretical work to his more widely disseminated writings in his capacity as a general cultural commentator.

But what if we were to dispense with this typical style of dealing with Žižek—with its incessant accusations (he does not adequately theorize the value-form, the proletariat, the commodity, the historical development of Marxist theory, the history of Marxism, the lived actuality of communism, etc.) and its economy of resentment? What if we were instead to ask: What relation, on the level of theory as such, can we draw between the actually existing work of Žižek—a real and living body of work—and the Marxist theoretical project? It is here that we might find something decisive, something useful, and above all, something productive. And this in turn concerns a doubling—of course, the double is an essential figure of Žižek's thought—in relation to Hegel: Hegel as mediated by Marx (or even the reverse); Hegel as mediated by Lacan.

Here I will attempt to elucidate in particular what is at stake in Marx within Žižek's work, by focusing on the theoretical complexity of another doublet: the relation between the form of capital and the form of the subject. Žižek has long alerted us to something essential as it pertains to this relation: working-class subjectivity in capitalist society only emerges precisely at the point wherein the innermost essence of the worker's body—the specific form of *labor power* (*Arbeitskraft*)—is reduced to a disposable or excremental "almost nothing" and exchanged for a wage, which is then itself utilized simply to reproduce this cycle in which the presumed subject of exchange "dwells in the sphere of pauperism." The specific wager made by Žižek is that this insight of Marx simultaneously provides us with a theoretical physics through which we see how the Cartesian subject, in order to emerge as the subject of the enunciation, must be reduced to "a disposable piece of shit" in the form of the subject of the enunciated. My thesis here is that this splitting (*Spaltung*) of the subject is also an intervention in the critique of political economy: that Žižek's work, rather than merely appealing to a certain Marxist politics on the level of gesture, enacts or performs a significant intervention by focusing on the *splitting* of capital as a social relation, forever torn between its history and its logic, a splitting in which the concept of the outside is returned to us as a central term in the Marxian problematic, precisely around the category of labor power.

This takes us back to the decisive question: the question of the outside, the question of where something, unbeholden to the existing scenario, could exert its own force, where it could intervene, where and in what ways it could *force* its way into existence. In other words, it is a question of the relationship between Marxist theory—the critique of political economy—and the possibility of a Marxist *politics*.

Topologies of the Subject

Let us focus on an exceptional passage from one of Žižek's major theoretical works, one in which the precise problem we are concerned with is rigorously developed, or "called what it is":

> For Marx, the emergence of working class subjectivity is strictly co-dependent on the fact that the worker is compelled to sell the very substance of his being (his creative power) as a commodity on the market—that is, to reduce the *agalma*, the treasure, the precious core of his being, to an object that can be bought for money: there is no subjectivity without the reduction of the subject's positive-substantial being to a disposable "piece of shit." In this case of correlation between Cartesian subjectivity and its excremental objectal counterpart, we are not dealing merely with an example of what Foucault called the empirico-transcendental couple that characterizes modern anthropology, but rather, with the split between the subject of the enunciation and the subject of the enunciated: if the Cartesian subject is to emerge at the level of the enunciation, he must be reduced to the "almost-nothing" of disposable excrement at the level of the enunciated content.[1]

This intensive and dense argument has two crucial elements. First, it expresses something essential that Žižek has long attempted to explicate regarding the status of the subject in capitalist society. Second, it constitutes an intervention in a crucial question of Marxist theory, the question of the relation between the history of capitalism and the logic of capital, and moreover, between Marxist *theory* and a Marxist *politics*.

But what sort of a conception of subjectivity are we here dealing with? First and foremost, I must point out that the subject is a complex and elusive category in Marx's work. Is the subject in question the proletariat? As Étienne Balibar and others have pointed out, the very term "proletariat" is nearly entirely absent in the text of *Capital*, the culmination of the mature Marx's work in the critique of political economy. Is capital itself the "self-moving subject" of capitalist society? Where then is a Marxist politics to be located? Could Marxism merely be the description and critical reconstruction of the inner dynamics of capitalist society, with a view to simply lapsing into defeatism, quietism, and abstentionism, faced with the extraordinary capacity of capital to renew itself? Or would Marxism instead also hold within it a "practical discourse for sustaining the subjective advent of a politics"?[2]

For Žižek, the question of the subject remains always in this split relation, torn between the instance of subjectivation and the possibilities of politics. And it is here that there is an essential Marxian thesis, one that allows us to think carefully about the "parallax" between history and logic. In Marx, the working class appears in two registers: (1) as the active agent of radical political upheavals, the class called on to develop the historical form of class struggle into an irreversible political threshold, and (2) the social stratum from which capital draws its perverse dynamism, unable to create the necessary labor-power inputs it requires without indirect mechanisms of control, such as the form of population, and an entire series of corollary forms of the management of the human body. In a sense, between these two instances exists a vast gulf. How can the one insight be articulated to the other?

In Marx's work, on the one hand the subject must be the concentrated expression of the explosive energy of the masses, wholly contingent on the "evental" nature of politics (in the sense of "all hitherto existing history is the history of class struggle"),[3] and on the other hand the subject must somehow simultaneously be the distillation or concentrated product of the transition from the antagonism (*Gegenstand*) between labor and capital to the contradiction (*Widerspruch*) between the development of the productive forces and their corresponding relations of production, and in this latter sense, must therefore be merely the expression or result of this inevitable historical contradiction, just a sign of the metahistorical process itself. This ruptural space, in which the rare or abyssal space of the subject flickers in and out of presence, between the "iron necessity" of capital's logic and the "random order of computation" in which capital encounters a preexisting semiotic and territorial field, always exists in a paradoxical or nonverifiable relation to the "reified" human being as political expression of the problem of the commodification of labor power.

In a recent and important work, Etienne Balibar writes:

> in *Capital*, Marx did not study one but two distinct structures, both stemming from the critique of political economy, but having divergent logical and therefore political implications, even if historically one encounters them in combination. The one concerns the circulation of commodities and the "value-form," the other the integration of labour power into the production process under the directive of capital and under conditions that enable its indefinitely expanding accumulation (hence exploitation and its diverse "methods"). But the implications of each structure for conceptualizing the tendency towards communism and the forms of its realization are totally different, alternatively brought up by Marx in different texts (notably in the descriptions in *Capital* of "commodity fetishism," on the one hand, and of "cooperation" or "polytechnics" on the other).[4]

Žižek's answer to this conundrum is as follows. In order for the subject of politics, the subject of class struggle (the "subject of the enunciation") to emerge, a situation must exist in which this subject expresses already in its structural position the *negative* limits and openings that it will exploit *affirmatively* in its interventions. That is, the political subject in capitalist society must be already *subjected by* capital or *subjected to* its domination (the enunciated), the working class immiserated by the acceleration of the development of the productive forces and consequently shifting relations of production. In order for the proletarian subject of the enunciation to emerge, Žižek points out, it must first "discover what it is," and this it discovers in a very specific manner. Marx reminds us:

"by heralding the *dissolution of the hitherto existing world order*, the proletariat merely proclaims the *secret of its own existence*, for it is the factual dissolution of that world order. By demanding the negation of private property, the proletariat merely raises to the rank of a principle of society what society has raised to the rank of *its* principle, what is already incorporated in *it* as the negative result of society without its own participation."[5]

That is, the proletariat is the void, the hole, the absence in the fullness of capitalist society, an existence that *forces* capital itself to disclose its weaknesses, its Achilles' heel. This outside to capital, this force called the proletariat, is a force of resistance. It is an outside that is only constituted as an outside insofar as capital traces the outer limits of its own spectral body by deploying this outside within itself in order to seal its ruptures. The important question here is precisely the parallax—to use a term extensively developed by Žižek following the influential formulation of Kōjin Karatani[6]—between the negative force of subjectivation of the working class as a merely passive part of capital itself (the "self-conscious instruments of production") and the affirmative force of inversion contained in the proletarian political capacity to wage class struggle, itself a field not of necessity but of absolute undecidability.

When Žižek therefore reminds us that the proletarian political subject can only emerge at the level of enunciation insofar as it is reduced to the "shit/agalma" or "alpha and omega" of capital at the level of the enunciated content, he is attempting to provide a point of entry into this most centrally difficult question of the Marxian theoretical system. Rather than showing us the violent reduction to shit of the ideological veil of the individual endowed with rights and so forth, the capture of heterogeneity and formation of labor power in the process of primitive accumulation or transition from feudalism to capitalism shows us that revolutionary politics and the break with this (im)probable history of capital, which is perversely also ours, consists in the political potential of our original state of being as shit, as refuse, as waste, as useless. That is, insofar as we are, at the level of capital's own "circuit process," the spectral substance called labor power that is circulated on capital's surface, the body, which lies outside the sphere of circulation and is instead in a direct relationship to the production process (mediated by the consumption of means of subsistence), reprocesses these means of subsistence as human waste, and thus is not only conceptually but concretely in a constant process of "shitting" on capital's supposedly pure interior. This labor power as shit exposes the contamination at the center of capital that capital itself would narrate away in its own dream of pure interiority without excess, without remainder. Yet capital must traverse this shit-outside every time it undertakes a production cycle, calling the labor power commodity into life from its exteriority in the unreliable, erratic, hazardous human body. By means of this eternal return of shitting, capital must pollute itself, contaminating its laboratory by repressing the fact that this laboratory is one big toilet, one vast "relative surplus population." Our essence as shit/excess is always-already contaminating the interior of capital's supposedly "clean" and "sterile" circuit process, and it is this weakness that the form of labor power discloses.[7] Žižek frequently reminds us, throughout his work, that the proletariat is famously described by Marx as a "substanceless subjectivity." But what does this mean precisely?

The Extimacy of Labor Power

The subject here is something that cannot be grasped as itself, so to speak. The subject comes to be grasped as itself only in being retrospectively projected back on to its own *presupposed* substantiality. That is, the subject is the original "semblance" because, paradoxically, it is only discovered and made concrete in the act of admitting its nonidentity. That is, when I try to discover myself as a subject, I can discover this, but only in as much as the subject's existence is guaranteed by the condition of being posited itself. Wherever the subject is posited, there remains the undecidability of practice, a certain impossibility that characterizes its very possibility: labor power does not exist as such. Labor power is called into being when its use-value, labor, is employed in the process of production. At that point, labor power is retrospectively made to have existed; in other words, its basic temporality is exactly the future anterior ("it will have been"). When capital needs to expand, it presumes the existence of a supply of labor power, but it conceals to itself the hazard of securing this supply. It posits for itself a semblance that fills the void and allows the circular logic of its cycle to smoothly continue. We should recognize that this entire schematics shows us something critical not only about the way in which capital operates, but about the *production of subjectivity* more broadly. In turn, the development of a political response to capitalist society depends not only on going deeper into what we might call here the "impossibility" of the commodification of labor power,[8] but also, following Žižek, on going deeper into what we might call the "impossibility of the subject," precisely because the entire question of what labor power is, how it is produced, and how it operates "signals the radical *scission* that marks the constitution of subjectivity in capitalism."[9]

This is capital's basic wager—the possibility that social relations could be managed as relations among things—in which something unquantifiable must be made to behave as if it were reducible to number, countability, and stability, and thus always contains within itself an infinite regress: the value of labor power can only be determined by means of the value of the means of subsistence utilized to indirectly "reproduce" it. In turn, the means of subsistence—which would include not only food, clothing, and shelter but also necessary regimes of training, medical care, education, forms of subjectivation, and so forth—must contain or encompass numerous qualitative aspects that exceed quantity or cannot be reduced purely to it. Here it should be emphasized that, like all commodities (save labor power and land), the means of subsistence must be produced by its own process of production. This process of production, through which the means of subsistence could be furnished for the reproduction of labor power, itself requires the labor power input. In this sense, we are already in a preliminary moment of infinite regress. With Žižek, we must then ask:

> Is then capital the true Subject/Substance? Yes and no: for Marx, this self-engendering circular movement is—to put it in Freudian terms—precisely the capitalist "unconscious fantasy" that parasitizes on the proletariat as the "pure substanceless subjectivity"; for this reason, capital's speculative self-generating dance has a limit, and it brings about the conditions of its own collapse.[10]

It is this parasitism of capital, whereby the living proletariat is "translated" into the form of variable capital, in which the worker becomes merely the "self-conscious instrument of production," in Marx's terrifying phrase. Yet because capital must imagine to itself that this variable capital is a stable reserve to be utilized—its "unconscious fantasy"—

capital must also constantly traverse its own limits, a circuit through which the proletarian position as this "interior exteriority" of capital discovers its subjective potential to overturn the entire order of its being. In this sense, the "exchange" (or "intercourse," *Verkehr*) produced by the circulation of capital gives rise to a situation through which a *politics proper*, no less than the complete "inversion" (*Verkehrung*) of capital itself, has the *potential* to develop. But the only thing that strictly speaking emerges here is a situation in which the limits of this "unconscious fantasy" are traced: the political response to such a situation can never merely be a direct outgrowth of this perverse movement but must instead be enacted.

Labor power, which cannot be assumed to be available when it is required, must be reproduced indirectly through the production of the means of subsistence, whose production itself must assume the existence of labor power inputs. This infinite regressive spiral of the logic inherent in the dynamics of capital returns us, therefore, to the ultimate paradox of the subject, a paradox that is at the heart of the problem of capital as a social relation: the problem of continuity. How is it that something that merely masquerades as a substance, something that cannot be assumed to be stable, something that is punctuated at every moment by breaks, interruptions, and contingencies, nevertheless remains in a state capable of subsisting, capable of presenting itself *as if* it were a continuity? What this irrational substratum shows us is not that it constitutes the moment at which things break down or cease functioning. The true paradox is that this irrationality is precisely what allows capital to appear as a continuity, as an organizing and perspectival force through which it *traverses* or *passes through* its own boundaries or borders. Labor power, in this sense, is something *extimate* for capital, intimate but axiomatically exterior, or "on the outside within," so to speak.

In the representation of the subject that would be considered "typical" or "usual," the subject is understood as a psychic island existing within a field in flux. This field would be outside or exterior to the boundaries of the island, and the island in turn would constitute an inside with regard to itself. Thus the subject would be imagined in this way as something in which interiority and exteriority could be strictly separated. Lacan's intervention in the 1950s in his Seminar 9 concerns an attempt to provide the theory of the subject with a different topology—a topology of the subject in the shape of the torus or Klein bottle. In other words, for Lacan, this rigid differentiation of inside and outside leads us to incorrectly assume that there is a hard kernel of interiority within the subject that would be the "evidence" or "proof" of the subject's self-identity. Rather, he argues, because the "I" as a subject emerges through the "traversing of the primal fantasy," in which the "I" as subject of the enunciation is presumed to be identical with the subject of the enunciated, already at the most primal stage of identification, this I would be exposed to some "other" outside its expected boundaries. Since, therefore, this other that is absolutely internal to me is simultaneously exterior to me as a subject, it follows that the subject can never be a given, but must rather be a production of this splitting—a splitting, however, that never appears as a split but is smoothly traversed as if it would never constitute a boundary or gap. This structure of putativity, this "as-if condition," irrevocably or irredeemably structures the subject, to the extent that we might even say: "the subject" names this simultaneous gap and suture understood in the form of the "as-if." What is paradoxical, or gives us pause, is the fact that this form in which the subject must occur is also a description of the microscopic internal physics of capitalist society, and it is here that we can connect this problem to that of the critique of political economy itself.

In order to undertake this point and locate Žižek's intervention around the relation of labor power and the subject, let us return to the following statement of Lacan, quoted in the epigraph: "the fact is that science, if one looks at it closely, has no memory. Once constituted, it forgets the circuitous path by which it came into being [elle oublie les péripéties dont elle est née]."[11] Here, we need to pay close attention to the term *péripéties*—the "circumstances," the "adventures," the "incidents" or "events," the "twists and turns" of the plot, so to speak. But this seemingly unimportant or cursory term in Lacan's statement turns out to be nothing less than the pivotal term around which the putatively "scientific" circle of capital's logic operates. *Peripeteia* in classical Greek narrative analysis refers to the sudden or dramatic change in circumstances, a *reversal*, an instantaneous and unexpected "plot twist." In other words, it connotes the tragic, comic, or absurd moment when an expected set of relations or phenomena is suddenly revealed to have transformed into its inverse, when a set of circumstances has somewhat *folded inside out*.

The pretensions to "science" of economics, as a pure cyclical set of laws of motion mirroring the exchange process, must always violently "forget" the contingencies of the historical process in order to imagine itself as a rationality, as a pure logic. That is, once constituted, the "science" of political economy "forces" itself to ignore or elide the fact that it came into being by imitating in its theoretical structure the "deranged" nature of capital itself, which pretends to be a pure interiority while constantly having recourse to the historical process in order to retain and reproduce its dynamism. In this sense, the critique of political economy consists in the *restoration* or "re-remembering" of these péripéties that "science" would seek to exclude from its image of itself, in the taking of these "secret" undercurrents and rather than erasing them instead raising them up to the level of the "world of principle" itself.

A very specific term in Marx's work functions in the style of this *peripeteia*, a term that links together the deranged logic of capital with the pretensions to "rationality" of the "dismal science" of economics. This term is also at first glance something cursory or unremarkable: the term *Umschlag*. In Marx's work, this term is used in two divergent senses: on the one hand it simply means the "turnover" of capital, that is, the process through which capital is advanced and subsequently returns; on the other hand this term is utilized in the *Grundrisse* manuscripts to indicate the movement of "inversion" or "reversal" whereby, through "a peculiar logic, the right of property is dialectically inverted [dialektisch umschlägt], so that on the side of capital it becomes the right to an alien product, or the right of property over alien labour, the right to appropriate alien labour without an equivalent, and, on the side of labour capacity [Arbeitsvermögens], it becomes the duty to relate to one's own labour or to one's own product as to *alien property*."[12]

This Umschlag, in other words, is a *topological* description of the traversal of capital's "primal fantasy" of completeness, a description of *how* something that appears as a limit is recreated, recoded, and redeployed as a *gradient* of intensity for capital's functioning. This Umschlag, also simply the term for an "envelope," literally "envelopes" the outside by turning it "inside out," torsionally folding it in on itself, so that what should operate as a gap can be dialectically "leaped," but also burrowed into, emptied out, transformed from an *apparent* depth into a volatile surface. It is no accident that the exchange process, the process of the buying and selling of labor power, is not something punctuated by limits as such: these limits or gaps between seller and buyer are torsionally inverted or penetrated into only in order to recalibrate themselves as one smooth surface on which will occur "der flüssige Umschlag von Verkauf und Kauf" ("the fluid 'reversal' or 'inversion' of sale and purchase").[13] It is a topological *folding* and *unfolding*, through which the interior surface and the exterior surface can be interlocked in a planar field, it appears therefore as a *torus*: "capital appears as this dynamic unity [prozessierende Einheit] of production and circulation, a unity which can be considered both as the totality [Ganze] of its production process and as the particular process through which capital goes during a single turnover [bestimmter Verlauf eines Umschlags des Kapitals], a single movement returning to itself [einer in sich selbst zurückkehrenden Bewegung]."[14] That is, *capital itself* is, in essence, this Umschlag, this inversion or torsion on itself, which names the cyclical course by which it goes through a single motion of its torsional pattern, its "circuit process" (*Kreislaufsprozeß*), not merely in a flat circle but in a topological opening out onto and simultaneous folding into itself. But, and this again is why capitalism is so purely demented, deranged, and de-ranged, capital is only capable of expressing itself as the logic toward which it is compelled in a *single* cycle. Once the cycle ends, this torsional movement of inversion finds that, in order to repeat itself, it must traverse the historical outside, it must appeal to the "apparatuses" for the traversal of this impossibility that lies at the boundary or edge of every circuit-process, every cycle of exchange in capitalist society, the hole at the center of the torus. Therefore, capital's compulsion to repeat always undermines its own attempt to appear as a logic, precisely because this logic is only able to legitimate itself in the form of a single circuit. This is exactly what Marx identifies in the question of "turnover," this moment of inversion/turnover that traces the outline of the maximal limit of capital's ability to grasp its outside *as if* it were a pure moment of the inside: "the production process itself is posited as determined by exchange, so that the social relation and the dependence on this relation [die gesellschaftliche Beziehung und Abhängigkeit von dieser Beziehung] in immediate production is posited not merely as a material moment, but as an *economic* moment, a determination of form [Formbestimmung]." This moment that should be impossible, the presentation of the social relation *as if* it were a derivation from the exchange process, in which social relationality is simply determined as the exchange of things, in this sense also expresses "the maximum of circulation [Das Maximum der Zirkulation], the limit [die Grenze] of the renewal of the production process through it."[15]

It is in turn this "torsion" or inversion that reminds us to torsionally invert this de-ranged logic back upon "economics," back upon the simple mirroring of capital's quasi logic as a "rational" explanatory mechanism. It is in fact this Umschlag that economics, following capital's own model faithfully, generally conceals or covers over. That is, when confronted with a "sudden inversion" (*plötzliche Umschlagen*), something that appears as the glimmer of the irrational outside within the putatively rational inside, the "agents of circulation" (*die Zirkulationsagenten*), or perhaps "economic fantasists," become overawed by "the impenetrable mystery surrounding their own relations" (*dem undurchdringlichen Geheimnis ihrer eignen Verhältnisse*).[16] This is not only because the confrontation with the problems of the subject and of labor power exposes the insanity of the image of capitalist society as a mere enlargement of the supposedly smooth and rational exchange process, it is also because Marx's critique is aimed not at capital's logic itself but at *the discourse of political economy*. This discourse is not itself "an" economics. It is a critical explosion of the way in which political economy "buys into" capital's own fantasy, its dream-like attempt to arrogate itself a logic. Thus

> the economic is in this sense the object itself of Marx's "critique": it is a representation (at once necessary and illusory) of real social relations. Basically it is only the fact of this *representation* that the economists abstractly explicate, which is inevitably already shared *practically* by the owners-exchangers [propriétaires-échangistes] of commodities, that the "economic" relations appear as such, in an apparent natural autonomy. The representation is implicated in the very form of the *manifestation* of social relations. This is precisely what enables producers-exchangers to *recognize themselves* in the image that the economists present of them. The "representation" of the economic is thus for Marx essential to the economic itself, to its real functioning and therefore to its conceptual definition.[17]

Marx himself reminds us that the scientificity of critique should never be confused with the pretension to "scientific rationality," but rather indicates an entirely different modality of analysis: "the weak points [die Mängel] of the abstract materialism of natural science, from which the historical process is excluded, are at once evident from the abstract and ideological conceptions [Vorstellungen] of its spokesmen, whenever they venture out beyond their own speciality."[18] Thus, we see precisely how the systematic and demented structure of capital also furnishes the theoretical architecture of the system of political economy. That is, because political economy itself relies on the same "deranged forms" as capital itself but "de-ranges" them into its motion, the same "forgetting" of the "circuitous path by which it was born," the critical restoration of these péripéties that are desperately erased from the inside serves to *politically* undermine the entire expression of political economy itself. This, in turn, is why Žižek reminds us:

> Again, to quote Lacan, truth has the structure of a fiction: the only way to formulate the truth of capital is to render this fiction of its "immaculate" self-generating movement. And this insight also allows us to locate the weakness of the "deconstructionist" appropriation of Marx's analysis of capitalism: although it emphasizes the endless process of deferral which characterizes this movement, as well as its fundamental inconclusiveness, its self-blockade, the "deconstructionist" retelling still describes the FANTASY of capital—it describes what individuals believe, although they don't know it.[19]

When we confront the de-ranged origin and reproduction of capital's logical functioning, we are also confronting the political physics and boundaries of our own theoretical representations of these phenomena, representations that are implicated already in the inner laws of capital's movement, in its demented forms of presupposition (*Voraussetzung*). In turn, it is precisely through the recurrent and endless analysis of the *genesis* of this dementia that we are constantly reminded of the volatile force, both dangerous and precious, of the historical outside, the space wherein the political capacity to implode capital's circuit-process remains an ever-present undercurrent of all social existence.

In a well-known text, Balibar reminds us: "it is the concrete configurations of the class struggle and not 'pure' economic logic which explain the constitutions of nation-states."[20] Without doubt, this is correct. But is it not also the case that the entire schematic of Marx's *critique* of political economy is devoted to showing us precisely that the "concrete con-figurations of the class struggle" always haunt and contaminate the sup-posedly "pure" interiority of the logic of capital, the apparently smooth and clean "rationality" that can never erase its "excremental" excess? The labor power commodity, the product of a historical accident in the form of a contingent encounter (the "so-called primitive accumulation"), is given a central role within the *logical drive* of capital. How could the relation of self-expanding value form itself as a circuit, as a cyclical and repeating process, without *presupposing* the presence of the labor power commodity, which is precisely that which can *never* be strictly presup-posed in capital's interior? In other words, from the very outset of the form of exchange relations, the labor power commodity, which is a prod-uct of a volatile and purely contingent history, is made to function *as if* it could be assumed to be a "pure economic logic." This is exactly where, in Žižek's terms, the secretive role of the "phantasmic semblance that fills the irreducible ontological gap" comes into the most inner moment of the logic of capital,[21] a moment that behaves as if historical consider-ations are axiomatically excluded. In this sense, we ought to push Bali-bar's argument slightly further by emphasizing that the "concrete con-figurations of the class struggle" and "pure economic logic" are in fact *always contaminated with each other* in the historical experience of capi-talist society.[22]

As Žižek has recently argued, "class struggle is a unique mediating term that, while mooring politics in the economy (all politics is 'ulti-mately' an expression of class struggle), simultaneously stands for the irreducible political moment at the very heart of the economic."[23] Let us recall that "class struggle" is not exclusively a political term, or even merely a political instance within the broader social situation, but is, as Žižek argues, the very essence of the mediation or parallax between the political and the economic, a correspondence that furnishes nothing less than the center of Marx's own work. After all, Marx himself reminds us:

> At last we have arrived at the *forms of manifestation* that serve as the start-ing point in the vulgar conception: rent, coming from the land; profit (interest), from capital; wages, from labour. But from our standpoint things now look different. The apparent movement is explained. . . . Since those 3 items (wages, rent, profit (interest)) constitute the sources of in-

come of the 3 classes of landowners, capitalists and wage labourers, we have the *class struggle*, as the conclusion in which the movement and disintegration of the whole shit resolves itself.[24]

Here the "whole shit" of the critique of political economy is "resolved" in the question of class struggle, itself a moment in which politics only emerges insofar as we ourselves are reduced to the specific and singular partial "shit," this non-whole or non-all (*pas-tout*) "shit," the "almost-nothing" of labor power—the "disposable excremental objects" of capital's inner workings. And it is Žižek who has most comprehensively reminded us today: the critique of political economy in Marx is reducible neither to a simplistic political doctrine nor to a purely scientist theory of exploitation but is instead devoted to the concept "class struggle." More than anything else, it is this renewal of focus on the concept of class struggle that gives us a new insight into the question of the possibilities of new subjective interventions, new possibilities of politics as such.[25] But as Žižek's body of work teaches us, this politics will only emerge into being at the level of enunciation if we understand the torsional logic of capital that overwhelms us at the level of the enunciated content, the situation in which we find ourselves, a situation in which the logic of capital remains something repeated at the daily level of the indirect formation of labor power, and its psychoanalytic correlate in the split of the subject.

Notes

1   Slavoj Žižek, *The Ticklish Subject: The Absent Centre of Political Ontology* (London: Verso, 1999), 157.
2   Alain Badiou, *Theory of the Subject*, trans. Bruno Bosteels (London: Continuum, 2008), 129.
3   Karl Marx and Friedrich Engels, "Manifesto of the Communist Party" in *Marx-Engels Collected Works*, vol. 6 (Moscow: Progress Publishers, 1984), 482.
4   Balibar, "Occasional Notes on Communism," *Krisis: Journal for Contemporary Philosophy*, no. 1 (2011), 7–8.
5   Karl Marx, "Contribution to the Critique of Hegel's *Philosophy of Law*." Introduction in MECW, vol. 3 (Moscow: Progress, 1975), 187.
6   See Kōjin Karatani, *Transcritique: On Kant and Marx*, trans. Sabu Kohso (Cambridge, MA: MIT Press, 2003).
7   Following this reading, we might "flip the script" on Henri Lefebvre by affirmatively

inverting and strategically misreading his declaration that existentialism was simply "the magic and metaphysics of shit," here reminding ourselves that the metaphysics of shit, as the torsional impossibility present in the labor power form, is exactly the motor force of the historical process; see Lefebvre, *L'existentialisme*, 2nd ed. (Paris: Anthropos, 2001), 63. In this sense, what is at stake in the "shit-question" is nothing less than the ontology of social being and its uncanny anterior in the form of labor, the endless loop of the putative "origin."

8   This term is central to the theoretical work of Uno Kōzō. On this point see Gavin Walker, "The Absent Body of Labour Power: Uno Kōzō's Logic of Capital," *Historical Materialism* 21, 4 (Fall 2013), 201–34, and the further developments in Gavin Walker, *The Sublime Perversion of Capital: Marxist Theory and the Politics of History in Modern Japan* (Durham, NC: Duke University Press, forthcoming).

9   See Sandro Mezzadra, "Forces and Forms: Governmentality and Bios in the Time of Global Capital," trans. Gavin Walker, in *The End of Area: Biopolitics, Geopolitics, History*, a special issue of *positions: asia critique*, ed. Gavin Walker and Naoki Sakai (Durham, NC, Duke University, forthcoming).

10   Žižek, *Less Than Nothing: Hegel and the Shadow of Dialectical Materialism* (London: Verso, 2012), 251–52.

11   Jacques Lacan, "La science et la vérité" in *Écrits*, t. 2 (Paris: Seuil, 1966), 349–50. The formulations in the following paragraphs are developed at greater length in Gavin Walker, "The World of Principle, or Pure Capitalism: Exteriority and Suspension in Uno Kōzō," *Journal of International Economic Studies* 26 (2012), 15–37, and in Walker, *The Sublime Perversion of Capital*.

12   Karl Marx, "Economic Manuscripts of 1857–1858 [Grundrisse]" in *Marx-Engels Collected Works*, vol. 28 (Moscow: Progress Publishers, 1986), 386–87; Marx, "Grundrisse der Kritik der politischen Ökonomie" in *Marx-Engels Werke*, Bd. 42. Berlin, Institut für Marxismus-Leninismus beim ZK der SED: Dietz Verlag, 1983), 370–71.

13   Marx, "Capital, vol. 1" in *Marx-Engels Collected Works*, vol. 35 (New York: International Publishers, 1996), 144; Marx, "Das Kapital," bd. 1 in *Marx-Engels Werke*, Bd. 23, Berlin, Institut für Marxismus-Leninismus beim ZK der SED: Dietz Verlag, 1962), 140.

14   Marx, "Economic Manuscripts of 1857–1858 [Grundrisse]" in *Marx-Engels Collected Works*, vol. 29 (Moscow: Progress Publishers, 1987), 8; Marx, "Grundrisse der Kritik der politischen Ökonomie" in *Marx-Engels Werke*, Bd. 43. Berlin, Institut für Marxismus-Leninismus beim ZK der SED: Dietz Verlag, 1983), 520.

15   Marx, "Economic Manuscripts of 1857–1858 [Grundrisse]" in *Marx-Engels Collected Works*, vol. 29 (Moscow: Progress Publishers, 1987), 16; Marx, "Grundrisse der Kritik der politischen Ökonomie" in *Marx-Engels Werke*, Bd. 43. Berlin, Institut für Marxismus-Leninismus beim ZK der SED: Dietz Verlag, 1983), 528.

16   Marx, "Economic Manuscripts of 1857–1858 [Grundrisse]" in *Marx-Engels Collected Works*, vol. 28 (Moscow: Progress Publishers, 1986), 365; Marx, "Grundrisse der Kritik der politischen Ökonomie" in *Marx-Engels Werke*, Bd. 43. Berlin, Institut für Marxismus-Leninismus beim ZK der SED: Dietz Verlag, 1983), 378–79.

17   Balibar, "Sur la dialectique historique: Quelques remarques critiques à propos de Lire le capital" in *Cinq études du matérialisme historique* (Paris: Maspero, 1974), 213.

18   Marx, "Capital, vol. 1" in *Marx-Engels Collected Works*, vol. 35 (New York: International Publishers, 1996), 375–76 n. 2; Marx, "Das Kapital," bd. 1 in *Marx-Engels Werke*, Bd. 23, Berlin, Institut für Marxismus-Leninismus beim ZK der SED: Dietz Verlag, 1962), 393n89.

19   Slavoj Žižek, ". . . Ce seul objet dont le néant s'honore" in *Filozofski vestnik* 26, no. 2 (2005), 12.

20   Balibar and Wallerstein, *Race, Nation, Class* (London: Verso, 1991), 90.

21   Slavoj Žižek, *The Ticklish Subject* (London: Verso, 1999), 238.

22   For an expansion of this point, see Gavin Walker, "Citizen-Subject and the National Question: On the Logic of Capital in Balibar." *Postmodern Culture* 22, no. 3 (Baltimore: Johns Hopkins University Press, 2012).

23   Slavoj Žižek, *The Year of Dreaming Dangerously* (London: Verso, 2012), 29.

24   Letter of Marx to Engels, April 30, 1868, in *Marx-Engels Collected Works*, vol. 43 (Moscow: Progress Publishers, 1988), 20.

25   Such a possibility of politics also would involve a necessary rethinking of the question of political organization and political invention. I attempt to develop this point in Gavin Walker, "The Body of Politics: On the Concept of the Party," *Theory and Event* 16, no. 4 and in Gavin Walker, "The Reinvention of Communism: Politics, History, Globality" in *South Atlantic Quarterly* 113, no. 4 (forthcoming).

13

Žižek as a Reader of Marx, Marx as a Reader of Žižek

Geoff Pfeifer

One very productive way of understanding Žižek's Marxism is to read it as an extended attempt to flesh out the meaning and implications of the famous line from the beginning of *The Eighteenth Brumaire of Louis Bonaparte* where Marx writes: "men make their own history, but they do not make it just as they please; they do not make it under circumstances chosen by themselves, but under circumstances directly encountered, given, and transmitted from the past."[1] In this we see, in an extremely condensed form, the two main components of Marx's thought on history and social change: on the one hand individual subjects are who and what they are as a result of the material circumstances and social structures—culture, traditions, government, economies, class, and so on—in which they find themselves; here there is very little actual agency for individuals. On the other hand, however, Marx claims, it is out of this determinism that individuals and groups become able to "make history" or bring about change in the social world and thus have the potential to break the hold of the weight of such history and circumstance. Many commentators when discussing Žižek's Marxism tend to focus primarily on his emphasis on the theory of ideology or his Leninism.[2] I want to begin with something lesser noted but equally important (and ultimately foundational for both the conception of ideology and Žižek's overall philosophical view), namely the importance Žižek places on Marx's analysis of the commodity form and its nature as an abstraction.

In *The Sublime Object of Ideology*, Žižek argues that Marx's conception of the commodity form has been so influential because it

> offers a kind of matrix enabling us to generate all other forms of the "fe-
> tishistic inversion": it is as if the dialectics of the commodity form presents
> us with a pure—distilled so to speak—version of a mechanism offering us
> a key to the theoretical understanding of phenomena which, at first sight,
> have nothing whatsoever to do with the field of political economy (law,
> religion, and so on). In the commodity form there is definitely something
> more at stake than the commodity form itself and it was precisely this
> "more" which exerted such a fascinating power of attraction.[3]

He goes on to argue, in reference to the work of Alfred Sohn-Rethel on this particular topic, that the commodity form as analyzed by Marx reveals the: "skeleton of the Kantian transcendental subject. . . . Herein lies the paradox of the commodity form: it—this inner-worldly "pathological" (in the Kantian meaning of the word) phenomenon—offers us the key to solving the fundamental question of the theory of knowledge: objective knowledge with universal validity—how is this possible?"[4]

What the commodity form, as analyzed by Marx, gives us is a glimpse into the material foundation of subjectivity (and of the society in which subjectivity finds itself) as well as the objective (in a Kantian sense) forms of knowing through which subjects grasp their world. There is no need to rehearse Marx's detailed analysis of the commodity form here (as it is well-worn territory), but in order to understand the point being made, we should recall briefly that on Marx's reading of it, a thing is a commodity insofar as it comes to have not merely use-value but also exchange-value, which ultimately becomes its defining feature over against use-value.[5]

Since it is the case that exchange-value is not connected to (and dominates) use-value, the commodity form itself is, as Marx argues, "characterized by a total abstraction from use-value," reflecting only quantity (or a monetarily quantifiable value)—a quantity that can be measured against other commodities and their value-as-quantity—and not quality.[6] Further explaining this point Marx writes: "Could commodities themselves speak, they would say: our use-value may be a thing of interest to men. It is no part of us as objects. What however does belong to us as objects is our value. Our natural intercourse as commodities proves it. In the eyes of each other, we are nothing but exchange-values."[7] Both

exchange-value and the commodity that results from it are born of a
social relation, or an act, namely, the exchange of commodities. This act
is itself born in a particular social context (capitalism). In this act, the
abstraction that is the commodity is, as Marx describes in the passage
above, treated *as if* it is the bearer of value in-itself (and not simply of
use to individuals) and it ultimately becomes this "as-if." It is here that
Sohn-Rethel's analysis of Marx becomes important, according to Žižek.
Sohn-Rethel shows us that this "as-if" does not arise in the consciousness
of those who engage in the exchange of commodities, but it is the structure inherent to this that determines the very being of that consciousness.
Here is Sohn-Rethel:

> The essence of commodity abstraction, however, is that it is not thought-
> induced; it does not originate in men's minds, but in their actions. And
> yet this does not give "abstraction" a merely metaphorical meaning. It is
> an abstraction in its precise literal sense. The economic concept of value
> resulting from it is characterized by a complete absence of quality, a dif-
> ferentiation purely by quantity and by applicability to every kind of com-
> modity and service which can occur in the market. . . . It exists nowhere
> other than in the human mind but it does not spring from it. Rather it is
> purely social in character, arising in the sphere of spatio-temporal human
> relations. It is [again] not people who originate these abstractions, but
> their actions.[8]

There are two important features of the Marxian analysis that Sohn-
Rethel seeks to clarify here (and that Žižek both agrees with and wishes
to extend). First, the abstraction inherent in the commodity form is, as
noted, founded on human action. The point here is similar to the point
that Louis Althusser makes in his view that it is action, or social practice,
that is primary and consciousness is built on this.[9] Second, as also noted,
it is the result of a particular form of social existence (namely the capitalist form). It is this abstraction that does the determining of the form of
thought for individuals who exist under capitalism and capitalist modes
of production with their attendant social relations.

Though we can see broad agreement between Sohn-Rethel and Althusser, insofar as both see social practice as being prior to and determi-
native of the consciousness of individuals, Sohn-Rethel criticizes por-
tions of Louis Althusser's reading of Marx's analysis of commodity

abstraction in that Althusser, rather than taking Marx's analysis literally, sees it as metaphorical.[10] Žižek also agrees broadly with the Althusserian thesis regarding the primacy of practice.[11] In *The Sublime Object*, however, Žižek opts for Sohn-Rethel's analysis over against that of Althusser insofar as it radicalizes the Althusserian "distinction between the real object and the object of knowledge" and allows us to view abstraction as a "third element which subverts the very field of this distinction; the form of thought previous and external to thought—in short: the symbolic order."[12] I will return to a discussion of Žižek's linking of Sohn-Rethel's critique of the commodity form to the Lacanian concept of the symbolic order later. For now, the important point is that abstraction, as Marx understands it, is not to be thought of as metaphorical, something that has no reality or, finally, a distortion of an underlying nonabstract existence; the abstraction that is the commodity form, its attendant act, and the forms of consciousness that are derived from it are very real and, as just pointed out, ultimately foundational.

I should pause for a moment here to point out that the conception of abstraction under consideration is that of Marx's mature, post-1857 renovation of the Feuerbachian notion of abstraction—what Alberto Toscano (with reference to Roberto Finelli) calls the "real-abstract" or "real-abstraction"—which is, as Toscano puts it,

> a break with a generic, humanist, or anthropological concept of abstraction: the passage to a notion of *real abstraction*—abstraction not merely as a mask, fantasy, or diversion, but as a force operative in the world . . . the crucial theoretical revolution would then be one that passes through this fundamentally intellectualist notion of abstraction—which presumes liberation as a "recovery" of the presupposed genus (putting Man where God, qua distorted humanity, had once stood)—to a vision of abstraction that, rather than depicting it as a structure of illusion, recognizes it as a social, historical, and "transindividual" phenomenon.[13]

There is no illusion. The "abstraction" of the commodity form and the web of human relations that determine it are what is "real" full-stop. The real-abstraction that is the commodity form is, as Toscano argues, the "transindividual" phenomenon that acts to determine both capitalist society and the ways in which individual capitalist subjects come into being (from capitalist subjectivity to proletarian subjectivity, and every other possible subject of capital). Or, as Toscano puts it (giving it a proper Hegelian inflection): "this real-abstract movement of totalization is capital qua substance becoming 'Subject.'"[14]

Furthermore, in referring to real-abstraction as "transindividual," Toscano points us to Balibar, who argues in *The Philosophy of Marx* that though Marx did not have the terminology to name the "transindividual phenomena" as such, it is a concept that captures Marx's meaning when he writes in the *Theses on Feuerbach* of the human essence as nothing more than the "ensemble of social relations" that exists at a given time (of which the abstraction that is the commodity-form, and the act of exchange on which it is based, is a part under capitalism).[15] Balibar continues: "The words Marx uses reject *both* the individualist point of view (the primacy of the individual, and especially the fiction of an individuality which could be defined *in itself*, in isolation, whether in terms of biology, psychology, economic behavior or whatever), *and* the organicist point of view (which today, following the *Anglo-American* usage, is also called the holistic point of view: the primacy of the *whole*, and particularly of society considered as an indivisible unity of which individuals are functional members)."[16] Here we begin to see a link back to the first part of Marx's claim from the *Eighteenth Brumaire*, quoted at the beginning of this chapter. Individual subjects and the form of thought that attends these subjects are—pace the real-abstraction founded in the act of commodity exchange—what they are as a *result* of the social relations in which they are enmeshed. The social form of commodity exchange (and the social practice that supports it) is *prior to* subjective constitution, and it is that through which individuals become the subjects that they are.

Returning now to Žižek's introduction of the Lacanian concept of the symbolic into this reading of Marxian abstraction so as to supplement Balibar's and Toscano's linking of the real-abstract to transindividuality, as Balibar himself notes, Lacan is one of those who offers us a theoretics that allows for a conception of transindividuality that condenses and clarifies what is at stake in Marx's analysis of abstraction and of the commodity form.[17] Elaborating on this, Žižek shows us how the symbolic order functions in the same manner as Marxian "real-abstraction": "insofar as Lacan defines the symbolic order as neither objective nor subjective, but precisely as the order of *intersubjectivity*, is not the perfect candidate for this third logic of intersubjectivity the psychoanalytic 'log of the signifier' that deploys the strange structure of the subject's relationship to the Other qua his symbolic substance, the space in which he interacts with other subjects?"[18] In fact, this should not only help us further make sense of both the argument that real-abstraction and the commodity form are themselves foundational to the production of subjectivity under capitalism but also give us some insight into how such a foundation is itself not an illusion, while at the same time it remains an abstraction. What intervenes between the objective, taken as the "brute" empirical fact, and the subjective—thought—is precisely the symbolic order. Take Žižek's example of this in relation to how we, as sociolinguistic subjects, come to hear "meaning" in what are otherwise nothing more than brute linguistic utterances: "When I hear a word, not only do I immediately abstract from its sound and 'see through it' to its meaning (recall the weird experience of becoming aware of the non-transparent vocal stuff of a word—it appears as intrusive and obscene . . .), but I have to do it if I am to experience meaning."[19]

As with the practice of commodity exchange, language is a transindividual, intersubjective, real-abstract *thing* that is formed out of the relations between various historically grounded linguistic meanings and practices that exist in a given sociohistorical space, the totality of which can be likened to a social substance or Spirit (*Geist*) in Hegelian parlance. Such a substance is, as Žižek argues, the third moment in the triad and acts to interpellate (to use an Althusserian term) individuals as its subjects insofar as individuals enter into the preexisting meanings—and the practices that support them—of a given sociohistorical community, so much so that, as in the example given above, even our very physical apparatuses (hearing in this instance) are trained by this substance in its constituting us as subjects. Returning now to the real-abstraction of the commodity form, here again is Žižek echoing much of what I have said already while at the same time reiterating the Marxian analysis of the violent nature of capital: "this 'abstraction' . . . is the 'real' in the precise sense of determining the structure of material social processes themselves: The fate of whole swaths of the population and sometimes whole countries can be decided by the 'solipsistic speculative dance of capital, which pursues its goal of profitability with blessed indifference to how its movements will affect social reality. Therein lies the fundamental systemic violence of capitalism . . . [it is] no longer attributable to concrete individuals and their "evil" intentions, but is purely "objective, systemic, anonymous." Žižek continues: "here we encounter the Lacanian difference between the reality and the Real: 'Reality' is the social reality of the actual people involved in interaction and the productive process, while the Real is the inexorable 'abstract' spectral logic of Capital that determines what goes on in social reality."[20] So, putting all of this together, we might say that the "Reality" of systemic violence is imposed on individual subjects of capital by the "Real," which is itself the result of the social practices (such as the act of commodity exchange). These practices in turn, make up the real-abstract, intersubjective, transindividual, symbolic substrate within which such subjects are founded.

What now of the second moment in the quotation from *The Eighteenth Brumaire*? How do we go from a seemingly all-encompassing lack of subjective freedom to a conception of the possibility of that subjective freedom and further, the possibility of revolutionary change? We can see this most fully if we now—with Lacan in view—turn for a moment to Žižek's materialist reading of Hegel.

In the opening pages of *The Parallax View* Žižek renders his materialist position in this way:

> materialism is not the direct assertion of my inclusion in objective reality (such an assertion presupposes that my position of enunciation is that of an external observer who can grasp the whole of reality); rather, it resides in the reflexive twist by means of which I am included in the picture constituted by me—it is this reflexive short circuit, this necessary redoubling of myself as standing both outside and inside my picture that bears witness to my "material existence." Materialism means that the reality I see is never "whole"—not because a large part of it eludes me, but because it contains a stain, a blind spot, which indicates my inclusion in it.[21]

The "redoubling of myself" that Žižek refers to here can be understood in relation to what I have said above. It is the redoubling that occurs in my awareness of myself (and my world) as built for me out of the material of the historico-communally grounded (transindividual) symbolic order that exists for me (that is, my *inclusion* as a being that is itself constructed by that symbolic universe and its relations) *and at the same time* my awareness of (in a properly materialist awareness anyway) the fact that my awareness of this is itself partial and limited. Adrian Johnston puts this point in this way: "what appears as external reflection (i.e. the gaze of the subject on substance) is not confined to an epistemological field separated off from the reflected-upon reality of being. Rather than being external, this reflection is inscribed in the reality of being upon which it reflects as an internal inflection, an immanent folding-back of substance on itself; the gaze of the subject upon substance is substance-as-not-all gazing upon itself."[22]

In this way, Žižek's materialism is not a rejection of the ideal altogether, or a relegating of it to another realm, but an embracing of the existence—and determining power—of the ideal qua subjectivity in a quasi–Kantian sense, but with a Lacanian-Hegelian twist in which the ideal itself is located as emerging *in*, and out of, the real-abstraction of the material symbolic. As such, subjectivity is itself (even in its ideality), materially generated, universally always-already partial, limited, and not-All there is.

If this is correct, if the finite, pathological, and limited ideal—even though it is that through which reality is constituted for us—emerges, as I have shown, out of the material, if the subject is, in Hegelian fashion (as Toscano has asserted), simultaneously substance, the question is then *how* does such a split, such a redoubling emerge? Or, as Žižek himself asks the question in *The Parallax View*, "how, from within the flat order of positive being, [does] the very gap between thought and being, the negativity of being, emerge?"[23]

One way Žižek works to make sense of this is by looking to Hegel's conception of "habit"—which here functions as a nice stand-in for the conception of social practice explored above—as our naturally extant "second nature": "it is not that the human animal breaks with nature through a creative explosion of Spirit, which then gets habituated, alienated, turned into mindless habit: the reduplication of nature in 'second nature' is primordial, that is, it is only this reduplication that opens up the space for spiritual creativity."[24]

The argument here goes as follows (echoing, again, much of what I have said already): the distinction between first nature and second nature is, for the human, *not really a distinction*—we are beings whose first nature is to be beings who have a second nature. This second nature—signified here as a collection of historically contingent and changing "habits" that are built out of what is communally acceptable and founded—is what organizes and constructs subjectivity's appearance. In this way, subjectivity is the internalization of that which is originally external and communal.

These subjective habits are truly habits insofar as they are experienced *by the individual subject* not as contingent chosen activities but rather as the necessary features of existence. One such set of habits is, as I have shown, linguistic habits, in which we become habituated to hear meaning. (Another is, obviously, the habits generated by the act of commodity exchange.) In this way, through habituation to and in historico-cultural practices (linguistic and otherwise), the actions themselves are "freed" from their material foundations, and this is reduplicated at a second level, which becomes the most important level. (Note once more the structural similarity here with how Marx describes the liberation of the commodity from its value-as-use in the creation of exchange-value.) Again referencing Hegel, Žižek argues: "Hegel emphasizes again and again that . . . habit provides the background and foundation for every exercise of freedom . . . through habits, a human being transforms his body into a mobile and fluid means, the soul's instrument, which serves as such without us having to focus consciously on it. In short, through habits, *the subject appropriates the body*."[25]

The freedom Žižek speaks of here is the emergent freedom of thought out of being, the transcendent out of the material, the "inner" out of the "outer" in which the outer (the body) comes to be regulated and controlled by this inner (the subject), which itself is first found externally to the individual (in the material real-abstract of the transindividual symbolic): "The conclusion to be drawn is thus that the only way to account for the emergence of the distinction between the 'inside' and 'outside' constitutive of a living organism is to posit a kind of self-reflexive reversal by means of which—to put it in Hegelese—the One of an organism as a whole retroactively 'posits' as its result, as that which dominates and regulates, the set of its own causes (i.e., the very multiple processes out of which it emerged)."[26]

I am enmeshed in the real-abstract social practices and structures that exist at a given time. These become the inner structure of my subjectivity as they are internalized by me and become part of who and what I am. At the same time this inner structure is then imposed on the world—by me—and is what acts as the "virtual" or "immaterial" limit of the world itself. In other words, I experience this limit—set by me in my subjective conceptual presuppositions—as an externally imposed limit. In this way my own positing activity is what imposes the limits and the concepts through which I understand my world: "In this way—and only in this way—an organism is no longer limited by external conditions, but is fundamentally self-limited—again, as Hegel would have articulated it, life emerges when the external limitation (of an entity by its environs) turns into self-limitation."[27]

Returning to Kant, Žižek continues: "there is a link to Kant here, to the old enigma of what, exactly Kant had in mind with his notion of 'transcendental apperception,' of self-consciousness accompanying every act of my consciousness (when I am conscious of something, I am thereby always also conscious of the fact that I am conscious of this)? Is it not an obvious fact that this is empirically not true, that I am not always reflexively aware of my awareness itself?"[28]

I am, in a very precise way, *not* aware of the presuppositions that I extend to my world in my everyday quotidian dealings with it, but it is these presuppositions that act as the very frame and filter of my cognition. This frame, however—and this is the important point—though it is ideal, in the sense of being the immaterial imposition of the subject-as-constructed out of the material, has a concrete effect on the reality that I experience. It is here that we can best see the link between the Žižekian reading of the Marxian notion of real-abstraction via the commodity form that I have been discussing and the theory of ideology: my world is an ideological construction insofar as it is retroactively posited (by me, in the already described subjective reduplication, without my awareness) as a closed whole, but as just mentioned, this positing activity is not merely imaginary: it has real consequences for the world as it exists. In further delineating this point Žižek invokes Deleuze:

> the solution to this dilemma is precisely the notion of virtuality in a strict Deleuzian sense, as the actuality of the possible, as a paradoxical entity, the very possibility of which already produces/has actual effects. One should oppose Deleuze's notion of the virtual to the all-pervasive topic of virtual reality: what matters to Deleuze is not virtual reality, but the *reality of the virtual* (which in Lacanian terms, is the Real). *Virtual reality* in itself is a rather miserable idea: that of imitating reality, of reproduc-

ing its experience in an artificial medium. *The reality of the virtual*, on the other hand, stands for the reality of the virtual as such, for its real effects and consequences.[29]

"Virtual" here is, of course, the term signifying the "inner" immaterial product—the subjective posits/presuppositions—of the "outer" material structures—historically bound social practices—that in turn, comes to have a decisive effect on the material world.

If the story I have told accounts for the material generation and constraint of individual conscious awareness, as it offers an explanation of the ways in which subjectivity is constructed by, supports, and reproduces the existing set of social practices (especially those under capitalism such as commodity exchange) and habits—via a retroactively posited virtualized totalization—it also, as I have begun to show, offers us a brief sketch of the ways in which the possibility of revolutionary change appears on the scene, according to Žižek. That there are "subjects" at all is a change (as the subject is the immaterial shift that arises out of the material). Further, Žižek's account of subjectivity's nature as self-limiting makes its own action the foundation for change, to the extent that individual subjects can become aware of their own power as the self-limiting entities that they have become as a result of the material processes in which they find themselves (and out of which they were first constructed).

This is a point not to be missed. In the contemporary moment of the reemergence of a radical politics and a theoretical "return to Marx," Žižek's Marxism offers us a way to see that the materially emergent subjective act of self-limitation can be put into the service not only of the existing transindividual constellation of social practices but also of a vital oppositional force. This is to say, that we can come to realize that the real-abstract out of which we were first formed is not all there is, that subjectivity itself is, in its very nature, already a break with that which determines its form, insofar as it is the very example of a more-than-material thing.

This, again, offers the demonstration that the existing real-abstract (which is conditioned in large part by the commodity form and the act of exchange) is not all there is and the hope (and possibility) of some kind of social existence that is radically other than the current one. We should, thus, reassert that famous claim that Marx and Engels make in the *Manifesto* but with a slightly different tone. It really is true that capitalism and capitalist social relations create "the weapons that bring death to itself"; not only in the classical sense of the revolutionary potential of the proletariat but also insofar as the capitalist real-abstract creates a more than material subjectivity itself.[30]

Notes

1   Karl Marx, *The Eighteenth Brumaire of Louis Bonaparte*, in *Karl Marx: Selected Writings*, 2nd ed., ed. David McLellan (Oxford: Oxford University Press, 2006), 329.
2   See, for instance, Matthew Sharpe, "Žižek," in *From Agamben to Žižek*, ed. Jon Simons (Edinburgh: Edinburgh University Press, 2010), and Ian Parker, *Slavoj Žižek: A Critical Introduction* (London: Pluto Press, 2004).
3   Slavoj Žižek, *The Sublime Object of Ideology* (London: Verso, 2008), 9.
4   Žižek, *The Sublime Object of Ideology*, 10.
5   See Karl Marx, *Critique of Political Economy*, trans. N. I. Stone (Chicago: Charles Kerr, 1904).
6   Marx, *Capital*, vol. 1, in *Karl Marx: Selected Writings*, 460.
7   Marx, *Capital*, 480.
8   Alfred Sohn-Rethel, *Intellectual and Manual Labor: A Critique of Epistemology*, trans. Martin Sohn-Rethel (London: MacMillan, 1978), 20.
9   For Althusser's own description of the foundational nature of social practice, see Louis Althusser, "Ideology and Ideological State Apparatuses," in *Lenin and Philosophy and Other Essays*, trans. Ben Brewster (New York: Monthly Review Press, 1971).
10   Sohn-Rethel, *Intellectual and Manual Labor*, 20.
11   For a detailed account of this relation see Geoff Pfeifer, *The New Materialism: Althusser, Badiou, and Žižek* (New York: Routledge, forthcoming), especially chapter 2.
12   Žižek, *The Sublime Object of Ideology*, 19.
13   Alberto Toscano, "The Open Secret of Real Abstraction," in *Re-thinking Marxism: A Journal of Economics, Society, and Culture* 20, 2 (2008), 273–87.
14   Toscano, "The Open Secret of Real Abstraction."
15   Marx, *Theses on Feuerbach*, in *Karl Marx: Selected Writings*, 172.
16   Etienne Balibar, *The Philosophy of Marx*, trans. Chris Turner (New York: Verso, 1995), 31.
17   Balibar, *The Philosophy of Marx*. He points this out directly after the passage just cited.
18   Slavoj Žižek, *The Ticklish Subject: The Absent Centre of Political Ontology* (London: Verso, 2000), 81.
19   Slavoj Žižek, "Discipline between Two Freedoms: Madness and Habit in German Idealism," in Markus Gabriel and Slavoj Žižek, *Mythology, Madness, and Laughter: Subjectivity in German Idealism* (New York: Continuum, 2009), 106.

20 Slavoj Žižek, *Less Than Nothing: Hegel and the Shadow of Dialectical Materialism* (London: Verso, 2012), 244.
21 Slavoj Žižek, *The Parallax View* (Cambridge, MA: MIT Press, 2006), 17.
22 Adrian Johnston, *Žižek's Ontology: A Transcendental Materialist Theory of Subjectivity* (Evanston: Northwestern University Press, 2008), 166.
23 Žižek, *The Parallax View*, 6.
24 Žižek, "Discipline between Two Freedoms," 100.
25 Žižek, "Discipline between Two Freedoms," 101.
26 Žižek, "Discipline between Two Freedoms," 106.
27 Žižek, "Discipline between Two Freedoms," 106.
28 Žižek, "Discipline between Two Freedoms," 109.
29 Žižek, "Discipline between Two Freedoms," 109. Emphasis in the original.
30 Karl Marx and Friedrich Engels, "The Communist Manifesto," in *Karl Marx: Selected Writings*, 250.

14

A Plea for

Agon Hamza | **Žižekian Politics**

Theoretical work, I am more convinced each day, brings to the world more than practical work; once the world of ideas is revolutionized, actuality cannot remain as it is.
—G. W. F. Hegel, letter to Friedrich Immanuel Niethammer, October 28, 1808

Is it possible to think politics based on the premises of the Žižekian philosophy, which is to say, is it possible to think of a particular ring of the Borromean knot (constituted of philosophy, psychoanalysis, and politics, as proposed by Žižek himself) and thus attempt to think *the* Žižekian politics as such? Žižekian politics, first and foremost, means a politics that is not so much a politics as a procedure of identifying and solving real and concrete (actual) problems. The preliminary task is constructing a politics based on the premises of what the Žižekian philosophy is: politics is the name of the problem, rather than the name of the solution. Therefore, when thinking about it, what is required is the "courage to conceive of theorizing not only as interpretation, which in itself cannot break through the social fantasy and its endless chain of alibis, but also as a reorientation of the subject in its relation to the fundamental fantasy."[1] The reorientation should be read as separation, that is to say, as a procedure of drawing lines of demarcation (in Althusser's terms) not only between the Left and the Right but also within the Left itself. In this regard, if we maintain our fidelity to Žižek's work, the result is what Hegel would have called *the patience of the concept*: that is to say, the orientation in the thought that renders possible the emergence of the New, through an immanent critique of the problem itself or from within the coordinates of the problem itself. In Schelling's terms, which Žižek likes to quote: the beginning is the negation of that which begins with it. This enterprise manifests itself through different procedures/practices, but in this chapter I will focus on two important aspects of his political writings, as they are developed in his "communist writing series": the Idea of Communism and the critique of ideology, which in a certain instance of analysis, are correlative with one another.

Political Variants

The standard reproach to Žižek's conception of politics is that he constantly changes his positions in relation to concrete situations. Peter Hallward argues that depending on the situation, "Žižek may urge us to withdraw and '*do nothing*' (in moments when 'the truly violent act is doing nothing, a refusal to act'), or to embrace the impossible and thus '*do everything*' (as illustrated by Stalin's 'revolution from above'), or again (on the model of Aristide or Chávez) to adopt the more pragmatic posture of someone who is at least prepared to 'do *something*,' by accepting some of the compromises that accompany a readiness to take and retain state power."[2] In the first reading, Hallward's critique points toward Žižek's inconsistencies—however, the problem with it is that this is Žižek's own position with regard to his own work. That is to say, whatever the concrete situation, the relation of the subject to itself is always one of cutting off whatever ties one to the dominant ideology. Or, to put it differently, we could argue that the Žižekian-Hegelian thesis, underlying the political orientation, is that the way a situation doesn't work as the mere "case" of a universal idea is precisely how the universal is grounded in that situation. In other words, Žižek treats conjunctures not as cases but as examples.

How should this be read? In *Seminar XVIII*, Lacan provided what can be called the truth of interpretation: according to him, "interpretation is not tested by a truth that would decide by yes or no, it unleashes truth as such. It is only true inasmuch as it is truly followed."[3] Žižek reads this as the dialectical unity of theory and practice, that is to say, "the 'test' of the analyst's interpretation lies in the truth-effect it unleashes in the patient."

According to Žižek, this gives us the perspective for (yet another) reading of Marx's Thesis XI: "the 'test' of Marxist theory is the truth-effect it
unleashes in its addressees (the proletarians), in transforming them into
revolutionary subjects."[4] Here one should supplement this with Žižek's
other reading of Marx's Thesis XI: "the first task today is precisely NOT
to succumb to the temptation to act, to directly intervene and change
things . . . but to question the hegemonic ideological coordinates."[5]
This dialectical mediation of theory and practice, which is based in a
Hegelian matrix, goes against Hallward's concept of self-determination,
or "the will of the people," by which he understands "a deliberate, emancipatory and inclusive process of collective self-determination."[6] Žižek's
concept goes against that of Hallward's because in Hegel's position, voluntarism (albeit not denied its importance) is posited as a step toward
thinking. That is to say, we must act not in such a way as to change the
world but because practice itself is a moment of the concept. And just as
the truth-effect in Lacan's theory of interpretation is not superimposed
to the world but added to it, in Hegel's theory of the concept as the unity
of practice and theory, only the concept can be truly added to a world.
Unreflected practices cannot but handle what is already there. Therefore, the way to summarize Žižek's politics is through the title of his talk
in the first series of the *Idea of Communism* conferences: "to begin from
the beginning," that is to say, a ruthless insistence on theoretical (philosophical) rigor with a realistic and pragmatic intervention in our predicament. When Žižek calls us to "step back and think" it is not a call
of the "beautiful soul"—that position that presupposes the higher moral
position of a given subjectivity that will do no wrong. The urge to do
nothing doesn't imply a neutral position with regard to a certain political development, a political event, popular uprising, or even elections,
critique or even celebrate them from a certain (usually a safe) distance.
Žižek does not urge us to withdraw from acting into thinking, thus occupying a position that, from a higher "moral" position, is always afraid
of wrongdoings. What the beautiful soul tends to forget is that moral insights don't have a say in how the spirit actualizes itself and takes a given
form: in this enterprise, the moral insights fall into oblivion. But the fault
of the "'beautiful soul,' of this gentle, fragile, sensitive form of subjectivity which, from its safe position as innocent observer, deplores the
wicked ways of the world,"[7] is not its inactivity, the fact that it only com-

plains about the world around itself without doing anything to change or revolutionize it. The falsity of the "beautiful soul" is "in the very mode of activity implied by this position of inactivity—in the way the "beautiful soul" structures the "objective" social world in advance so that it is able to assume, to play in it, the role of the fragile, innocent, and passive victim."[8] When Žižek calls us to "do nothing" he is not calling us to occupy the position of a passive victim or that of a benevolent spectator, i.e., he's not urging us *not to take position*. "Do nothing" doesn't equal the "stubborn insistence on its own isolated self-existence, but only to bring forth the soulless, spiritless unity of abstract being."[9] In some situations "the pressure 'to do something' here is like the superstitious compulsion to make some gesture when we are observing a process over which we have no real influence. Are not our acts often such gestures? The old saying 'Don't just talk, do something!' is one of the most stupid things one can say, even measured by the low standards of common sense. Perhaps, rather, the problem lately has been that we have been doing too much, such as intervening in nature, destroying the environment, and so forth." Taking this into account, "perhaps it is time to step back, think and say the right thing. True, we often talk about something instead of doing it; but sometimes we also do things in order to avoid talking and thinking about them. Such as throwing $700 billion at a problem instead of reflecting on how it arose in the first place."[10] In some particular constellation, doing something can be more problematic than mere passivity. That is to say, sometimes it is

> better to do nothing than to engage in localized acts whose ultimate function is to make the system run smoother (acts like providing the space for the multitude of new subjectivities, etc.). The threat today is not passivity, but pseudo-activity, the urge to "be active," to "participate," to mask the Nothingness of what goes on. People intervene all the time, "do something," academics participate in meaningless "debates," etc., and the truly difficult thing is to step back, to withdraw from it. Those in power often prefer even a "critical" participation, a dialogue, to silence—just to engage us in a "dialogue," to make it sure our ominous passivity is broken.[11]

In this regard, "doing nothing" in itself implies two different stances in the political struggle: a) in a given situation, the most subversive and violent act is to resist the temptation to act, and b) not involving ourselves in those struggles that are not ours, that is to say, in the pseudostruggles that do not possess any emancipatory potential. In sum, there is "a doing nothing" that is an activity, an act, that marks a negativity, and there is a "doing nothing" that means simply not doing anything and thereby recognizing that nothing in fact took place. By occupying this political position, that is, by refusing to participate in a struggle that at its best will be carried out under the terms determined by the present, we engage in a much more difficult process: that of thinking. In a situation where basic coordinates are too opaque and obscure, we are offered an expert-knowledge as solution: the knowledge based on the problematic defined by the ruling ideology. Against this, we should return to pure theory, that is, philosophy. Žižek's favorite example is Lenin's act: when the revolution failed in 1914, he went to Switzerland and studied Hegel's *Logic*. Today, we must return from Marx to Hegel. More than the shift between two particular names, the "return to Hegel" should be understood as the return to philosophy, to pure thinking. When Žižek writes that "we must trust theory," what he means is that "today, more than ever, one should bear in mind that Communism begins with the 'public use of reason,' with thinking, with the egalitarian universality of thought."[12] When we think of examples of real practical political movements, we always find something weirdly void or negative about them—and for Hegel and Žižek, this negative aspect is thinking itself, which exists as a real abstraction in "pure" practice as well. This insight ties Žižek back with Badiou, because for both of them thinking is the ground that encompasses both "reflective" and "immanent" abstractions, both thinking that appears to itself as such and thinking as implicated immanently in true practice.[13] That being said, we could say that even those who think they espouse the opposite position, of advocating a "pure practice," are also unconsciously in agreement with Žižek regarding the primacy of thought (i.e., "purity") as the index of politics.

The Dirty Hands of Politics

The other fundamental aspect of a Žižekian political orientation is its pragmatic approach to taking state power. Unlike Badiou, who argues that "Marxism, the workers' movement, mass democracy, Leninism, the proletarian party, the Socialist state—all these remarkable inventions of the twentieth century—are no longer of practical use,"[14] Žižek responds that not only the apparatus of the party form and the orientation of taking state power but also the failure of twentieth-century communism was due to its distancing, not its proximity, to power. He stands against the all too comfortable position of self-organization movements, which lack a central body or authority to regulate their movement, and their (frequent) refusal of the idea of the party or of the taking over of state power, as such movements are always reduced to some form of civil society movement that tries to exert pressure onto those in power. According to Žižek, it is "the tetrad of *people—movement—party—leader*"[15] that can accomplish the next step; that is to say, we need a strong body or authority to reorganize or restructure our entire social and political life, from making the harsh and difficult decisions to implementing them. In this regard, Žižek puts forward another highly polemic thesis: although "anti-capitalism cannot be directly the goal of political action— in politics, one opposes concrete political agents and their actions, not an anonymous 'system,' nevertheless, it should be its ultimate aim, the horizon of all its activity."[16] This strategy can be summarized by distinguishing between two types of politics: we should leave Politics (with a capital *P*) for thinking, and in this way we will be able to be more realistic about what politics (with a small *p*) can in fact accomplish. This does not mean that we shouldn't do it, but it means that though pragmatism today is in line with the inherently corrupted and dirty work of politics, we should have no illusions there. The best example here of what Žižek himself would not go for is the former president of Brazil, Lula da Silva; one should rather go for Jean-Bertrand Aristide. Lula is the best example of confusing Politics with politics, that is to say, in his use of real-politics he was quite successful, until the moment he referred to politics as Politics, for example referring to basic rent not as a step in a larger socialist program but as its accomplishment. Aristide presents a more or less successful story: with his constant references to Christianity and liberation theology, he managed to safeguard the truly emancipatory dimension of Politics, while at the same time engaging on the work necessary to assure immediate victories for the people. Because the transcendental status of politics was safe through Christianity, Aristide could get his hands dirty without it leading to a corrosion of the very ideals that led him to action. In this way, he showed that nothing gets done in corrupted countries without politicians and militants engaging with the actually existing logic of corruption, but the crucial move was that he proved that this could be done without corrupting Politics as such in the process. In other words, it is part of a true political act to distinguish between Politics and politics, and to show that "corruption" is not a true political category but a particular way of structuring the relation between the law and the lawful transgression of a situation. There is no emancipatory potential in denouncing corruption itself. When we shed the Left's illusion of its own righteousness, we can clearly see that the situation in which the Left finds itself when it takes the power is not optimistic. The "historical tendencies" are against us, there is no big Other on whom we can rely. In this sense,

> is this not the predicament of the Morales government in Bolivia, of the former Aristide government in Haiti, and of the Maoist government in Nepal? They came to power through "fair" democratic elections, not through insurrection, but once in power, they exerted it in a way which was (partially, at least) "non-statal": directly mobilizing their grassroots supporters and bypassing the party-state representative network. Their situation is "objectively" hopeless: the whole drift of history is basically against them, they cannot rely on "objective tendencies"; all they can do is to improvise, do what they can in a desperate situation. Nevertheless, does this not give them a unique freedom? One is tempted to apply here the old distinction between "freedom from" and "freedom for": does their freedom from History (with its laws and objective tendencies) not sustain their freedom for creative experimentation? In their activity, they can rely only on the collective will of their supporters.[17]

This opens up the space for further complications: the difference between Politics and politics is not that of Event and nonevent. The event, in Žižekian terms, is "something shocking, out of joint, that happens all of a sudden and interrupts the usual flow of things; something that appears out of nowhere, without discernible causes, and whose ontological status is unclear—an appearance without solid being as its foundation." That is to say, in politics perhaps "we should effectively renounce the myth of a Great Awakening—the moment when (if not the old working class then) a new alliance of the dispossessed, multitude or whatever, will gather its forces and master a decisive intervention. So what if, in politics, an authentic Event is not the Event traditional Marxists are waiting for (the big Awakening of the revolutionary Subject), but something that occurs as an unexpected side-event?"[18]

Žižek's understanding of an Event is far from postmodern relativism. An event should be understood as a momentary opening of that which before it happened appeared impossible, an opening that renders possible (but not effective on its own) the entire transformation of the political, economic, and social bodies. This is how one should read protests like Occupy Wall Street, the Arab Spring, the ongoing demonstrations in Spain, Greece, and elsewhere: far from looking to history or context for rendering them meaningful, one should realize that they gain their meaning only if analyzed from the perspective of communism. In this sense, the communist hypothesis is the truly evental point: without it, these political protests around the world are indistinguishable from the physiology of the crisis/stability that is proper to capital itself. Once more, the true point of novelty is negative, that of a hypothesis, and therefore of the order of thought. This enables us to further explore Žižek's understanding of institutional and party politics, or more precisely the crisis of the Left in two dimensions: first, the problem of its notion, and second, one of the main ideological and political paradigms that characterizes the Left today. Žižek's assertion that we must "get our hands dirty" is of crucial importance but nevertheless not sufficient (and he is well aware of this). Party politics, which functions under the constraints of the state, finds its limits not only in the structure of the state apparatuses but also in the discourse of the Left itself. The ongoing protests in Europe and other parts of the world are the best examples of the poverty of our discourse and analysis of our predicament, that is to say, it renders visible very clearly the traps in which we are caught. We are fighting wrong enemies: the Left is criticizing neoliberalism and its effects, instead of capitalism. When faced with the limits of neoliberalism as a critical category, we jump into the safe moralizing position: "of course the problem is capitalism, but we have to have a name in order to grasp and criticize what is going on today. Neoliberalism designates our situation." Here we encounter the pure ideological mystification of our predicament: far from being a critical concept, neoliberalism is an ideological category/tool of analysis.[19] The important question is: What do we get as a result after completely dismantling neoliberalism? And this is where the Left stands today: in a desperate attempt to articulate itself, its positions, and its emblems, in order to convince itself and others that this is what leftism is. Paraphrasing Lacan's statement about desire, in *Subversion of the Subject*, we should rather maintain that leftism is not articulable, because it is always articulated (within the situation). That's why true leftists are not afraid to get their hands dirty: if leftism is always articulated, then it can articulate itself through whatever other name is needed—neoliberal, conservative, totalitarian, radical, whatever—such that the only trace indicating that a trajectory was in fact a leftist one will be that the adjectives it will gather may be contradictory of one another. What in Badiou's mathematical ontology is called a "generic set," a trajectory that treats a situation so immanently that no intensional property, can be ascribed to name its totality.[20]

Communism Again!

But why should we return to communism? Isn't communism a "doomed" word, discredited both intellectually and politically, especially after the terrible failure of the twentieth-century socialist experiments throughout the world and the impotence of the Left in the contemporary predicament, especially during the ongoing financial crisis? Evocation of the word "communism" is usually accompanied by two predominant reactions: (1) anticommunist paranoia, or (2) nostalgia for "good old socialist times."[21] The latter is easily accounted for: nostalgia stands for the depoliticized subjectivity, a stage of gently accepting and adapting to the new rules of the "new society." On the other hand the rise of anticommunist sentiment, not only in the East, is what should concern us, as it is accompanied by the rise of the new rightist populism, which substitutes class struggle for a more comfortable compromise formation and which is accompanying the rise of national and religious fundamentalism. The impasses of today's radical politics find their most profound elaboration in Žižek's *First as Tragedy, Then as Farce* and *Living in the End Times*, both written at the wake of the 2008 financial meltdown. Although in both books he explicitly calls for the reinvention of the idea of communism, he warns us that a blind fidelity to the Idea is not sufficient.

According to Žižek, since communism is an "eternal idea," it works as a Hegelian "concrete universality": "it is eternal not in the sense of a series of abstract-universal features that may be applied everywhere, but in the sense that it has to be reinvented in each new historical situation."[22] Therefore, communism is "not just one of the solutions but, first of all, a unique formulation of the problem as it appears within the Communist horizon."[23] Far from being a tool or the means to a solution, communism is rather the name of an impasse. It is precisely as an enigma that communism can today help us grasp certain unthought dimensions of our political situation. As Chesterton says in his *Orthodoxy*, "man can understand everything by the help of what he does not understand,"[24] communism is, today, precisely such a common useful problem. With this in mind, I can sum up Žižek's idea of communism by presenting the following four aspects of it.

The most important aspect (at the level of setting up the stage) is the question of fidelity to the idea of communism. It is not sufficient to evoke the idea of communism as an ideal;

> one has to locate within historical reality antagonisms which give this Idea a practical urgency. The only true question today is: do we endorse the predominant naturalization of capitalism, or does today's global capitalism contain antagonisms which are sufficiently strong to prevent its indefinite reproduction? There are four such antagonisms: the looming threat of an ecological catastrophe; the inappropriateness of the notion of private property in relation to so-called "intellectual property"; the socio-ethical implications of new techno-scientific developments (especially in biogenetics); and, last but not least, the creation of new forms of apartheid, new Walls and slums. There is a qualitative difference between this last feature—the gap that separates the Excluded from the Included—and the other three, which designate different aspects of what Hardt and Negri call the "commons"; the shared substance of our social being, the privatization of which involves violent acts which should, where necessary, be resisted with violent means.[25]

This constitutes the primary antagonisms within which the idea should be localized. It also gives communism its necessary Kantian aspect: communism should not be understood as being needed because we, the Left, envision a better world; rather, communism is needed because we cannot do otherwise. The real contradictions, which give the hypothesis "its practical urgency," allow us to think of communism as something like

Kantian moral law, equally empty and equally removed from our subjective aspirations and beatitudes. These first contradictions are followed by the secondary antagonisms, which are presented as the problems of the commons: the *commons of culture*, the *commons of external nature*, and the *commons of internal nature*. Note that from the perspective of the principle of contradiction, the commons is a negative category, while in the secondary antagonisms, the commons becomes a localized and positive category. And since communism is the name (at the level of the commons) of a concrete problem, Žižek identifies "four horsemen of the Apocalypse" (ecology, intellectual property, biogenetics, apartheids), whose existence is strictly connected to the radical reinterpretation of the notion of the "proletariat." The basic Marxist understanding of the proletariat is as subjectivity devoid or deprived of its substance. This notion is of extreme importance in analyzing our contemporary predicament: "we should certainly not drop the notion of the proletariat, or of the proletarian position; on the contrary, the present conjuncture compels us to radicalize it to an existential level well beyond Marx's imagination. We need a more radical notion of the proletarian subject, a subject reduced to the evanescent point of the Cartesian cogito."[26] This brings us to the third aspect of Žižek's polemical stance with regard to the "communist state." When Marx defined communism as "the *real* movement which abolishes the present state of things," he had in mind that "bourgeois cannot exist without constantly revolutionising the instruments of production, and thereby the relations of production, and with them the whole relations of society."[27] It is on this point that Žižek follows Marx, and asks the pertinent question:

> How, then, are we to revolutionize an order whose very principle is constant self-revolutionizing? . . . The Hegelian answer is that capitalism is already in itself communism, that only a purely formal reversal is needed. My surmise is: what is contemporary dynamic capitalism, precisely insofar as it is "wordless," a constant disruption of all fixed order, opens up the space for a revolution which will break the vicious cycle of revolt and its re-inscription, i.e., which will no longer follow the pattern of an evental explosion after which things return to normal, but will assume the task of a new "ordering" against the global capitalist disorder? Out of revolt we should move on shamelessly to enforcing a new order.[28]

On this point, he gives two proposals, or "axioms concerning the relationship between the State and politics":

> (1) The failure of the Communist State-Party politics is above all and primarily the failure of anti-statist politics, of the endeavor to break out of the constraints of the State, to replace statal forms of organization with "direct" non-representative forms of self-organization ("councils"). (2) If you do not have an idea of what you want to replace the State with, you have no right to subtract/withdraw from the State. Instead of withdrawing into a distance from the State, the true task should be to make the State itself work in a non-statal mode.[29]

So, how are we to do this? Can (or should) people, organized in plural rhizomatic networks, or people as such, need a central body that would do the work for them? In his *Phenomenology*, Hegel writes that "the share in the total work of mind that falls to the activity of any particular individual can only be very small."[30] This leads us to the fourth aspect of the idea of communism in Žižek's work, for we must ask: How is this to be reconciled with Žižek's call for "a new Master"? The Master here doesn't have the Lacanian status of the "subject supposed to know"—if anything, the psychoanalytic process is to dissolve the status of the Master qua the *subject supposed to know*. The concept of the Master should not be reduced to an individual (i.e., Stalin) but should be understood more as a central body that (to put it in Badiou's terms) makes it possible for the individuals to become subjects. Therefore, a true Master doesn't stand for the Father (the figure of discipline or punishment, that is, setting the coordinates of the possible and impossible); a true

> Master is a vanishing mediator who gives you back to yourself, who delivers you to the abyss of your freedom: when we listen to a true leader, we discover what we want (or, rather, what we always-already wanted without knowing it). A Master is needed because we cannot accede to our freedom directly—for to gain this access we have to be pushed from outside since our "natural state" is one of inert hedonism, of what Badiou called "human animal." The underlying paradox is here that the more we live as "free individuals with no Master," the more we are effectively non-free, caught within the existing frame of possibilities—we have to be pushed/disturbed into freedom by a Master.[31]

In this regard, the Žižekian politics, with all its vicissitudes, can be
thought only insofar as it is subjected to reinventing the idea of communism, this radical drive toward emancipation. And when we think
about the idea of communism, one has to locate the cause of a desire for
communism beyond the contingencies of one's own personal wishes or
dreams of utopia. We have to engage with the contradictions that allow
us to put the communist hypothesis to the test of the problem of the commons, its localized dimension. In doing so, we should bravely move from
the problem of the commons to a new conception of the state, and finally
we must get rid of the unilateral connotation of mastery as an alienating
force, in order to conceive of a notion of mastery that reveals, rather than
sutures, what is common.

Notes

1   Fabio Vighi, *On Žižek's Dialectics: Surplus, Subtraction, Sublimation* (New York: Con-
    tinuum, 2010), 163.
2   Peter Hallward, "Communism of the Intellect, Communism of the Will," in *The Idea
    of Communism*, ed. C. Douzinas and S. Žižek (London: Verso, 2010), 115.
3   Jacques Lacan, *D'un discours qui ne serait pas du semblant* (Paris: Seuil, 2007), 13.
4   Slavoj Žižek, *Living in the End Times* (London: Verso, 2010), xiii.
5   Slavoj Žižek, *Repeating Lenin*, 2001, *Marxists Internet Archive*. Accessed June 2014.
    www.marxists.org/reference/subject/philosophy/works/ot/zizek1.htm.
6   Peter Hallward, "The Will of the People: Notes Towards a Dialectical Voluntarism,"
    Radical Philosophy 155 (May/June 2009), 17.
7   Slavoj Žižek, *The Sublime Object of Ideology* (London: Verso, 2008), 244.
8   Žižek, *The Sublime Object of Ideology*, 244.
9   G. W. F. Hegel, *Phenomenology of Spirit* (Oxford: Oxford University Press, 1977), 407.
10 Slavoj Žižek, *First as Tragedy, Then as Farce* (London: Verso, 2009), 11.
11 Slavoj Žižek, "The Impasses of Today's Radical Politics," *Crisis and Critique* 1, 1
    (2014), 28, http://materializmidialektik.org/wp-content/uploads/2014/01/Zizek
    _Politics.pdf.
12 Slavoj Žižek, *The Year of Dreaming Dangerously* (London: Verso, 2012), 3.
13 See Alain Badiou, "Philosophy and Psychoanalysis," in *Infinite Thought: Truth and the
    Return to Philosophy*, trans. and ed. O. Feltham and J. Clemens (London: Continuum,
    2004), 79–90.
14 Alain Badiou, *The Meaning of Sarkozy* (London: Verso, 2008), 113.
15 Slavoj Žižek, "Answers without Questions," in *The Idea of Communism*, vol. 2, ed. Sla-
    voj Žižek (London: Verso, 2013), 188.
16 Žižek, "Answers without Questions," 195.

17 Žižek, *First as Tragedy, Then as Farce*, 155.

18 Slavoj Žižek, *Event: Philosophy in Transit* (London: Penguin, 2014), 184.

19 It is crucial to note that neoliberalism is a consensual notion: everybody uses it to de-nounce what is going on in the present: from the so-called far Left to neofascists like Golden Dawn.

20 In this regard, Žižek's and Badiou's support for SYRIZA remains problematic: Badiou writes that "it is better to do nothing than to contribute to the invention of formal ways of rendering visible that which Empire already recognizes as existent." Badiou is here at his Žižekian best, that is to say, he takes a profound Žižekian position. Nevertheless, the problem that arises here with regard to their support of SYRIZA is that neither of them remains faithful enough to his respective propositions or thesis. In this respect, the problem of both Žižek and Badiou is that they are not Žižekian enough: the pragmatism of SYRIZA, especially with regard to the European Union, renders impossible any possibility of opening up of the situation, of interrupting the normal flow of things and creating a vacuum that could then be filled in with a radi-cal Left program. In psychoanalytic terms, SYRIZA occupies the position of the ob-sessional neurotic: they are active all the time (which equals continuous "pragmatic" compromises) to make sure that the state of the situation in Greece will always remain the same.

21 It is interesting to note and compare the approach of Western scholarship to nostal-gia with regard to the former Socialist bloc: nostalgia for former Yugoslavia is almost normal; many Western scholars, activists, etc. still mourn the breakdown of the "great multicultural, authentic form of Yugoslav socialist management." However, the same doesn't hold for the Soviet Union: it is as if it is prohibited to express any form of nos-talgia for the post-Lenin Soviet Union.

22 Žižek, *First as Tragedy, Then as Farce*, 6.

23 Žižek, *The Impasses of Today's Radical Politics*, 16.

24 G. K. Chesterton, "Orthodoxy," in *The Everyman Chesterton*, ed. Ian Ker (London: Everyman's Library, 2011), 282.

25 Žižek, *First as Tragedy, Then as Farce*, 90–91.

26 Žižek, *First as Tragedy, Then as Farce*, 90–91, 92. Žižek gives a more detailed elabo-ration of this notion in a dispute with Catherine Malabou's *Les Nouveaux Blésses* in *Living in the End Times*, 313–14.

27 Karl Marx and Friedrich Engels, *The Communist Manifesto*, 1848, *Marxists Internet Archive*. Accessed June 2014. www.marxists.org/archive/marx/works/1848/communist -manifesto/ch01.htm#007.

28 Slavoj Žižek, "How to Begin from the Beginning?," in *The Idea of Communism*, 219.

29 Žižek, "How to Begin from the Beginning," 219.

30 Hegel, *Phenomenology of Spirit*, 45.

31 Žižek, *The Impasses of Today's Radical Politics*, 42.

PART IV | **religion**

15

The Problem of Christianity and Žižek's "Middle Period"

Adam Kotsko

Žižek repeats himself. Throughout his sprawling body of work, he returns again and again to the same problems, the same thinkers, the same concepts. Examples, jokes, and even verbatim passages recur across multiple books and articles.[1] Yet it would be overhasty to look at this repetitious style and conclude, as some have, that Žižek is essentially saying the same thing over and over. Though it can be difficult to see, Žižek's repetition is very often "nonidentical"—he is returning to recurring problems again and again in order to keep them open as problems and attack them from new directions. Hegel and Lacan remain constant points of reference, for instance, but his reading of each of them, and of the two thinkers' relationships to one another, continually evolves. The same could be said of his approach to film, his politics, or any other major theme in his work.

Perhaps nowhere else is this nonidentical repetition more evident than in Žižek's treatment of Christianity. While Christian references played a role in his arguments from the very beginning, they often functioned merely as cultural background, as for instance when he discussed Pascal and other Christian thinkers in *The Sublime Object of Ideology* as a way of elaborating on Althusser's Christian references.[2] In the late 1990s and early 2000s, however, Christianity emerges quite suddenly as a central preoccupation of his thought. One of the most important chapters of *The Ticklish Subject* is taken up with a critique and reappropriation of Badiou's theory of the truth-event, centered on Badiou's reading of Saint

Paul.[3] In the years that followed, Žižek devoted no less than three books to a deeper exploration of Christianity—books that served as crucial preparatory work for important sections of his self-declared "magnum opus," *The Parallax View*.[4]

A careful reader of all three books on Christianity cannot help but notice continual shifts, both in substantive position and in emphasis. The place of Freud's reading of Christian origins changes significantly over the course of the three books, as Žižek struggles to find a way to remain faithful to the psychoanalytic heritage while still focusing on the concerns that he finds most urgent. The theme of sacrifice plays a major role in *The Fragile Absolute* and *On Belief*, while it recedes in importance in *The Puppet and the Dwarf*. His stance toward Judaism changes perhaps most significantly, as he begins with a somewhat simplistic traditional reading of the relationship between Judaism and Christianity and winds up embracing Pauline Christianity as a radicalization of Judaism that is betrayed by the subsequent mainstream of gentile Christianity. It is clear that Žižek is using the books to work out ideas that are rapidly evolving over a short period of time.

The question I set out to answer in my book *Žižek and Theology* was why Christianity arose as a major theme in Žižek's work and why the development of his ideas on the issue was apparently such an urgent concern for him in those years.[5] Taking my cue from the undeniable changes in his position on Christianity, I have read Žižek's body of work as characterized by a series of decisive shifts that allow it to be divided into periods each of which ends in some kind of conceptual deadlock. In the period immediately preceding Žižek's engagement with Christianity, I argued, he had become caught in a deadlock on the question of revolution. On the one hand he adamantly believed that revolution was necessary and that one of the most important tasks of theory is to think through the conditions of possibility and elaborate at least the overall "shape" of a genuine revolution. On the other hand he seemed to have no convincing answer as to why a revolution would be ultimately worthwhile. This is because his previous work had made the structure of ideology, governed by a meaningless master-signifier, seem like an ineluctable feature of human experience—such that any revolution would wind up replacing one master with another. At times it seemed that the best justification that Žižek could offer was that the moment of authentic revolution was inherently worthwhile, regardless of how it turned out.

The period that began with Žižek's critique of Badiou in *The Ticklish Subject* was an attempt to get out of that deadlock, setting aside the notion of "revolution for revolution's sake" in order to think through the possibility of a more thoroughgoing revolution that could displace the deep structure of ideology itself. In this chapter, I would first like to discuss the alternative that began to emerge in Žižek's work on Christianity. I will then explore the development of this possibility of a "nonideological" social order in his subsequent works. Finally, I will conclude by suggesting that Žižek's work may be entering into a new period where he is beginning to lose sight of this problem—a development that I would view as a significant regression compared to the hard-won insights forged in the crucible of his reading of Christianity.

Žižek's position on Christianity reaches its more or less final form in the third of his books on the topic, *The Puppet and the Dwarf*. I have undertaken a detailed reading of his argument in this book and the writings that lead up to it elsewhere, but in the present context it seems most helpful to provide a broad overview of the key conceptual moves at work. The first is a shift in position on the relationship between Christianity and Judaism. Whereas Badiou had followed the traditional reading that associates Judaism with legalism and particularity as opposed to the grace and universality of Christianity, Žižek claims that we must recognize paganism and Judaism as fundamentally different *stances* toward the law.

For Žižek, the pagan subject is caught in the deadlock of law and transgression. For subjects in this deadlock, violating the law is in no way opposed to the law, and this is because the law already presupposes and in fact requires the transgression that supposèdly subverts it. This dynamic is what Žižek calls the "obscene superego supplement." In contrast to the popular notion of the superego as something analogous to the guilty conscience, Žižek follows Lacan in arguing that the superego actually incites the subject to enjoy. Transgression is a kind of built-in "release valve" that actually ties subjects more closely to the law, insofar as it not only gives them implicit permission to indulge in their extralegal pleasures but actually seems necessary to the very existence of those pleasures—how would jouissance be possible without the thrill of transgression?

Žižek believes that this logic has been carried to its extreme point in contemporary Western culture, where transgression itself becomes the mandate. He finds the same logic at work in "actual existing Christianity," particularly in its Catholic form. His discussion of Chesterton is meant to prove this point, as Chesterton views Catholicism not as forbidding "pagan pleasures" but as providing the only stable access to them. Both the Catholic view and the contemporary Western view are thus "perverse" in the Lacanian sense. While many have read Žižek's invocations of "perversion" as indicating something subversive or potentially revolutionary, he believes that the perverts are actually more invested in sustaining the law than anyone—after all, their access to jouissance depends on the ability to violate the law. At its worst, this perverse logic leads subjects to believe that upholding the law directly requires the worst violations of the law, as when it is argued that the only way to save liberal values from terrorists is to engage in torture and aggressive war. He finds this same perverse logic at work in Stalinism, where the ultimate goal of establishing the communist utopia justified the most inhuman crimes.

The place to attack the hold of law on the subject is thus not in the content of law but in its very form. This is where Judaism is all-important. Following Eric Santner's reading of Judaism in *The Psychotheology of Everyday Life*, Žižek argues that the Jewish subject's stance toward the law is not structured by the "obscene superego supplement." In Judaism, the law's role in regulating community life and rendering it intelligible has somehow been "decoupled" from the libidinal dynamics that end in the deadlock of perversion. Žižek attempts to account for how this could have come about by turning to the Book of Job. For Žižek, God's appearance to Job at the end of that book is, for all God's boasting, a tacit confession of God's own impotence. Job's silence, then, has to be reinterpreted: "he remained silent neither because he was crushed by God's overwhelming presence, nor because he wanted thereby to indicate his continuous resistance . . . but because, in a gesture of solidarity, he perceived the divine impotence." The Jewish subject, then, always lives in the wake of the acknowledgment of the nonexistence of the Other (i.e., the powerlessness of God). The Jewish community's relationship to the law is thus free of the superego supplement; instead of being stuck in the cycle of the prohibition generating the transgression, they follow God's law in order to hide God's powerlessness: "the paradox of Judaism is that it maintains fidelity to the founding violent Event [of confronting the impotence of God] precisely by not confessing, symbolizing it: this 'repressed' status of the Event is what gives Judaism its unprecedented vitality." At the same time, despite the "unplugged" character of the Jewish experience of law, precisely this shared, disavowed secret binds the Jewish nation together in a form of "pagan love" directed toward one's in-group.[6]

Based on this reading of Job, Žižek develops what amounts to an entire Christology, which he then appears to tacitly attribute to Paul. Where Job, symbolizing here the Jewish community as a whole, expresses his solidarity with the divine impotence by remaining silent about it, Christ as God-become-man directly reveals the divine impotence through his death on the cross and particularly in his cry of dereliction, meaning that Christianity is essentially "the religion of atheism." For this reason, Žižek argues (against Badiou) that cross and resurrection are dialectically identical, insofar as Christ's death immediately is the foundation for the new community, which Žižek calls the "Holy Spirit." This is because the public disclosure of what Judaism kept secret makes the Jewish "unplugged" stance toward the law available to everyone, resulting in a new, universal form of love to go along with the Jews' "new" (from the pagan perspective) experience of law. This combination is illustrated by Paul's logic of the "as if not" in 1 Corinthians 7, in which the subject does not simply maintain a vague distance toward symbolic obligations—which for Žižek is how the symbolic order normally works—but enacts "the disavowal of the symbolic realm itself: I use symbolic obligations, but I am not performatively bound by them." That is to say, I am freed from the logic of the "obscene superego supplement" that binds me to the law through enjoyment. Referring to Agamben's idea of the messianic law as a further state of emergency above and beyond the "normal" Schmittian state of exception, Žižek argues that "what the Pauline emergency suspends is not so much the explicit Law regulating our daily life, but, precisely, its obscene unwritten underside: when, in his series of as if prescriptions, Paul basically says: 'obey the laws as if you are not obeying them,' this means precisely that we should suspend the obscene libidinal investment in the Law, the investment on account of which the Law generates/solicits its own transgression."[7] Thus Paul radicalizes the Jewish tradition by "betraying" it—that is, revealing its secret through his reference to the cross—and universalizing it precisely by forming particular communities founded in this new experience of law and love.

Overall, one can state the inner logic of Žižek's reading of Paul in a fairly straightforward schematic form. Judaism represents an "unplugged" stance toward the law that Žižek valorizes, but it is combined with a "pagan" form of love that is bound to one's own in-group. Actual Existing Christianity represents a universal love that cuts across differences, but it is combined with a "pagan" form of law that generates its own transgression through the obscene superego supplement. What the letters of Paul present to us is a fragile moment of emergence, when pagans are inducted directly into the Jewish "unplugged" stance toward the law, not through adherence to the positive law of the Jewish community but through participation in the love beyond the law. Yet, tragically, it is precisely that "love beyond the law" that necessarily collapses back into the obscene superego supplement, generating a return to the perverse pagan stance toward law.

Hence the model of Pauline Christianity holds out the promise of a nonideological form of community, a social bond not structured by the master-signifier and its obscene superego supplement. More important, the model seems to present us with a form of communal life that is livable and sustainable beyond a moment of authentic revolutionary fervor. The challenge then becomes that of finding conceptual resources for thinking through the ways in which this apparently sustainable model could *actually* be sustained, rather than reverting to the perverse structure.

Žižek's later works on theology contribute to the effort to fill out this account of a nonideological order by reaffirming and deepening his reading of Christianity, in part by taking the rare step of engaging in the contemporary theological debate. This was manifested most dramatically in the publication of *The Monstrosity of Christ: Paradox or Dialectic?*[8] which consists of a dialogue between Žižek and the Anglican theologian John Milbank, founder of the "Radical Orthodoxy" school of theology. In his opening piece, "The Fear of Four Words," Žižek puts forward what he calls "a modest plea for the Hegelian reading of Christianity," a reading in which God the Father empties himself irreversibly into the Son, whose death on the cross opens up the way for a new social bond called the Holy Spirit. In other words, he "translates" his Lacanian Christology into Hegelian terms, deepening its connection to his overall theoretical project of synthesizing Lacan and Hegel.

The essay does more than simply translate his position from Lacanese to Hegelese, however. It deepens his position on two fronts. First, it advances a critique of trinitarian orthodoxy, characterizing it as an attempt to avoid the radical consequences of the death of God by preserving "God-Father" as the one who "continues to pull the strings [and] is not really caught in the process" of divine kenosis. The second way that Žižek's first contribution to *The Monstrosity of Christ* advances his position is by continuing the work, begun in *The Parallax View*, of clarifying the ontological consequences of his view. Rejecting the Roman Catholic attempt to harmonize faith and reason by putting forth God as the "constitutive exception" or master-signifier that allows us to perceive a harmoniously ordered universe, Žižek contends that modern science at its most radical presents us with a universe without a master-signifier guaranteeing its order. This radical materialism "has thus nothing to do with the assertion of 'fully existing external reality'—on the contrary, its starting premise is the 'non-all' of reality, its ontological incompleteness."[9] The "death of God," then, does more than allow us to conceive of a nonideological social order—it allows us to face the universe as the internally inconsistent and incomplete thing it is.

Prior to this, Žižek had deepened his position in another way in *The Parallax View*, where he rearticulates this notion of the "Holy Spirit" in more explicitly Lacanian terms by raising the possibility of thinking about a new collectivity in terms of Lacan's "discourse of the analyst"— further integrating the insights of his reading of Christianity into the core of Žižek's theoretical enterprise. While the discourse of the analyst is often conceived as a purely transitional one that is basically limited to the literal analytic session, Žižek makes broader claims for it: "Lacan's aim is to establish the possibility of a collective of analysts, of discerning the contours of a possible social link between analysts (which is why, in his schema of four discourses, he talks about the discourse of the Analyst as the 'obverse' of the Master's discourse)." For Žižek, this notion of a "collective of analysts"—which he explicitly links to the Pauline collectives—

opens up the possibility of a social order that would not be structured by a master-signifier. If successful, a revolution based on the discourse of the analyst would represent *"a sociopolitical transformation that would entail the restructuring of the entire field of the relations between the public Law and its obscene supplement."*[10]

In other words, with the collective of the "Holy Spirit" or the collective of analysts, Žižek claims to have found a way out of the deadlock of revolution as the moment between the old boss and the new boss—a radically new way of structuring human subjects' relationship to language and jouissance. Nevertheless, it remains unclear what such an order might look like in practice. The closest he comes to discussing this question in detail comes in Žižek's response to Milbank in *The Monstrosity of Christ*.[11] His discussion centers on Agota Kristof's novel *The Notebook*, which for him is "the best literary expression" of an ethical stance that goes beyond the sentimentality of moralism and instead installs "a cold, cruel distance toward what one is doing." The novel follows two twin brothers who are "utterly immoral—they lie, blackmail, kill—yet they stand for authentic ethical naivety at its purest." He gives two examples. In one, they meet a starving man who asks for help and get him everything he asks for, while claiming that they helped him solely because he needed help, not out of any desire to be kind. In another, they urinate on a German officer with whom they find themselves sharing a bed, at his request. Žižek remarks, "if ever there was a Christian ethical stance, this is it: no matter how weird their neighbor's demands, the twins naively try to meet them."[12] After going through some additional examples, including various punishments of malicious characters and an assisted suicide, Žižek summarizes the ethical core that he takes away from Kristof's novel as follows: "this is where I stand—how I would love to be: an ethical monster without empathy, doing what is to be done in a weird coincidence of blind spontaneity and reflexive distance, helping others while avoiding their disgusting proximity. With more people like this, the world would be a pleasant place in which sentimentality would be replaced by a cold and cruel passion."[13] This passage does fill in some detail as to what the nonideological order Žižek is hoping for would look like, yet it is only a first step. Even assuming that one agrees with him that the world would be a better place with "more people like this," significant work is required to develop a convincing account of how a social order based around such ethics might be structured and of how we get there from here.

Unfortunately, further development of this question does not appear to be forthcoming. While his later work includes scattered references to the "Holy Spirit" as an alternative social form, the attempt to elaborate the concept has become more and more marginal in his work. One can see this most clearly in *Less Than Nothing*, where the discussion of Christianity is mainly limited to the preparatory section titled "The Drink Before." What was arguably the culminating insight of *The Parallax View* has become an obscure byway in his intellectual project. This is perhaps not surprising, because it can often appear that *The Parallax View*—once put forward as his "magnum opus"—has more or less disappeared down the memory hole. While he responds to Jameson's review of *The Parallax View*,[14] and makes scattered references to the concept of parallax, one gets the sense that *Less Than Nothing* is being offered up as a replacement for *The Parallax View*, as the real "magnum opus" that makes up for the failure of his first attempt.

The most salient difference between the two books from this perspective is that *The Parallax View* was an attempt by Žižek to put forward his system in his own voice. The governing ambition is not the synthesis of Hegel and Lacan but the development of an authentic "dialectical materialism" that can reinvigorate Marxist politics.[15] The guiding concept of "parallax" is drawn not from Hegel or Lacan but from the Japanese philosopher Kojin Karatani, whose book *Transcritique* argues for a Kantian rather than Hegelian reading of Marx.[16] While Hegel and (especially) Lacan feature prominently in *The Parallax View*, the presentation and structure of the book combine to give the sense that Žižek has finally "arrived," finally wrested a consistent philosophical position from his synthesis of Lacan and Hegel.

By contrast, *Less Than Nothing* implicitly walks back this claim. In a passage outlining his intellectual trajectory in the book's introduction, Žižek claims that all along, "the theoretical work of the Party Troika to which I belong (along with Mladen Dolar and Alenka Zupančič) had the axis of Hegel-Lacan as its "undeconstructible" point of reference: whatever we were doing, the underlying axiom was that reading Hegel through Lacan (and vice versa) was our unsurpassable horizon." Žižek then opens the possibility that they are now on the brink of surpassing that horizon: "Recently, however, limitations of this horizon have appeared: with Hegel, his inability to think pure repetition and to render thematic the singularity of what Lacan called the *objet a*; with Lacan, the fact that his work ended in an inconsistent opening: *Seminar XX (Encore)* stands for his ultimate achievement and deadlock—in the years after, he desperately concocted different ways out (the *sinthome*, knots . . .) all of which failed."[17]

The answer, however, is not to give up on "the axis of Hegel-Lacan" but to insist on it all the more: "my wager was (and is) that, through their interaction (reading Hegel through Lacan and vice versa), psychoanalysis and Hegelian dialectics mutually redeem themselves, shedding their accustomed skin and emerging in a new unexpected shape."[18] The previous attempt to shed the skin of the Hegel-Lacan axis in *The Parallax View* is not actually disavowed. Instead, its disappearance is almost akin to a party purge, where the offender is so radically erased from history as to have never existed.

The problems broached in *The Parallax View* do continue to cast a shadow, but they do not present themselves as clearly *as* core problems. Concepts closely akin to the discourse of the analyst—such as the so-called feminine, non-all, or (as I would prefer to translate the Lacanian *pas-tout*) non-whole structure of reality, which implies that the "masculine" structure of the master-signifier is always a secondary and fundamentally false imposition—are very frequently placed in a subordinate or purely transitional role. This is clearest in his discussion of quantum physics, where he makes the radical claim that contemporary science is empirically verifying that the universe as such is non-whole, but at the same time argues that the intervention of some kind of master-signifier is necessary to create a livable or intelligible reality.

Now it is possible that things would be different at different ontological levels. More specifically, what is necessary to kickstart some kind of concrete reality out of the primal quantum void may not be necessary to structure a livable or intelligible social order. Indeed, one could even conceive of humanity's surpassing of the ideological structure from which human society emerged as the ultimate example of the overcoming of "natural" limitations that Žižek has always associated with both Hegelian dialectics and Lacanian psychoanalysis. There are passages of

Less Than Nothing that could be open to that type of interpretation, most notably in his discussions of the "Holy Spirit,"[19] but a clear emphasis on the nonideological order as a genuinely *livable* option is absent.

More ambiguous is his discussion of the Occupy movement at the end of the book, where he discusses the relationship between the intellectual and the protestor:

> faced with the demands of the [Occupy Wall Street] protestors, intellectuals are definitely not in the position of the subjects supposed to know: they cannot operationalize these demands, or translate them into proposals for precise and realistic measures. With the fall of twentieth-century communism, they forever forfeited the role of the vanguard which knows the laws of history and can guide the innocents along its path. The people, however, also do not have access to the requisite knowledge — the "people" as a new figure of the subject supposed to know is a myth of the Party which claims to act on its behalf. . . . There is no Subject who knows, and neither intellectuals nor ordinary people are that subject.[20]

Having laid out the dilemma, he then argues for a relationship structurally similar to that between the hysteric and the analyst: "is this a deadlock then: a blind man leading the blind, or, more precisely, each of them assuming that the other is not blind? No, because their respective ignorance is not symmetrical: it is the people who have the answers, they just do not know the questions to which they have (or, rather, are) the answer. . . . Intellectuals should not primarily take [the protestors' demands] as demands, questions, for which they should produce clear answers, programs about what to do. They are answers, and intellectuals should propose the questions to which they are answers."[21] Again, though, there is no clear statement on whether this is merely a transitional phase that will culminate in the imposition of a new master-signifier — perhaps a "better," more humane, less destructive one but a master-signifier nonetheless — or if this movement can *itself* "directly" become a new order and *a new kind of order*.

It may be that Žižek veered off-path in *The Parallax View*. Indeed, I assume that many readers of Žižek would be willing to dismiss the work on Christianity that led up to *The Parallax View* as an unnecessary detour and would be relieved to see his theological reflections taking on a more subordinate role in *Less Than Nothing*. It could even turn out to be the case that Žižek now includes the notion of a "collective of analysts" among those failed solutions put forward in Lacan's final seminars. In my view, though, his forceful return to the narrow path in *Less Than Nothing* risks backtracking on all that he has achieved since the apparent detour.

Before *Less Than Nothing* appeared, I worried that Žižek's attempt to develop the concept of the "Holy Spirit" could lead him back into the dilemma that motivated his engagement with Christianity in the first place: if no positive account of the new community seemed possible, he could easily fall into the trap of either sneaking the master-signifier back in or valorizing the moment of revolution in itself with no reference to future sustainability. In both cases, the implicit message would be that there is no hope, no real alternative to ideology: the revolutionary outburst would be ultimately parasitic on the existing order and would have no concrete outcome other than the installation of a new ideological order. In that case, he would be falling back into the position of perversion, of encouraging violation of the existing order as a "release valve" that serves finally to reinforce order—or, in other words, he would be repeating the very betrayal of which he accuses historical Christianity.

For now, it seems that Žižek has avoided that outcome by simply side-stepping the question. If I am correct about that, then the appearance of *Less Than Nothing* truly opens a new period in his work, the first one to begin with the evasion of a deadlock rather than a head-on confrontation—the "late Žižek." If that is the case, then I will be forced to follow the example of Žižek's own preference for the fraught "middle period" of great thinkers (such as Heidegger and Schelling), lingering on the "middle Žižek" of the writings on Christianity and *The Parallax View*. My reason will be the same as Žižek's: the "middle period" names that pregnant moment just when thinkers first begin to grasp the full magnitude of the problem they have set themselves and yet before they come up with an all-too-easy solution—or worse, lose track of the problem altogether.

Notes

1   I have followed Žižek's example in this chapter, which includes passages adapted from "Politics and Perversion: Situating Žižek's Paul," *Journal for Cultural and Religious Theory* 9, 2 (2008), 43–52; "The Christian Experience Continues: On Žižek's

Work since *The Parallax View,*" *International Journal of Žižek Studies* 4, 4 (2010), 1–9; "On Materialist Theology: Thinking God beyond the Master Signifier," *Revue Internationale de Philosophie* 66, 3 (2012), 347–57; and "Out of the Woods? On Žižek's *Less Than Nothing,*" *Journal for Cultural and Religious Theory* 13.2 (2014): 96–101.

2 Slavoj Žižek, *The Sublime Object of Ideology* (New York: Verso, 1989).

3 Slavoj Žižek, *The Ticklish Subject: The Absent Center of Political Ontology* (New York: Verso, 1999); Alain Badiou, *Saint Paul: The Foundation of Universalism*, trans. Ray Brassier (Stanford: Stanford University Press, 2003).

4 Slavoj Žižek, *The Fragile Absolute: Or, Why Is the Christian Legacy Worth Fighting For?* (New York: Verso, 2000); *On Belief* (New York: Routledge, 2001); *The Puppet and the Dwarf: The Perverse Core of Christianity* (Cambridge, MA: MIT Press, 2003); *The Parallax View* (Cambridge, MA: MIT Press, 2006).

5 See my *Žižek and Theology* (New York: T & T Clark, 2008).

6 Eric Santner, *On the Psychotheology of Everyday Life: Reflections on Freud and Rosenzweig* (Chicago: University of Chicago Press, 2001), 120, 126, 128.

7 Santner, *On the Psychotheology of Everyday Life*, 112, 113, 171.

8 Slavoj Žižek and John Milbank, *The Monstrosity of Christ: Paradox or Dialectic?*, ed. Creston Davis (Cambridge, MA: MIT Press, 2009). My review of this volume is in *Political Theology* 11.1 (2010): 141–44.

9 Žižek and Milbank, *Monstrosity*, 29, 97.

10 Žižek, *The Parallax View*, 305, 305–6, 308 (italics in original).

11 Žižek and Milbank, *Monstrosity of Christ*, 297–303.

12 Žižek and Milbank, *Monstrosity of Christ*, 301.

13 Žižek and Milbank, *Monstrosity of Christ*, 303.

14 Slavoj Žižek, *Less Than Nothing: Hegel and the Shadow of Dialectical Materialism* (New York: Verso, 2012), 268.

15 Žižek, *The Parallax View*, 4.

16 Kojin Karatani, *Transcritique: On Kant and Marx*, trans. Sabu Kohso (Cambridge, MA: MIT Press, 2005).

17 Žižek, *Less Than Nothing*, 18.

18 Žižek, *Less Than Nothing*, 18.

19 Žižek, *Less Than Nothing*, 112, 202, 230–31. In the first passage in particular, Žižek identifies Jesus with *objet a* as opposed to the master-signifier, which can be read in terms of the difference between the analyst's and master's discourse.

20 Žižek, *Less Than Nothing*, 1007–8.

21 Žižek, *Less Than Nothing*, 1008.

Richard Wagner's Hegelian insight in *Parsifal*, "the wound can be healed only by the spear that smote it," provides one of the more substantive reasons that explains Žižek's engagement with the "authentic" Christian legacy. The return of the religious dimension in postmodern thought, this "massive onslaught of obscurantism," creates a wound that, paradoxically, can only be healed and countered by retrieving the precious Christian legacy from the "fundamentalist freaks."[1]

The return of religion is equally a problem for Islam. In this context the question is: Is there an authentic emancipatory kernel in Islam that can heal the wound that its return in the form of obscurantism and fundamentalism has caused? Does Žižek's Hegelian insight that the wound can be healed only by the spear that smote it apply to Islam? And if there is an emancipatory kernel in Islam, what is it and how do we extract it from the shell that mystifies it? This chapter argues that Žižek's reading of Christianity is problematic in its relation to Islam but that nonetheless he provides indispensable insights that can be repeated in the Islamic contexts. Žižek's trajectory of thought can be constructively employed to reclaim the emancipatory legacy of Islam, and Islam, whatever Žižek may tell us about it, shares with Christianity a *struggling* universality where there are no Jews and no Greeks, and neither Christians nor Muslims for that matter.[2] But Žižek's reading of Christianity raises daunting and—within his framework—insoluble problems regarding Islam; particularly regarding its inscription in the emancipatory space represented by the name of Judeo-Christianity: there is no place for Islam in this space.

The Emancipatory Kernel of Christianity

The emerging idea from Žižek's reading is relatively simple and can be stated succinctly: Christianity represents the idea of the death of God of the Beyond. It is God himself, the God of the Beyond and not only Jesus, who dies on the cross. The God of the Beyond dies and is resurrected as the Holy Spirit, and the Holy Spirit is the community of the believers "deprived of its support in the big Other."[3] The death of God leads to the only possible conclusion that follows from that premise: Christianity is *the* religion of atheism: "while in all other religions, there are people who do not believe in God, only in Christianity does God not believe in himself."[4] God dies and is resurrected as a Holy Spirit, "the egalitarian emancipatory collective which cancels any organic-hierarchal social link."[5] What sets Christianity apart from Judaism and Islam is the idea of atheism, an atheism that is unlike any other atheism: "in the standard form of atheism, God dies for men who stop believing in him; in Christianity, God dies for *himself*."[6] To become a true atheist, one has to do more than merely renounce God—God can still be invoked under different guises, history, nature, and so on—ultimately, one must pass through the Christian experience, and renounce the very possibility of the big Other.

This reading of Christianity is at odds with Islam, in that Islam *affirms* what Christianity denies: for Islam, and to a certain extent Judaism, God is still the big Other. In Judaism, this is somehow understandable, because it comes *before* Christianity, but with Islam this is less apparent: "no wonder that, to many a Western historian of religion, Islam is a problem—how could it have emerged *after* Christianity, the religion to end all religions?"[7]

This description holds true, not only of many Western historians and philosophers of religion but also of Žižek himself. Žižek's fundamental problem with Islam is precisely: "how could it have emerged *after* Christianity, the religion to end all religions?" What follows from this is a rather disconcerting consequence, namely that Islam is *not* a continuation to the unfolding story of the Spirit of Christianity as a Holy Spirit but rather a concrete negation of it: Islam is a step backward. Moreover, Islam *cannot* accomplish a synthesis, whatever deadlock it may perceive in the unfolding of the *linear* Judeo-Christian story. There is no way for Islam to insert itself in this trinity that never became trinity, because Islam provides a counternarrative: it does not tell the story of the death of God but reasserts God all the more powerfully. Hence Islam's radical break with and exclusion of itself from the Judeo-Christian tradition: Islam's exclusion transpires not because the West wants it but because it is a self-incurred exclusion.

What differentiates Judaism from Christianity is its relation to God's impotence, as in the story of Job's meaningless suffering. Judaism conceals this secret and refuses to give up the ghost, while Christianity *reveals* it: the breakthrough of Christianity, however, is that it makes God realize his own impotence. Christ's suffering—"Father, why hast thou forsaken me"—is a redoubling of Job's suffering, with the noted difference that in Christ "the gap that separates the suffering, desperate man (Job) from God is transposed into God Himself, as His own radical splitting or, rather, self-abandonment."[8] There is thus not only a historical but also a conceptual and logical *continuity* between Judaism and Christianity: Christianity could only occur *after* Judaism, because "it reveals the horror first confronted by the Jews."[9] From this perspective Islam seems to try the impossible, namely to *undo* the Christ event. Islam goes so far as to deny the crucifixion and resurrection took place: the Qur'an disavows crucifixion and asserts that those who maintain otherwise are merely offering ignorant conjectures: "and for their saying, 'We slew the Messiah, Jesus son of Mary, the Messenger of God'—yet they did not slay him, neither crucified him, only a likeness of that was shown to them. Those who are at variance concerning him surely are in doubt regarding him; they have no knowledge of him, except the following of surmise; and they slew him not of a certainty—no indeed" (4:15).

Crucifixion is unthinkable in Islam, and that is why Islam can only treat it as a conjectural whim without any basis in reality. Without crucifixion or, to be more precise, Christ's dereliction on the cross and the resurrection, however, Christianity is unthinkable, because it represents the moment that discloses God's self-abandonment, God's *realization* that he does not exist, and the passage of his resurrection as a Holy Spirit. The breakthrough of Christianity is the public proclamation of the death of God—the public space is by definition atheistic—which is necessary from the standpoint of the break with Judaism, where the big Other still survives in the community of the believers in the form of the prescribed way of life.[10] "There is no Holy Spirit without the squashed body of a bird (Christ's mutilated body)" is how Žižek describes the necessity of the passage from a community where the big Other still survives to a community where the big Other is dead.[11] By trying to obliterate first the monstrosity of Christ and then the passage from in-itself to for-itself, Islam commits itself to a naïve pre-Christian ontology, an ontology of fullness, a seamless flaw of causes and events, a rational universe that remains tied to a masculine logic of universality and its constitutive exception, a true "God of Reason" who is wholly transcendent and "who knows and directs everything."[12] In this universe, freedom is not possible. In contrast to Islam, Christianity is committed to a feminine logic of non-All:[13] it "*is the miraculous Event that disturbs the balance of the One-All; it is the violent intrusion of Difference that precisely throws the balanced circuit of the universe off the rails.*"[14] It is only in/with Christianity that freedom becomes possible. In other words, the death of God confronts us with "the terrible burden of freedom and responsibility for the fate of divine creation,"[15] a responsibility that Islam has shirked. Is it any wonder how, Žižek writes in another context, "Islam ends up with the *worst* of both worlds . . . in Islam, we find BOTH, narrative and superego?"[16]

In yet another context, Žižek presents the problem of Islam through the work of the great French anthropologist Claude Lévi-Strauss, who laments: "today, it is behind Islam that I contemplate India; the India of Buddha, prior to Muhammad who—for me as a European and because I am European—arises between our reflection and the teachings which are closest to it . . . the hands of the East and the West, predestined to be joined, were kept apart by it."[17]

What we are shown here is a conception of Islam caught in the space between the East and the West. It is properly neither of the East nor of the West, and so it interposes itself in between the two geographical poles, making their union improbable, preventing the West from achieving its own identity and "in a sense which would have been all the more Christian insofar as we were to mount beyond Christianity itself."[18] However one looks at Islam, its very being is an unaccommodatable surplus, a "disturbing excess," whose only seeming function is to demarcate borders and keep separate what belongs together. Žižek remains a part of this philosophic-anthropological imagery, and despite his occasional praises,[19] his conceptual resources prevent him from engaging Islam the way he has engaged Judaism. Nevertheless, there is a significant shift occurring here: for Lévi-Strauss, Islam's foreignness was geographically external, while for Žižek this foreignness of Islam is not merely geographical—though it presupposes that—but *conceptual*. Islam is no longer an external screen that separates the East from the West, it is a much more ominous thing. In the Straussian version, Islam's obstacle is merely contingent, and as such, one can safely assume, it can be inscribed within the space of the Western narrative of itself. In Žižek's version, this is conceptually impossible: Christianity has revealed *all* that was there to be revealed: God is dead, there is no big Other. The relation of Islam and Christendom thus goes from bad to worse: Islam's foreignness is so foreign that there is no possibility to inscribe it within the emancipatory space of the Judeo-Christian tradition. Islam's very presence is an unassimilable foreign object at the very heart of Christendom.[20] If Lévi-Strauss's problem might have morphed into how to domesticate, assimilate, Islam's strangeness so that the unity of the East and West could occur, today the reverse problem occurs, namely how to estrange Islam, how to eject it from the West, and how to make it keep its distance so the West can become one with itself, which is the political fantasy of all right-wing and populist parties across Europe. An *unintended* consequence of his reading is that it inadvertently endorses what it deliberately excludes from his horizon of thinking. It is unintended because it goes against his unreserved endorsement of all progressive issues today and his basic ontology of the incompleteness of reality.[21] Nonetheless, when he speculates that perhaps one of the reasons for there being so much anti-Semitism in the Muslim world might be explained by the *proximity* of Judaism and Islam and continues to propose that perhaps we should begin to talk about *"Jewish Muslim civilization* as an axis opposed to Christianity,"[22] he comes dangerously close to such a fantasy. Perhaps we should talk of "Jewish-Muslim civilization," but why? And particularly, why talk about it as *opposed* to Christianity?[23]

As a result of Žižek's reading of Christianity as the religion that ends all religions, Islam becomes superfluous. The attribution of superfluousness to Islam is neither accidental nor something that pertains only to Žižek; he is a part of a more general trend. It also partly explains the almost total absence—its presence is noted only in the mode of its absence—of Islam from the canon of the Western scholarly traditions. In philosophical books, one rarely finds references to Islam, or one finds them in obscure footnotes. Western philosophers' concepts go only as far as Christianity, and then they turn silent, making the usual historical and conceptual leap that reads Christianity as having always been consubstantial with the West. Between the early Christianity and the modern West, there is only uninhabitable desert. This unaccounted leap, which leaves a tradition like Islam out of its purview, renders all attempts at reading Christianity as the only true religion, and the notions of universality they propagate, provincial. In a sense, these readings have not been updated historically and have not considered the changes that have occurred since, at least, the end of colonialism and the vertiginous speed with which capitalism has spread globally. The guiding assumption of these readings of Christianity is that civilizations are fixed entities; thus one can unproblematically theorize about Christianity as the universal religion. However, when civilizations become fluid entities and borders porous, when pluralism is the prevalent condition and Capital is the only Real force to be reckoned with, this anachronistic assumption becomes problematic.[24]

Islam, as would be expected, reads Christianity differently: it elevates itself to the position of being the *final* religion, and thus creates the place for itself *after* Christianity. This is not done haphazardly: Islam opens this space for itself by reading Christianity, its main events, both *theologically* and *politically* differently from the way Žižek reads it. It is not that Islam does not recognize the fact that Christianity might have been the last religion, as much as the fact that Christianity *failed* to be what effectively was the last religion. Islam purports to be an eloquent articulation of the failure of Christianity to be the last religion. If Christianity revealed what Judaism was trying to keep secret, namely that there is *nothing* to reveal, then what Islam revealed is the failure of Christianity to *stabilize* into a tradition of emancipation and/or community not grounded in some form of the existence of the big Other. To his key question, "Is the Holy Spirit still a figure of the big Other, or is it possible to conceive it outside of this frame?"[25] Žižek gives a negative answer: the "Holy Spirit" is not a figure of the big Other because it is a "collective link of love."[26] Islam palpably doubts that collectives can sustain themselves on links of love alone without any support in the big Other; it questions the viability of such a community. The key question of Islam is the opposite one, namely: Is the figure of the Holy Spirit conceived outside the frame of the big Other sustainable as an emancipatory political collective?[27]

What follows from conceiving the Holy Spirit outside the frame of the big Other is that Islam is not part of that emancipatory story that Christianity is. The question that I posed at the outset of this chapter thus gets a negative answer from Žižek. Confronted with this conundrum, Muslims' choices narrow down to an either-or choice: either they find a way to erase the big Other from Islam and thus insert Islam into the Judeo-Christian tradition, or they find a way to demonstrate the impossible—that there can be an emancipation within the coordinates of the existence of the big Other—and thus relativize and contextualize Žižek's reading. The latter option seems to be the option that Islam opts for. And the critique of Islam, which is not so much theological as political, is that the Holy Spirit without support in the big Other can only stabilize in small groups but not large political groups, or it can stabilize in communities that function as vanishing mediators between the old and the new. Incidentally this is not far from what Žižek himself argues with regard to the realization of the "Holy Spirit": "the true Idea of the Christian collective *was* realized, but outside of the Church as an institution—which, however does not mean that it survived in intimate, authentic religious experiences which had no need for the institutional frame; rather, it survived in *other* institutions, from revolutionary political parties to psychoanalytic societies."[28]

In this passage Žižek says more than what he probably intends to say, namely, that communities that have realized the Idea of Christianity are either temporally short-lived, that is, revolutionary parties, or extremely small communities, that is, psychoanalytic societies. If this is the case then emancipation is extremely limited in its scope, and very few, if any, are completely emancipated. This hardly constitutes a ground for building sustainable emancipatory political collectives. It brings into focus not the truth of Lacan's motto "Il n'y a pas de grand Autre" (There is no big Other) but the problem of its realization in durable and sustainable political institutions. Islam thus shifts the accent of emancipation from the question of the *in*existence of the big Other to the question of the modality of its *in*existence.[29]

Political communities organize around a certain cause that at a particular juncture quilts the whole range of other struggles into one primary struggle. There is no guarantee that things will turn out well, but nonetheless the struggle has to presuppose and keep the horizon of the expectation of success open, for otherwise it would not get off the ground. When the Qur'an, for example, says that the righteous shall inherit the earth (21:105), it is obvious that God does *not* guarantee this success, there is no hidden hand or Master-guarantor guiding the process, but the subject has to believe that his or her efforts are not all in vain. To put it slightly differently, it does not matter whether the big Other exists or not; what matters is that at a certain level it has to be presupposed for communities to function; it is a condition of their existence. The big Other in Islam functions as the *nonmessianic* Hope, a kind of "fidelity to the possibility opened by the event," to borrow Badiou's succinct formulation, which keeps the collective horizon of expectations open so that the struggle might succeed. There is no guarantee of the outcome of the struggle—it is not totally accidental that Islam is obsessed with jihad, which literally means struggle; indeed all that matters *is* the struggle itself, not the outcome—but the subject who struggles continues to do so under the horizon of the principle of Hope.

The Disappearance of Islam

There was a time when it was presumed that whatever was good for the West is good for the rest. Times have changed faster than philosophical notions that accompany them are able to keep pace with them. As a result we have an asymmetrical relation between what is happening on the ground and what philosophers are theorizing about what is happening on the ground. We have the case that Islam is expanding in the West, but there are no adequate theories to deal with it: an approach that renders Islam superfluous might have been feasible in the past, when the West was presumed to be homogenous, but when its condition changes to that of multiple heterogeneities, then these same approaches become inadequate for handling the multiplicity that the West has become.

In this context, although the postcolonial intellectual critique of Žižek misses the point,[30] it can nonetheless be reasserted under a different figure of thought. The deeper, albeit unarticulated, insight of these critiques is that Žižek's philosophy is incapable of being a genuine representative philosophy of the multiplicity that the West has become. Žižek is a European philosopher, and as such his philosophy is and remains confined solely to this tradition, and his universalism, as Maldonado-Torres argues, is *"universalized provinciality."*[31] It is a universalism that is premised on the assumption that other figures of thought are not capable of shouldering the burden of authentic thought or shouldering the responsibility of freedom. The conclusion is that Žižek's Eurocentrism or his Christian-centrism is an obstacle that prevents it from being a genuine universality. In other words, Žižek's sympathies may lie with the excluded and the immigrant, but his sympathies go only so far. In his defense, Žižek may argue that this criticism knocks on an open door, which is true, but nonetheless, it is still effective. An articulation of Christianity as the ultimate horizon of emancipation might be good news for Christians, even believing Christians, but this in a very profound sense remains a provincial philosophy.[32] Those who have not undergone the Christian experience will not find themselves in that horizon, or they will find themselves there only minimally, that is, their inclusion as well as the solidarity with them will be conditional.

Why Repeat Žižek?

A group of so-called Progressive Muslims,[33] and the movement of Islamic feminism,[34] have provided some interesting interpretations of Islam and addressed some of the problems and challenges that contemporary Muslims face, but their approaches suffer from the same defects and difficulties that liberal readings of religion do. There is also Tariq Ramadan, who clearly politically stands on the left and with the Left,[35] but who theologically stands for the continuation of the classical traditions of reformation and therefore cannot provide a way to subvert the system of reasoning that underpins and supports the current obscurantist theologies of Islam, which remain totally silent about the adventures of capitalism.[36] Neither Progressive Muslims nor Islamic feminism, nor Ramadan, have ever tackled the *philosophical* problems raised by Western philosophers in their interpretations of Christianity. In other words, neither Ramadan nor Progressive Muslims have provided the conceptual resources that would liberate Islam from its theological chains. Their methodologies undermine their progressive political aspirations. Moreover, both progressive Muslims and Ramadan provide us with depoliticized versions of Islam, the former in the hermeneutic direction and the latter in the direction of the ethicization of the political problems.

Roland Boer has argued that Žižek's engagement with Christianity happened because he could not find the basis for a viable politics in psychoanalysis, so that his Pauline Christianity enabled him "to get out of the closed circuit of Lacan's psychoanalysis, to dispense in particular with the constitutive exception."[37] This makes it sound as though Žižek's only interest in Christianity is tactical and instrumental. Regardless of the reasons that motivate Žižek's engagement with Christianity, there is an undeniable consistency between the struggle for liberation from capitalism and the struggle for liberation from obscurantism of theology. Islam needs both. Repeating Žižek means repeating his struggle under different conditions and laying the ground for the emergence of a true universal solidarity that renders all our attachments to our traditions that obstruct the struggle for equality and emancipation obsolete. With Žižek, finally, one can read Islam *politically* while avoiding its shallow and counterproductive politicization in the guise of the demand for the application of sharia. Islam desperately needs to free its spirit from its theological shackles, and Žižek, more than any other, provides it with the intellectual help that it needs.

Notes

1   Slavoj Žižek, *The Fragile Absolute: Or, Why Is the Christian Legacy Worth Fighting For?* (London: Verso, 2008), xxix.

2   It is worth remembering that at its origin Islam spoke of believers indistinctively; it included Jews, Christians, and those who were yet to be Muslims. Islam did not yet have the sense of confessional distinctness that is now associated with it. See Fred M. Donner, *Muhammad and the Believers: At the Origins of Islam* (Cambridge, MA: Harvard University Press, 2010).

3   Slavoj Žižek, *The Puppet and the Dwarf: The Perverse Core of Christianity* (Cambridge, MA: MIT Press, 2003), 171.

4   Slavoj Žižek and John Milbank, *The Monstrosity of Christ: Paradox or Dialectic?*, ed. Creston Davis (Cambridge, MA: MIT Press, 2009), 49.

5   Slavoj Žižek, *Less Than Nothing: Hegel and the Shadows of Dialectical Materialism* (London: Verso, 2012), 114.

6   Žižek, *The Monstrosity of Christ*, 48.

7   Žižek, *The Monstrosity of Christ*, 85.

8   Žižek, *The Puppet and the Dwarf*, 126.

9   Žižek, *The Puppet and the Dwarf*, 129. To what do Jews remain faithful and refuse to reveal? "The secret to which the Jews remain faithful is the horror of the divine impotence—and it is this secret that is revealed in Christianity," 129.

10 Žižek, *The Monstrosity of Christ*, 74.

11 Žižek, *The Monstrosity of Christ*, 76. In *Less Than Nothing*, 104, Žižek says something similar: "So why did Christ have to die? The paradox is that in order for the virtual Substance (the big Other) to die, the price had to be paid in the real of flesh and blood. In other words, God is a fiction, but for the fictions (which structures reality) to die, a piece of the real had to be destroyed. . . . The fiction has to be destroyed from within, that is its inherent falsity has to be brought out. To put it in descriptive terms, it is not enough to prove that God does not exist—the formula of true atheism is that God himself must be made to proclaim his own inexistence, must stop believing in himself." See also 232: "if the God were to morph directly into the Holy Ghost then we would still have the symbolic big Other. But the monstrosity of Christ, this contingent singularity interceding between God and man, is proof that the Holy Ghost is not the big Other surviving as the spirit of community after the death of the substantial God, but a collective link of love without any support in the big Other."

12 Žižek, *The Monstrosity of Christ*, 85.

13 "'Non-All' designates the feminine position, a field which is not totalized because it lacks the exception, the Master Signifier." Žižek, *Less Than Nothing*, 112.

14 Žižek, *The Fragile Absolute*, 112.

15 Žižek, *The Monstrosity of Christ*, 25.

16 Slavoj Žižek, *On Belief* (New York: Routledge, 2001), 165.

17 Quoted in Žižek, *The Monstrosity of Christ*, 85.

18 Žižek, *The Monstrosity of Christ*, 85.

19 "What all this means," Žižek writes about the 2009 uprising in Iran, "is that there is a genuinely liberatory potential in Islam: we don't have to go back to the tenth century to find a 'good' Islam, we have it right here, in front of us." "Berlusconi in Tehran," *London Review of Books*, July 23, 2009. www.lrb.co.uk/v31/n14/slavoj-Žižek /berlusconi-in-tehran.

20 This in fact should count as a positive contribution of Islam to the West because in its very presence as a radical alterity, a foreign body, it ensures that the political space remains open.

21 Žižek, *Less Than Nothing*, chapter 11 (739–802) and chapter 14 (905–61).

22 Žižek, *The Monstrosity of Christ*, 86.

23 The answer is, of course, obvious: he cannot accommodate Islam within the space of the Christian emancipation.

24 Inadequacy of these frameworks for the study or interpretation of Christianity always

and without exception favors Christianity as the religion of Europe: Christianity is consubstantial with the West, and the relation does not seem to hold only contingently but necessarily. Referring to the work of Marcel Gauchet, Charles Hirschkind reminds us how a "certain post-Reformation understanding of Christianity is valorized as true religion in its undistorted form, while all other religious traditions and forms of religiosity are recognized as incompatible with modernity"; Hirschkind, "Religious Difference and Democratic Pluralism: Some Recent Debates and Frameworks," *The Finnish Society for the Study of Religion, Temenos* 44, 1 (2008), 70. The naturalization of Christianity is also part of Žižek's agenda: in *On Belief*, Žižek writes: "Christianity is from its very inception, THE religion of modernity"; 150.

25   Žižek, *Less Than Nothing*, 232.

26   Žižek, *Less Than Nothing*, 232. In *The Fragile Absolute*, Žižek writes that love "enjoins us to 'unplug' from the organic community into which we were born"; 111.

27   We must remember here that Islam was originally conceived as a political movement, which sought to redress issues of equality and justice. Islam's critique of Christianity must also be conceived as a political critique, and its failure not as a religious failure but as a political failure.

28   Žižek, *Less Than Nothing*, 115.

29   In *Less Than Nothing*, Žižek defines the big Other as a "virtual order which exists only through subjects 'believing' in it," 92; "an ideal structure of reference," "which exists only insofar as it is continuously sustained by the work of 'all and everyone,'" 185.

30   Walter D. Mignolo, "Yes We Can: Non-European Thinkers and Philosophers," *Al-Jazeera*, last modified February 19, 2013. www.aljazeera.com/indepth/opinion/2013/02/2013267274732089I.html; Hamid Dabashi, "Slavoj Žižek and Harum Scarum," *Al-Jazeera*, last modified November 11, 2011, www.aljazeera.com/indepth/opinion/2011/11/2011111011283172950.html.

31   Nelson Maldonado-Torres, "Liberation Theology and the Search for the Lost Paradigm: From Radical Orthodoxy to Radical Diversality," in *Latin American Liberation Theology: The Next Generation*, ed. Ivan Petrella (Maryknoll, NY: Orbis Books, 2005). Žižek has argued that Christian universalism is not all-inclusive, that those who are excluded from it are thoroughly excluded, but their particular identities of those who are included are suspended, rendered irrelevant to the fact of being a Christian, so one can be both a Greek and a Christian, and so on. One can, in other words, directly participate in the Christian community, bypassing all particular identities. The problem with this is that it is equally true of Islam. One can participate in the Muslim community regardless of what other identity one may have. The crucial question that imposes itself here is: Is Christianity a generic name for emancipation (there are neither Greeks nor Jews . . . logic)? If it is a generic name for emancipation would this then mean that there is only one way to emancipation or are there other ways that lead to emancipation? Identification of Christianity with emancipation is problematic because it excludes many other potentially emancipatory traditions.

32   A notable exception is Alain Badiou's *Saint Paul: The Foundation of Universalism* (Stanford: Stanford University Press, 2003). Badiou also does not address Islam, but his

nontreatment of it is not exclusionary as such: in fact on a purely formal level Islam easily finds its place in a Badiouian politics. In fact Badiou, with his reading of Jesus as "the name for what happens to us universally" (60), and of Paul as the founder of the universal "through the termination of communitarian particularisms" and the consideration of "the production of equality and the casting off, in thought, of differences [as] the material signs of the universal," effectively provides the frame for an emancipatory reading of Islam.

33 Omid Safi, ed., *Progressive Muslims: On Justice, Gender and Pluralism* (Oxford, UK: Oneworld, 2003).

34 For an introduction to Islamic feminism see Margot Badran, *Feminism in Islam: Secular and Religious Convergences* (Oxford, UK: Oneworld, 2009); Ziba Mir-Hosseini, Islam and Gender (Princeton: Princeton University Press, 1999).

35 Tariq Ramadan, *What I Believe?* (New York: Oxford University Press, 2009).

36 Tariq Ramadan, *Radical Reform: Islamic Ethics and Liberation* (New York: Oxford University Press, 2008).

37 Roland Boer, *Criticism of Heaven: On Marxism and Theology* (Leiden: Brill, 2007), 336.

Afterword.

The Minimal Event:

From Hystericization to

Subjective Destitution

The reproach one often hears is that the Event Alain Badiou and me are talking about is some big shattering magic occurrence that changes everything, the very basic coordinates of a situation in which it occurs. To counter that misleading impression, I would like to focus on the Event at its most fragile, a barely perceptible shift in the subjective attitude.

Shakespeare: Music as "a Sign of Love"

Shakespeare's ability to prefigure insights that properly belong to the later epochs often borders on the uncanny. Was not, well before Satan's famous "Evil, be thou my Good?" from Milton's *Paradise Lost* the formula of the diabolical Evil provided by Shakespeare in whose *Titus Andronicus* the unrepentant Aaron's final words are: "if one good deed in all my life I did, / I do repent it from my very soul"?[1] Was not Richard Wagner's short-circuit between seeing and hearing in the last act of *Tristan*, which is often perceived as the defining moment of modernism proper (the dying Tristan *sees* Isolde's voice) clearly formulated already in *Midsummer Night's Dream*? In act 5, scene 1, Bottom says: "I see a voice; now will I to the chink, To spy if I can hear my Thisbe's face." (The same thought occurs later in King Lear: "Look with thine ears." *King Lear*, act IV, scene 6).

One should not shirk from asking the vulgar historicist question: Why was Shakespeare able to see all this? Part of the answer resides in his historical moment (late sixteenth, early seventeenth century), the moment at which the rise of melancholy overlaps with the prohibition and gradual disappearance of different forms of carnival, of manifestations of "collective joy" from public life—Hamlet, the ultimate Shakespearean hero, is clearly a melancholic subject.[2] What makes melancholy so deadening is that objects are here, available, the subject just no longer desires them. As such, melancholy is inscribed into the very structure of the modern subject (the "inner self"): the function of prohibition is to shatter the subject out of melancholic lethargy and to set alive its desire. If, in melancholy, the object is here, available, while the cause of the subject's desire for it is missing, the wager of prohibition is that, by depriving the subject of the object, it will resuscitate the cause of desire. The lesson of melancholy is thus that there is no "pure" subject, that such a subject is a fantasmatic position, since there is no subject simply dwelling in an external point with regard to universal reality: subject is simultaneously always-already "objectivized," relying on its impossible-real objectal counterpart.[3]

The void filled in by fantasmatic content (by the "stuff of the I," as Lacan called fantasy) is opened up by the ultimate failure of the subject's symbolic representation: it is not that every symbolic representation simply fails, is inadequate to the subject it represents ("words always betray me . . ."); much more radically, the subject IS the retroactive effect of the failure of its representation. It is because of this failure that the subject is divided—not into something and something else, but into something (its symbolic representation) and nothing, and fantasy fills in the void of this nothingness. And the catch is that this symbolic representation of the subject is primordially *not its own*: prior to speaking, I am spoken, identified as a name by the parental discourse, and my speech is from the very outset a kind of hysterical reaction to being-spoken-to: "Am I really then, that name, what you're saying I am?" Every speaker—every name-giver—HAS to be named, has to be included into its own chain of nominations, or, to refer to the joke often quoted by Lacan: "I have three brothers, Paul, Ernest, and myself." (No wonder that, in many religions, God's name is secret, one is prohibited to pronounce it.) The speaking subject persists in this in-between: prior to nomination, there is no subject, but once it is named, it already disappears in its signifier—the subject never is, it always *will have been*.

It is from this standpoint that one should reread the passages in *Richard II* that turn around *objet petit a*, the object-cause of desire. Pierre Corneille (in his *Medee*, act 2, scene 6) provided its nice description: "Souvent je ne sais quoi qu'on ne peut exprimer / Nous surprend, nous emporte et nous force d'aimer." ("Often an I-don't-know-what which one cannot express / surprises us, takes us with it and compels us to love.") Is this not the *objet petit a* at its purest—on condition that one supplements it with the alternate version: ". . . and compels us to hate"? Furthermore, one should add that the place of this "I-don't-know-what" is the desiring subject itself: "The secret of the Other is the secret for the Other itself"—but crucial in this redoubling is the self-inclusion: *what is enigmatic for the Other is* MYSELF, that is, I am the enigma for the Other, so that I find myself in the strange position (as in detective novels) of someone who all of a sudden finds himself persecuted, treated as if he knows (or owns) something, bears a secret, but is totally unaware WHAT this secret is. The formula of the enigma is thus: "What am I for the Other? What as an object of the Other's desire am I?"

Because of this gap, the subject cannot ever fully and immediately identify with his or her symbolic mask or title; the subject's questioning of his or her symbolic title is what hysteria is about:[4] "Why am I what you're saying that I am?" Or, to quote Shakespeare's Juliet: "What's in a name?" (*Romeo and Juliet*, Act II, scene 2). There is a truth in the word-play between "hysteria" and "historia": the subject's symbolic identity is always historically determined, dependent on a specific ideological constellation. We are dealing here with what Louis Althusser called "ideological interpellation": the symbolic identity conferred on us is the result of the way the ruling ideology "interpellates" us—as citizens, democrats, or patriots. Hysteria emerges when a subject starts to question or to feel discomfort in his or her symbolic identity: "You say I am your beloved— what is there in me that makes me that? What do you see in me that causes you to desire me in that way?" *Richard II* is Shakespeare's ultimate play about hystericization (in contrast to *Hamlet*, the ultimate play about obsessionalization). Its topic is the progressive questioning by the king of his own "kingness"—what is it that makes me a king? What remains of me if the symbolic title "king" is taken away from me?

> I have no name, no title,
> No, not that name was given me at the font,

> But 'tis usurp'd: alack the heavy day,
> That I have worn so many winters out,
> And know not now what name to call myself!
> O that I were a mockery king of snow,
> Standing before the sun of Bolingbroke,
> To melt myself away in water-drops!

In Slovene translation, the second line is rendered: "Why am I what I am?" Although this clearly involves too much poetic license (the link with the original is almost beyond recognition), it does render adequately the gist of it: deprived of its symbolic titles, Richard's identity melts like that of a snow king under sun rays. — The hysterical subject is the subject whose very existence involves radical doubt and questioning, his or her entire being is sustained by the uncertainty as to what he is for the Other; insofar as the subject exists only as an answer to the enigma of the Other's desire, the hysterical subject is the subject par excellence. In contrast to it, the analyst stands for the paradox of the desubjectivized subject, of the subject who fully assumes what Lacan calls "subjective destitution," that is, who breaks out of the vicious cycle of intersubjective dialectics of desire and turns into an acephalous being of pure drive. With regard to this subjective destitution, Shakespeare's *Richard II* has in store a further surprise in store for us: not only does the play enact the gradual hystericization of the unfortunate king; at the lowest point of his despair, before his death, Richard enacts a further shift of his subjective status that brings him to subjective destitution:

> I have been studying how I may compare
> This prison where I live unto the world:
> And for because the world is populous
> And here is not a creature but myself,
> I cannot do it; yet I'll hammer it out.
> My brain I'll prove the female to my soul,
> My soul the father; and these two beget
> A generation of still-breeding thoughts,
> And these same thoughts people this little world,
> In humours like the people of this world,
> For no thought is contented. The better sort,
> As thoughts of things divine, are intermix'd

With scruples and do set the word itself
Against the word:
As thus, "Come, little ones," and then again,
"It is as hard to come as for a camel
To thread the postern of a small needle's eye."
Thoughts tending to ambition, they do plot
Unlikely wonders; how these vain weak nails
May tear a passage through the flinty ribs
Of this hard world, my ragged prison walls,
And, for they cannot, die in their own pride.
Thoughts tending to content flatter themselves
That they are not the first of fortune's slaves,
Nor shall not be the last; like silly beggars
Who sitting in the stocks refuge their shame,
That many have and others must sit there;
And in this thought they find a kind of ease,
Bearing their own misfortunes on the back
Of such as have before endured the like.
Thus play I in one person many people,
And none contented: sometimes am I king;
Then treasons make me wish myself a beggar,
And so I am: then crushing penury
Persuades me I was better when a king;
Then am I king'd again: and by and by
Think that I am unking'd by Bolingbroke,
And straight am nothing: but whate'er I be,
Nor I nor any man that but man is
With nothing shall be pleased, till he be eased
With being nothing. Music do I hear?

(The music plays.)

Ha, ha! keep time: how sour sweet music is,
When time is broke and no proportion kept!
So is it in the music of men's lives.
And here have I the daintiness of ear
To cheque time broke in a disorder'd string;
But for the concord of my state and time

Had not an ear to hear my true time broke.
I wasted time, and now doth time waste me;
For now hath time made me his numbering clock:
My thoughts are minutes; and with sighs they jar
Their watches on unto mine eyes, the outward watch,
Whereto my finger, like a dial's point,
Is pointing still, in cleansing them from tears.
Now sir, the sound that tells what hour it is
Are clamorous groans, which strike upon my heart,
Which is the bell: so sighs and tears and groans
Show minutes, times, and hours: but my time
Runs posting on in Bolingbroke's proud joy,
While I stand fooling here, his Jack o' the clock.
This music mads me; let it sound no more;
For though it have helped madmen to their wits,
In me it seems it will make wise men mad.
Yet blessing on his heart that gives it me!
For 'tis a sign of love; and love to Richard
Is a strange brooch in this all-hating world.

It is crucial to properly grasp the shift in modality that occurs with the entrance of *music* in the middle of this monologue. The first part is a solipsistic rendering of a gradual reduction to nothingness, to the pure void of the subject ($): Richard starts with the comparison of his cell with the world; but in his cell, he is alone, while the world is peopled; so, to solve this antinomy, he posits his thoughts themselves as his company in the cell—Richard dwells in the fantasms generated by a mother (his brain) and father (his soul). The pandemonium he thus dwells in, in which the highest and the lowest coexist side by side, is exemplified by a wonderful Eisensteinian montage of two biblical fragments: "Come, little ones" (reference to *Luke* 18:16, *Matthew* 19:14, and *Mark* 10:14) counterposed to "It is as hard to come as for a camel to thread the postern of a small needle's eye" (reference to *Luke* 18:26, *Matthew* 19:24, and *Mark* 10:25). If we read these two fragments together, we get a cynical superego God who first benevolently calls us to come to him and then sneeringly adds, as a kind of second thought ("Oh, by the way, I forgot to mention that . . ."), that it is almost impossible to come to him. The problem with this solution is that, if Richard with his thoughts is a multitude of people, then, caught in this shadowy unsubstantial world, the substantial consistency of his Self explodes, he is forced to play "in one person many people." And, he concludes, he effectively oscillates between being a king, a beggar, the truth of it and the only peace to be found is in accepting to be nothing.

In the second part, music as an object enters, a true "answer of the Real." This second part itself contains two breaks. First, in his usual rhetorical vein, Richard uses this intrusion to, yet again, form a metaphor: the playing of the music out of tune reminds him how he himself was "disordered" (out of tune) as a king, unable to strike the right notes in running the country and thus bringing disharmony—while he has great sensitivity for musical harmony, he lacked this sensitivity for social harmony. This "out of joint" is linked to time—the implication being that not merely is time out of joint, but time as such signals an out-of-jointness, that is, there is time *because* things are somehow out of joint. Then, no longer able to sustain this safe metaphoric difference, Richard enacts a properly psychotic *identification with the symptom*, with the musical rhythm as the cipher of his destiny: like an alien intruder, music parasitizes, colonizes, him, its rhythm forcing on him the identification with time, a literal identification, psychotic, where he no longer needs a clock but, in a terrifying vision, he directly *becomes* the clock (in the mode of what Deleuze celebrated as "becoming-machine"). It is as if Richard is driven to such extreme of painful madness with this music that, for him, the only way to get rid of this unbearable pressure of music is to directly identify with it . . . In one of the episodes of the 1945 British horror omnibus *Dead of the Night*, Michael Redgrave plays a ventriloquist who becomes jealous of his dummy, gnawing with the suspicion that it wants to leave him for a competitor; at the episode's end, after destroying the dummy by way of thrashing its head, he is hospitalized; after reawakening from coma, he identifies with his symptom (the dummy), starting to talk and contorting his face like it. Here we get the psychotic identification as the false way out: what started out as a partial object (the dummy is a doll stuck on his right hand, it is literally his hand acquiring an autonomous life, like the hand of Ed Norton in *Fight Club*) develops into a full double engaged in a mortal competition with the subject, and since the subject's consistency relies on this symptom-double, since it is structurally impossible for him to get rid of the symptom, the only way out of it, the only way to resolve the tension, is to directly identify with the symptom, to become one's own symptom—in exact homology to Hitchcock's *Psycho*, at the end of which the only way for Norman to get rid of his mother is to identify with her directly, to let her take over his personality and, using his body as a ventriloquist uses his dummy, speak through him.

Finally, there occurs an additional shift toward the end of the monologue, in the last three lines: music, which first is experienced as a violent intrusion that drives Richard to madness, now appears as a soothing "sign of love"—why this shift? What if it simply stands for the return to real music that he hears: it is a "sign of love" when separated from the metaphoric dimension of recalling the disharmony of his kingdom. The designation of music as "a sign of love" has to be understood in its strict Lacanian sense: an answer of the Real by means of which the circular-repetitive movement of drive is reconciled with—integrated into—the symbolic order.

This moment of subjective destitution provides an exemplary case of what event is: not a big spectacular explosion, but just a barely perceptible shift in the subjective position. It is a shift that concerns the subject's relationship to a trauma, a traumatic intrusion: the shift toward reconciling with the trauma.

Beckett: A Scene from a Happy Life

The inner and constitutive link between trauma and subject is the topic of what is undoubtedly Beckett's late masterpiece: *Not I*, a twenty-minute dramatic monologue written in 1972, an exercise in theatric minimalism: there are no "persons" here, intersubjectivity is reduced to its most elementary skeleton, that of the speaker (who is not a person, but a partial object, a faceless MOUTH speaking) and AUDITOR, a witness of the monologue who says nothing throughout the play (all the Auditor does is that, in "a gesture of helpless compassion" (Beckett), he four times repeats the gesture of a simple sideways raising of the arms from the sides and their falling back. (When asked if the Auditor is Death or a guardian angel, Beckett shrugged his shoulders, lifted his arms, and let them fall to his sides, leaving the ambiguity intact—repeating the very gesture of the Auditor.) Beckett himself pointed to the similarities between *Not I* and

The Unnamable, with its clamoring voice longing for silence, circular narrative, and concern about avoiding the first person pronoun: "I shall not say I again, ever again." Along these lines, one could agree with Vivian Mercier's suggestion that, gender aside, *Not I* is a kind of dramatization of *The Unnamable*—one should only add that in *Not I*, we get the talking partial coupled/supplemented with a minimal figure of the big Other.

Beckettology, of course, did its job in discovering the empirical sources of the play's imagery. Beckett himself provided the clue for the "old hag," but also emphasized the ultimate irrelevance of this reference: "I knew that woman in Ireland. I knew who she was—not 'she' specifically, one single woman, but there were so many of those old crones, stumbling down the lanes, in the ditches, besides the hedgerows." But, replying the queries, Beckett said: "I no more know where she is or why thus than she does. All I know is in the text. 'She' is purely a stage entity, part of a stage image and purveyor of a stage text. The rest is Ibsen." As to the reduction of the body of the speaker to a partial organ (mouth), in a letter from April 30, 1974, Beckett gave a hint that the visual image of this mouth was "suggested by Caravaggio's Decollation of St John in Valetta Cathedral." As to the figure of the Auditor, it was inspired by the image of a djellaba-clad "intense listener" seen from a café in Tunis (Beckett was in North Africa from February to March 1972). James Knowlson conjectured that this "figure coalesced with [Beckett's] sharp memories of the Caravaggio painting," which shows "an old woman standing to Salome's left. She observes the decapitation with horror, covering her ears rather than her eyes" (a gesture that Beckett added in the 1978 Paris production).

Much more interesting are Beckett's own uncertainties and oscillation with regard to the Auditor (who is generally played by a male, although the sex is not specified in the text): when Beckett came to be involved in staging the play, he found that he was unable to place the Auditor in a stage position that pleased him, and consequently allowed the character to be omitted from those productions. However, he chose not to cut the character from the published script, and left the decision whether or not to use the character in a production to the discretion of individual producers. He wrote to two American directors in 1986: "he is very difficult to stage (light—position) and may well be of more harm than good. For me the play needs him but I can do without him. I have never seen him function effectively." In the 1978 Paris production he did reinstate the character but from then on abandoned the image, concluding that it was perhaps "an error of the creative imagination." From the Lacanian perspective, it is easy to locate the source of this trouble: the Auditor gives body to the big Other, the Third, the ideal Addressee-Witness, the place of Truth which receives and thereby authenticates the speaker's message. The problem is how to visualize/materialize this structural place as a figure on the imaginary of the stage: every play (or even speech) needs it, but every concrete figuration is by definition inadequate, that is, it cannot ever "function effectively" on stage.

The basic constellation of the play is thus the dialogue between the subject and the big Other, where the couple is reduced to its barest minimum: the Other is a silent impotent witness which fails in its effort to serve as the medium of the Truth of what is said, and the speaking subject itself is deprived of its dignified status of "person" and reduced to a partial object. And, consequently, since meaning is generated only by means of the detour of the speaker's word through a consistent big Other, the speech itself ultimately functions at a presemantic level, as a series of explosions of libidinal intensities. At the premiere in Lincoln Center, the Mouth was played by Jessica Tandy, the mother from Hitchcock's *Birds*. Debating the piece with her, Beckett demanded that it should "work on the nerves of the audience, not its intellect" and advised Tandy to consider the mouth "an organ of emission, without intellect."[5]

Where does this bring us with regard to the standard postmodern critique of dialogue that emphasizes its origin in Plato, where there is always the one who knows (even if only that he knows nothing), questioning the other (who pretends to know) so as to lead the other to admit he knows nothing. There is thus always a basic asymmetry in a dialogue—and does this asymmetry not break out openly in late Plato's dialogues, where we are no longer dealing with Socratic irony, but with one person talking all the time, with his partner merely interrupting him from time to time with "So it is, by Zeus!" "How cannot it be so?" . . . and so on It is easy for a postmodern deconstructionist to show the violent streak even in Habermas's theory of communicative action, which stresses the symmetry of the partners in a dialogue: this symmetry is grounded in the respect of all parts for the rules of rational argumentation, and are these rules really as neutral as they claim to be? Once we accept this and bring it to its radical conclusion—the rejection of the very notion of "objective truth" as oppressive, as an instrument of domination—the postmodern path to what Lyotard called *le différend* is open: in an authentic dialogue, there is no pressure to reach a final reconciliation or accord, but merely to reconcile ourselves with the irreducible difference of perspectives that cannot be subordinated to any encompassing universality. Or, as Rorty put it: the fundamental right of each of us is the right to tell his/her/their own story of life-experience, especially of pain, humiliation, and suffering. But, again, it is clear that people not only speak from different perspectives, but that these differences are grounded in different positions of power and domination: what does the right to free dialogue mean when, if I approach certain topics, I risk everything, up to my life? Or, even worse, when my complaints are not even rejected, but dismissed with a cynical smile? The left-liberal position here is that one should especially emphasize the voices that are usually not heard, that are ignored, oppressed, or even prohibited within the predominant field—sexual and religious minorities, and so on. But is this not all too abstract-formal? The true problem is: how are we to create conditions for a truly egalitarian dialogue? Is this really possible to do in a "dialogic"/respectful way, or is some kind of counter-violence needed? Furthermore, is the notion of (not naïvely "objective," but) universal truth really by definition a tool of oppression and domination? Say, in the Germany of 1940, the Jewish story of the Jews' suffering was not simply an oppressed minority view to be heard, but a complaint whose truth was in a way universal, that is, rendered visible what was wrong in the entire social situation.

Is there a way out of this conundrum? What about the dialogic scene of the psychoanalytic session, which weirdly inverts the coordinates of the late-Platonic dialogue? As in the latter case, here also one (the patient) talks almost all the time, while the other only occasionally interrupts him or her with an intervention that is more of a diacritical order, asserting the proper scansion of what was told. And, as we know from Freudian theory, the analyst is here not the one who already knows the truth and just wisely leads the patient to discover it himself/herself: the analyst precisely doesn't know it, his or her knowledge is the illusion of transference that has to fall at the end of the treatment.

And is it not that, with regard to this dynamic of the psychoanalytic process, Beckett's play can be said to start where the analytic process ends: the big Other is no longer "supposed to know" anything, there is no transference, and, consequently, "subjective destitution" already took place. But does this mean that, since we are already at the end, there is no inner dynamic, no radical shift, possible anymore—which would nicely account for the appearance of the circular movement in this (and other) Beckett's play(s)? A closer look at the content of the play's narrative, of what is told in this twenty-minute monologue, seems to confirm this diagnostic: the Mouth utters at a ferocious pace a logorrhea of fragmented, jumbled sentences that obliquely tells the story of a woman of about seventy who, having been abandoned by her parents after a premature birth, has lived a loveless, mechanical existence and who appears to have suffered an unspecified traumatic experience. The woman has been virtually mute since childhood, apart from occasional winter outbursts part of one of which constitutes the text we hear, in which she relates four incidents from her life: lying face down in the grass on a field in April; standing in a supermarket; sitting on a "mound in Croker's Acre" (a real place in Ireland near Leopardstown racecourse); and "that time at court." Each of the last three incidents somehow relates to the repressed first "scene," which has been likened to an epiphany—whatever happened to her in that field in April was the trigger for her to start talking. Her initial reaction to this paralyzing event is to assume she is being punished by God; strangely, however, this punishment involves no suffering—she feels no pain, as in life she felt no pleasure. She cannot think why she might be being punished but accepts that God does not need a "particular reason" for what he does. She thinks she has something to tell, though she doesn't know what, but believes if she goes over the events of her life for long enough she will stumble on that thing for which she needs to seek forgiveness; however, a kind of abstract nonlinguistic continued buzzing in her skull always intervenes whenever she gets too close to the core of her traumatic experience.

The first axiom of interpreting this piece is not to reduce it to its superficial cyclical nature (endless repetitions and variations of the same fragments, unable to focus on the heart of the matter), imitating the confused mumbling of the "old hag" too senile to get to the point: a close reading makes it clear that, just before the play's end, there IS a crucial break, a decision, a shift in the mode of subjectivity. This shift is signaled by a crucial detail: in the last (fifth) moment of pause, the Auditor DOESN'T intervene with his mute gesture—his "helpless compassion" has lost its ground. Here are all five moments of pause:

1. all that early April morning light . . . and she found herself in the—
   . . . what? . . . who? . . . no! . . . she! . . . [*Pause and movement 1.*]
2. the buzzing? . . . yes . . . all dead still but for the buzzing . . . when
   suddenly she realized . . . words were—. . . what? . . . who? . . . no!
   . . . she! . . . [*Pause and movement 2.*]
3. something she—. . . something she had to—. . . what? . . . who? . . .
   no! . . . she! . . . [*Pause and movement 3.*]
4. all right . . . nothing she could tell . . . nothing she could think . . .
   nothing she—. . . what? . . . who? . . . no! . . . she! . . . [*Pause and
   movement 4.*]
5. keep on . . . not knowing what . . . what she was–. . . what? . . . who?
   . . . no! . . . she! . . . SHE! . . . [*Pause.*] . . . what she was trying . . .
   what to try . . . no matter . . . keep on . . . [*Curtain starts down.*]

Note the three crucial changes here: first, the standard, always identical, series of words that precedes the pause with the Auditor's movement of helpless compassion (". . . what? . . . who? . . . no! . . . she! . . .") is here supplemented by a repeated capitalized "SHE"; second, the pause is without the Auditor's movement; third, it is not followed by the same kind of confused rumbling as in the previous four cases, but by the variation of the paradigmatic Beckettian ethical motto of perseverance ("no matter . . . keep on"). Consequently, the key to the entire piece is provided by the way we read this shift: does it signal a simple (or not so simple) gesture by means of which the speaker (Mouth) finally fully assumes her subjectivity, asserts herself as SHE (or, rather, as I), overcoming the blockage indicated by the buzzing in her head? In other words, insofar as the play's title comes from the Mouth's repeated insistence that the events she describes or alludes to did not happen to her (and that therefore she cannot talk about them in first person singular), does the fifth pause indicate the negation of the play's title, the transformation of "not I" into "I"? Or is there a convincing alternative to this traditional-humanist reading that so obviously runs counter to the entire spirit of Beckett's universe? Yes—on condition that we also radically abandon the predominant cliché about Beckett as the author of the "theatre of the absurd," preaching the abandonment of every metaphysical Sense (Godot will never arrive), the resignation to the endless circular self-reproduction of meaningless rituals (the nonsense rhymes in *Waiting for Godot*).

This, of course, in no way implies that we should counter the "theatre of the absurd" reading of Beckett with its no less simplified upbeat mirror image; perhaps a parallel with "Der Laienmann," the song that concludes Schubert's *Winterreise*, may be of some help here. "Der Laienmann" displays a tension between form and message. Its message appears to be utter despair of the abandoned lover who finally lost all hope, even the very ability to mourn and despair, and identifies with the man on the street automatically playing his music-machine. However, as many perspicuous commentators have noticed, this last song can also be read as the sign of forthcoming redemption: while all other songs present the hero's inward brooding, here, for the first time, the hero turns outward and establishes a minimal contact, an emphatic identification, with another human being, although this identification is with another desperate loser who has even lost his ability to mourn and is reduced to performing blind mechanical gestures. Does something similar not take place with the final shift of *Not I*? At the level of content, this shift can be read as the ultimate failure both of the speaker (Mouth) and of the big Other (Auditor): when the Mouth loses even the minimal thread of the content and is reduced to the minimalist injunction that the meaningless bubble must go on ("keep on . . . not knowing what"), the Auditor despairs and renounces even the empty gesture of helpless compassion. There is, however, the opposite reading that imposes itself at the level of FORM: the Mouth emerges as a pure (form of) subject, deprived of all substantial content (depth of "personality"), and, pending on this reduction, the Other is also depsychologized, reduced to an empty receiver, deprived of all affective content ("compassion," etc.). To play with Kazimir Malevitch's terms, we reach the zero-level of communication—the subtitle of the play's finale could have been "white noise on the black background of immobile silence" . . .

In what, then, does this shift consist? We should approach it via its counterpart, the traumatic X around which the Mouth's logorrhea circulates. So what happened to "her" on the field in April? Was the traumatic experience she underwent there a brutal rape? When asked about, Beckett unambiguously rejected such a reading: "How could you think of such a thing! No, no, not at all—it wasn't that at all." We should not take this statement as a tongue-in-cheek admission, but literally—that fateful April, while "wandering in a field . . . looking aimlessly for cowslips," the woman suffered some kind of collapse, possibly even her death—definitely not a real-life event, but an unbearably intense "inner experience" close to what C. S. Lewis described in his *Surprised by Joy* as the moment of his religious choice. What makes this description so irresistibly delicious is the author's matter-of-fact "English" skeptical style, far from the usual pathetic narratives of the mystical rapture. Lewis refers to the experience as the "odd thing"; he mentions its common location—"I was going up Headington Hill on the top of a bus"—and gives qualifications like "in a sense," "what now appears," "or, if you like," "you could argue that . . . but I am more inclined to think . . ." "perhaps," "I rather disliked the feeling":

The odd thing was that before God closed in on me, I was in fact offered what now appears a moment of wholly free choice. In a sense. I was going up Headington Hill on the top of a bus. Without words and (I think) almost without images, a fact about myself was somehow presented to me. I became aware that I was holding something at bay, or shutting something out. Or, if you like, that I was wearing some stiff clothing, like corsets, or even a suit of armor, as if I were a lobster. I felt myself being, there and then, given a free choice. I could open the door or keep it shut; I could unbuckle the armor or keep it on. Neither choice was presented as a duty; no threat or promise was attached to either, though I knew that to open the door or to take off the corset meant the incalculable. The choice appeared to be momentous but it was also strangely unemotional. I was moved by no desires or fears. In a sense I was not moved by anything. I chose to open, to unbuckle, to loosen the rein. I say, "I chose," yet it did not really seem possible to do the opposite. On the other hand, I was aware of no motives. You could argue that I was not a free agent, but I am more inclined to think this came nearer to being a perfectly free act than most that I have ever done. Necessity may not be the opposite of freedom, and perhaps a man is most free when, instead of producing motives, he could only say, "I am what I do." Then came the repercussion on the imaginative level. I felt as if I were a man of snow at long last beginning to melt. The melting was starting in my back—drip-drip and presently trickle-trickle. I rather disliked the feeling.[6]

In a way, everything is here: the decision is purely formal, ultimately a decision to decide, without a clear awareness of WHAT the subject decides about; it is nonpsychological act, unemotional, with no motives, desires, or fears; it is incalculable, not the outcome of strategic argumentation; it is a totally free act, although one couldn't do it otherwise. It is only AFTER-WARD that this pure act is "subjectivized," translated into a (rather unpleasant) psychological experience. From the Lacanian standpoint, there is only one aspect that is potentially problematic in Lewis's formulation: the traumatic Event (encounter of the Real, exposure to the "minimal difference") has nothing to do with the mystical suspension of ties that bind us to ordinary reality, with attaining the bliss of radical indifference in which life or death and other worldly distinctions no longer matter, in which subject and object, thought and act, fully coincide. To put it in mystical terms, the Lacanian act is rather the exact opposite of this "return to innocence": the Original Sin itself, the abyssal DISTURBANCE of the primeval Peace, the primordial "pathological" Choice of the unconditional attachment to some singular object (like falling in love with a singular person who, thereafter, matters to us more than everything else). And does something like THIS not take place on the grass in *Not I*? The *sinful* character of the trauma is indicated by the fact that the speaker feels punished by God. What then happens in the final shift of the play is that the speaker ACCEPTS the trauma in its meaninglessness, ceases to search for its meaning, restores its extrasymbolic dignity, as it were, thereby getting rid of the entire topic of sin and punishment. This is why the Auditor no longer reacts with the gesture of impotent compassion: there is no longer despair in the Mouth's voice, the standard Beckettian formula of the drive's persistence is asserted ("no matter . . . keep on"), God is only now truly love—not the loved or loving one, but Love itself, that which makes things go. Even after all content is lost, at this point of absolute reduction, the Galilean conclusion imposes itself: *eppur si muove*.

This, however, in no way means that the trauma is finally subjectivized, that the speaker is now no longer "not I" but "SHE," a full subject finally able to assume her Word. Something much more uncanny happens here: the Mouth is only now fully destituted as subject—at the mo-

ment of the fifth pause, the subject who speaks fully assumes its identity
with Mouth as a partial object. What happens here is structurally similar
to one of the most disturbing TV episodes of *Alfred Hitchcock Presents*,
"The Glass Eye" (the opening episode of the third year). Jessica Tandy
(again—the very actress who was the original Mouth!) plays here a lone
woman who falls for a handsome ventriloquist, Max Collodi (a reference
to the author of *Pinocchio*); when she gathers the courage to approach
him alone in his quarters, she declares her love for him and steps forward
to embrace him, only to find that she is holding in her hands a wooden
dummy's head; after she withdraws in horror, the "dummy" stands up
and pulls off its mask, and we see the face of a sad older dwarf who
starts to jump desperately on the table, asking the woman to go away . . .
the ventriloquist is in fact the dummy, while the hideous dummy is the
actual ventriloquist. Is this not the perfect rendering of an "organ without bodies"? It is the detachable "dead" organ, the partial object, which
is effectively alive, and whose dead puppet the "real" person is: the "real"
person is merely alive, a survival machine, a "human animal," while the
apparently "dead" supplement is the focus of excessive Life.

Notes

1   However, when Shakespeare speaks of "a sick man's appetite, who desires most that
    which would increase his evil" (*Coriolanus*, act I, scene I), the ambiguity is radical:
    this characterization holds for self-destructive evil as well as for the dedication to the
    Good that neglects one's own well-being.
2   Perhaps, the best way to account for the relationship between mourning and melan-
    choly would have been to apply to it Lacan's formula of psychosis: "what is foreclosed
    from the Symbolic, returns in the Real"—the loss whose symbolic process of mourn-
    ing is foreclosed returns to haunt us in the Real, as a superego guilt.
3   This is why the melancholic subject who displays his misfortune is a nice case of the
    dialectics of picture and stain: his aim is to inscribe himself into the picture of the
    (social) world, which he inhabits as a worthless stain or the stain of suffering; i.e., to
    make himself into a stain of the picture and thereby catch the Other's gaze.
4   Lacan identifies hysteria with neurosis: the other main form of neurosis, obsessional
    neurosis, is for him a "dialect of hysteria."
5   In the 2000 filmed production, directed by Neil Jordan, we see Julianne Moore come
    into view and sit down and then the light hit her mouth—this makes us aware that a
    young woman as opposed to an "old hag" is portraying the protagonist.
6   C. S. Lewis, *Surprised by Joy* (London: Fontana Books, 1977), 174–75.

Contributors

HENRIK JØKER BJERRE, PhD in philosophy, is Associate Professor, Aalborg University, Denmark. Main areas of interest: Kant, Kierkegaard, Freud, Lacan, Žižek. Author of *Kantian Deeds* (Continuum, 2010) and *The Subject of Politics* (HEB, 2010, with Carsten Bagge Laustsen), as well as numerous articles on German idealism, Kierkegaard, psychoanalysis, and politics. Member of the philosophical collective Centre for Wild Analysis.

BRUNO BOSTEELS is Professor of Romance Studies at Cornell University. He is the author of several books, including *Alain Badiou, une trajectoire polémique, The Actuality of Communism, Badiou and Politics*, and *Marx and Freud in Latin America* and the translator of numerous books by Alain Badiou, including *Theory of the Subject, Wittgenstein's Antiphilosophy, The Adventure of French Philosophy*, and *Philosophy for Militants*.

AGON HAMZA is a PhD candidate in philosophy at the Postgraduate School ZRC SAZU in Ljubljana, Slovenia. He is a cofounder and member of the international Dialectical Materialism Collective and serves as editor-in-chief of the international philosophical journal *Crisis and Critique*. His latest publications are *From Myth to Symptom: The Case of Kosovo* and *Louis Althusser* (2011), a book coauthored with Slavoj Žižek, and *Për Althusserin* (2012). Agon is currently working on a new book: *The Sublime Absolute: Hegel, Althusser and Žižek*.

BRIAN BENJAMIN HANSEN, PhD in philosophy, is Lecturer, University College, School of Continuing Education, Denmark. Researching in the themes of subjectivity and collectivity from the perspective of psychoanalysis and diagnostics of the contemporary. Member of the philosophical collective Centre for Wild Analysis.

ADRIAN JOHNSTON is Professor in the Department of Philosophy at the University of New Mexico, Albuquerque, and a faculty member at the Emory Psychoanalytic Institute in Atlanta. He is the author of *Time Driven: Metapsychology and the Splitting of the Drive* (2005), *Žižek's Ontology: A Transcendental Materialist Theory of Subjectivity* (2008), *Badiou, Žižek, and Political Transformations: The Cadence of Change* (2009), and *Prolegomena to Any Future Materialism*, vol. 1, *The Outcome of Contemporary French Philosophy* (2013), all published by Northwestern University Press. He is the coauthor, with Catherine Malabou, of *Self and Emotional Life: Philosophy, Psychoanalysis, and Neuroscience* (Columbia University Press, 2013). His most recent book is *Adventures in Transcendental Materialism: Dialogues with Contemporary Thinkers* (Edinburgh University Press, 2014). With Todd McGowan and Slavoj Žižek, he is a coeditor of the book series Diaeresis at Northwestern University Press.

KATJA KOLŠEK, PhD in Philosophy, is Research Associate at the Science and Research Centre, University of Primorska, Koper (Slovenia). She has published *The Other of Democracy: Problems of Immanence and Otherness in Contemporary Theories of Democracy* (Univerza na Primorskem, Založba Annales, Koper, 2011) and numerous articles on contemporary French philosophy (Althusser, Badiou, Rancière) and theoretical psychoanalysis, most recently "The Parallax Object in Althusser's Materialist Philosophy" (in *Encountering Althusser: Politics and Materialism in Contemporary Radical Thought*, edited by K. Diefenbach, S. Farris, K. Kirn, P. Thomas, Bloomsbury, 2013). She is also translating modern and contemporary Chinese literature into Slovenian.

ADAM KOTSKO is Assistant Professor of Humanities at Shimer College in Chicago. He is the author of *Why We Love Sociopaths, The Politics of Redemption, Awkwardness*, and *Žižek and Theology* and the translator of several of Agamben's works. His current research focuses on the potential place of the devil in political theology.

CATHERINE MALABOU is Professor in the Department of Philosophy at the Centre for Modern European Philosophy at Kingston University, UK. She is the author of several books translated into English, including *The Future of Hegel: Plasticity, Temporality and Dialectic; What Should We Do with Our Brain?; Plasticity at the Dusk of Writing: Dialectic, Destruction, Deconstruction; The New Wounded*; and *Changing Difference*.

BENJAMIN NOYS is Reader in English at the University of Chichester. He is the author of *Georges Bataille: A Critical Introduction* (2000), *The Culture of Death* (2005), *The Persistence of the Negative: A Critique of Contemporary Theory* (2010), and *Malign Velocities: Accelerationism and Capitalism* (2014) and editor of *Communization and Its Discontents* (2011).

GEOFF PFEIFER is Assistant Teaching Professor of Philosophy at Worcester Polytechnic Institute in Worcester, Massachusetts. His work has been published in *Human Studies, Journal of Global Ethics, European Legacy*, and *Current Perspectives in Social Theory*. He is also the author of *The New Materialism: Althusser, Badiou, and Žižek* (Routledge, forthcoming).

FRANK RUDA is Research Associate at the Collaborative Research Centre on Aesthetic Experience at the Free University of Berlin (Germany), Visiting Lecturer at the Institute of Philosophy, Scientific Research Centre, in Ljubljana (Slovenia), and Visiting Lecturer at Bard College Berlin (Germany). His publications include *Hegel's Rabble: An Investigation into Hegel's Philosophy of Right* (Continuum, 2011); *For Badiou: Idealism without Idealism* (Evanston: "Northwestern University Press, forthcoming), and "Remembering the Impossible: For a Meta-Critical Anamnesis of Communism," in *The Idea of Communism 2: The New York Conference*, ed. Slavoj Žižek (Verso, 2013), 137–65.

OXANA TIMOFEEVA, PhD in Philosophy, is a Senior Research Fellow at the Institute of Philosophy of the Russian Academy of Sciences, a Humboldt Fellow at Humboldt University in Berlin, and a member of the group Chto Delat (Russia). She is the author of *Introduc-*

tion to the Erotic Philosophy of Georges Bataille (*New Literary Observer*, Moscow, 2009; in Russian) and *History of Animals: An Essay on Negativity, Immanence and Freedom*, with a preface by Slavoj Žižek (Jan van Eyck Academy, Maastricht, 2012).

SAMO TOMŠIČ is Research Assistant at the Humboldt University in Berlin and at the Institute of Philosophy, Scientific Research Centre of the Slovenian Academy of Sciences and Arts (Ljubljana). He has published papers on psychoanalysis, contemporary French philosophy, and structuralism and has translated Kant, Freud, Lacan, Badiou, and others into Slovenian. His book on Marx and Lacan is forthcoming in 2015.

GABRIEL TUPINAMBÁ was born in Rio de Janeiro, Brazil. He is a practicing analyst, a member of the international collective Pensée, and Coordinator of the Circle of Studies of the Idea and Ideology. He has published the book *Hegel, Lacan, Žižek* (Atropos Press, 2013) as well as written chapters in *Žižek and Education* (forthcoming) and *The Žižek Dictionary* (Acumen, 2014). Gabriel is currently working on a new book: *Thinking, in Psychoanalysis*.

FABIO VIGHI teaches Critical Theory and European Cinema at Cardiff University. Among his recent books: *States of Crisis and Post-Capitalist Scenarios* (edited with Heiko Feldner and Slavoj Žižek, 2014), *Critical Theory and Film* (2012), *On Žižek's Dialectics* (2010) and *Sexual Difference in European Cinema* (2009).

GAVIN WALKER is Assistant Professor of History and East Asian Studies at McGill University. He works on topics in modern Japanese intellectual history, Marxist theory and historiography, and contemporary critical theory. Recent publications include "The Absent Body of Labour Power: Uno Kozo's Logic of Capital," *Historical Materialism* 21, 4 (2013); "The Body of Politics: On the Concept of the Party," *Theory and Event* 16, 4 (2013); and "On Marxism's Field of Operation: Badiou and the Critique of Political Economy," *Historical Materialism* 20, 2 (2012). He is currently finishing his book *The Sublime Perversion of Capital: Marxist Theory and the Politics of History in Modern Japan*.

SEAD ZIMERI studied Islamic philosophy and theology at the University of Damascus. Now he is studying continental philosophy at the University of Oslo. He has written on Marxism, German idealism, Islamic philosophy, and other topics. He is a cofounder and member of the Dialectical Materialism Collective, in Prishtina (Kosovo). His latest publications include *Islam without Islam* (Filosofisk Supplement, 2008), *Die Stellung der Frau im Islam aus der Sicht des Korans'* (Springer, 2003), *Transfer Projekt Damaskus: Urban orientation* (Springer, 2003), *Slavoj Žižek on the Dialectic of the Universal and Particular* (Filosofisk Supplement, 2010), *Sharia og misnøyen med det sekulære lovgivning* (Nytt Norsk Tidskrift, 2011), "Althusser sive Žižek" (in *Për Althusserin*, ed. Agon Hamza, 2012), and other works. Sead is currently working on a new book: *In Search of Islamic Equality*.

SLAVOJ ŽIŽEK, born March 21, 1949, in Ljubljana, Slovenia, Doctor of Arts (psychoanalysis, 1985) at the Universite Paris-VIII, Doctor Causa Honoris at the University of Cordoba, Argentina (2005), is Codirector of the International Center for Humanities, Birkbeck College, University of London (from 2005). He has been Visiting Professor at the Department of Psychoanalysis, Universite Paris-VIII (1982–1983 and 1985–1986), at Columbia University, New York (1995), at Princeton University (1996), at the New School for Social Research, New York (1997), at the University of Michigan, Ann Arbor (1998), at Georgetown University, Washington, DC (1999), and at the Film Department of New York University (2002). He is the founder and president of the Society for Theoretical Psychoanalysis (Ljubljana) and editor of the book series Shortcuts (MIT Press), Wo es war (Verso), and SIC (Duke University Press). His main works are *The Sublime Object of Ideology* (1989), *Tarrying with the Negative* (1993), *The Plague of Fantasies* (1997), *The Ticklish Subject* (1999), *The Fragile Absolute* (2000), *The Puppet and the Dwarf* (2004), *The Parallax View* (2006), and *Less Than Nothing* (2012).

Index

Printed and bound by CPI Group (UK) Ltd, Croydon, CR0 4YY

09/06/2025

14685753-0001